TIM
CONWAY
with Jane Scovell

What's So Funny?

· *My Hilarious Life* ·

HOWARD BOOKS
A DIVISION OF SIMON & SCHUSTER, INC.
New York · Nashville · London · Toronto · Sydney · New Delhi

Howard Books
A Division of Simon & Schuster, Inc.
1230 Avenue of the Americas
New York, NY 10020

First Howard Books hardcover edition October 2013

HOWARD and colophon are trademarks of Simon & Schuster, Inc.

For information about special discounts for bulk purchases,
please contact Simon & Schuster Special Sales at
1-866-506-1949 or business@simonandschuster.com.

The Simon & Schuster Speakers Bureau can bring authors
to your live event. For more information or to book an event,
contact the Simon & Schuster Speakers Bureau at
1-866-248-3049 or visit our website at www.simonspeakers.com.

Designed by Ruth Lee-Mui

Manufactured in the United States of America

1   3   5   7   9   10   8   6   4   2

Library of Congress Cataloging-in-Publication Data

Conway, Tim.
What's so funny? : my hilarious life / Tim Conway ; with Jane Scovell.
pages cm
1. Conway, Tim. 2. Comedians—United States—Biography. 3. Actors—United States—
Biography. I. Scovell, Jane, date. II. Title.
PN2287.C584A3 2013
792.702'8092—dc23
[B]   2013005868
ISBN 978-1-4767-2650-2
ISBN 978-1-4767-2651-9 (ebook)

I want to, well, what I really want to do is kiss my wife
and thank her for all the years of happiness
she has brought into my life.
She's what makes it fun to write a book.
With Charlene around I could fill our library shelves with ease.

Contents

Contents

Contents

Contents

Foreword

Let me start off with: I absolutely adore Tim Conway. Maybe there are other performers as funny, but in my opinion, I can't think of anybody funnier. Tim is a true original, with a comedic mind so brilliant that it's downright scary. His sketches with Harvey Korman deserve a spot in whatever cultural time capsule we're setting aside for future generations.

I first became aware of Tim in the early 1960s when he was a guest one week on *The Garry Moore Show*, where I was a regular performer. We didn't get to know each other very well at that time because he did a solo performance and appeared in a sketch that I wasn't in that week. He was also quite shy. However, when he did his routine, he killed the audience (and all the rest of us on the show!).

Our paths didn't cross until a few years later when I had my own variety show and we booked Tim as a guest. People assume he was a regular on the show from the get-go. Not so. He was a regular guest one or two times a month until the ninth year, when (*Duh!* How stupid were we?), we finally asked him to be on every week.

We would tape two shows on Friday in front of two different audiences. In the early show, Tim would perform a sketch exactly the way we rehearsed it all week. Then when we did the second show, he would pull out all the stops, improvising and coming up with hysterical bits of business none of us had seen before. Many times a four-minute sketch would stretch to ten minutes or more due to the bits he added, plus the added laughter from our audience. The second show was always the one that went on the air, because what Tim came up with was . . . pure gold. Sometimes we were accused of breaking up on purpose. Not true. We all tried our best to keep straight faces, but when Tim got on a roll that was all but impossible.

However, let me emphasize, he never tried to hog the spotlight. He would only improvise when it was suited to the character he was playing.

Tim is as wildly inventive in real life as he is on the screen. You never know what's going to happen when he gets going. In the fall of 1973, our show was chosen to be the first television show to open the newly completed Sydney Opera House. We put together the necessary personnel, crew, and performers and flew off to Sydney where we all stayed at the same hotel. During rehearsal time, we got together in the evenings and visited the restaurants around town. After a few days our group began to shrink as people split off, which often happens when you're working on location. Caution is thrown to the wind, and mini and major love affairs start popping up. Naturally, the various couples thought their rendezvous were big secrets. Wishful thinking. At the time, I was married to the show's producer/director, Joe Hamilton. We felt funny about the state of affairs, but these were adults and it was none of our business. Put it this way, we were a long way from home and people were assuming that what happened Down Under would stay Down Under.

A few nights before the show, Joe and I made a dinner date with Tim, who was traveling alone. He suggested that we pick him up at his suite. At the appointed time we went to get him. Joe knocked on the door, and Tim called out, "Come on in." The door was unlocked and we entered the living room. Tim was nowhere to be seen. "In here. C'mon in," he called from the bedroom. Joe and I walked over to the open door and looked into the dimly lit room. There was Tim, bare-chested, lying in the bed, with the covers pulled up to his waist. He was smoking a cigarette with his arm around a realistic, full-size toy sheep whose head was peeking out from underneath the comforter.

"Hi guys. Be right with you," he said, waving to us. Tim leaned over, kissed his bed partner on her polyester, wooly brow, and said sweetly, "Don't wait up, Barbara. I'll see you in the morning."

Turning to us with a big wink, he said, "I know you'll keep this to yourselves."

Since the show went off the air, we have remained close. His wife, Charlene ("Sharkey"), who is one of my dearest friends (she was an assistant on *The Garry Moore Show*), is the perfect companion, supportive and . . . funny in her own right. They are devoted to one another. Sometimes when we all go out to dinner together, we laugh so much that I've made myself learn how to do the Heimlich maneuver, just in case.

I've talked about his comedic genius. People often ask, "What's Tim Conway really like?" Did I mention that he sews? He's a tailor!

Not only can he whip up a new suit for himself, he can upholster furniture! He also builds furniture! I wouldn't be surprised if he could erect a suspension bridge with his bare hands.

More importantly, he's as nice as he is funny. I've never heard him say a bad thing about anybody. He's loyal to his friends, and he never fails to stick his neck out for those he loves.

In reading his story (both hilarious and thought-provoking) you'll gain a great deal of insight into the events that fashioned him into the kind and funny genius he turned out to be.

Did I mention that I adore him?

—Carol Burnett

Preface

I've written books with a number of celebrities; each experience was special, and yet I never enjoyed working with anyone as much as I enjoyed working with Tim Conway. He's a unique combination of a genuinely funny man and a real old-fashioned gentleman. At once bold as brass and, at the same time, disarmingly humble. There isn't a sanctimonious bone among all his funny ones. He never boasts about his accomplishments, and that's precisely why I'm using this Preface to say things about him (things the reader should know) that he'd never say about himself. So here goes.

At our first meeting in Los Angeles, Tim came to my hotel. The front desk called to say he was on his way up. I went into the hallway to wait for him. The elevator was at the opposite end of the corridor. In the middle of the hallway, a man, wearing headphones, was vacuuming. Tim stepped out of the elevator at the same moment the cleaning man left the vacuum running in the center of the hallway as he turned to dust a side table. Tim started down the corridor. He reached the upright vacuum and, without breaking stride, grabbed the handle with one hand and, waving to me with the other, called out, "I'll be right there, just have to finish my work." He put his head down and began to vacuum. The cleaning man, oblivious to what was happening, thanks to his headphones, finished dusting and turned around to recover his vacuum only to discover Tim pushing it around. For a moment, the man looked befuddled. Then, he got it. He smiled and gingerly tapped Tim on the shoulder. Immediately, Tim dropped the vacuum and threw himself against the wall with his arms spread above his head waiting to be frisked. That's when I learned that Tim Conway seizes any opportunity to amuse. Moreover, he is as delighted to make one or two people laugh as he is to entertain huge audiences.

Shenanigans aside, Tim is a really grounded person. For one thing, he's had the same friends for decades. Although their names read like a Who's Who of Emmy and Oscar winners, they, like Tim, are down-to-earth people leading normal lives in the abnormal world of show business. And here's another Hollywood anomaly: Tim's second marriage to Charlene Beatty has been going strong for nearly three decades. It's a match made in heaven, but it took Tim one divorce, and Charlene two, to find that out. They play off each other brilliantly. If you ask Tim what Charlene's father did for a living, he'll say, "He was a bookie." Ask Charlene the same question, and she'll tell you her father was a trumpet player who performed with the big bands until they went out of fashion. He still had to earn a living and the only other thing he knew was betting the horses. "My father was a musician for most of his life," says Charlene with a laugh. "But my husband calls him a bookie because it sounds funnier."

Charlene and Tim Conway are their own reality show with Charlene providing the reality. She's his leveler, the straight man who keeps him honest. Tim knows what a difference Charlene has made in his life and finds ample opportunities to acknowledge it.

While receiving one of his many awards, Tim stood at the podium and thanked everyone for the wonderful honor. "I wouldn't be standing in front of you right now," he said, "if it weren't for the way my wife looks out for me. She takes charge of everything, including my diet. She's been feeding me so much fiber, I'm now passing wicker furniture."

Tim's fundamentally a cheerful person yet he has a reflective side; a quiet wisdom informs his art and his life. The right comic conditions, however, will always conquer any guardedness, and he becomes totally playful. He is a combination clown and comic. Generally speaking, comedians pursue one tradition or the other. Tim has the funny bone to do slapstick and the wit to do stand-up. It's a rare gift.

"Funny" has become an archaic word; it's been replaced by "edgy." Once upon a time most comedians were not looking to shock you into laughter; they wanted you to enjoy yourself. Today's comics tend to be in your face. They'll sacrifice anything for the laugh and have no qualms about making someone else the butt of the joke. Too many rely on confrontational techniques. If nothing else works, hurl a vulgarity at a guy in the front row, and you'll get a laugh. Tim would never do that. He masterminds the gag and takes the onus upon himself, as illustrated by the vacuum cleaner story. He didn't need to make a fool of the cleaning man; he was content to make a fool of himself. That self-effacing modus operandi has characterized his career, with one glorious exception—his work with the late Harvey Korman.

While each of them performed successfully without the other, their transcendent partnership on *The Carol Burnett Show* was a genuine marvel. Professionally and personally, theirs was a remarkable relationship, one in which Tim, the runt, always got the better of Harvey, who towered over him. Though Tim Conway is the kindest of men, there was nothing he wouldn't stoop to in order to get Harvey Korman.

From the beginning, Tim was content with being an ensemble player. He didn't need to be the star. The networks did not feel the same and pushed him into a number of shows as the headliner. They all failed. Why was such an outrageously gifted man unable to carry his own show? In the opinion of those who know him best, and that includes Tim, he wasn't comfortable in the starring role. Tim Conway is a sublime second banana. Like Falstaff, he is not only witty in himself "but the cause that wit is in other men."

His solo failings notwithstanding, Tim reigned supreme as a cast member on *The Steve Allen Show, McHale's Navy,* and *The Carol Burnett Show.* During that time he became one of the most familiar and beloved figures of the entertainment world. "Beloved" is a much-bandied word in show business, but one that fits Tim Conway to a *T.*

In the years since the *Burnett* show Tim has appeared as a guest star on TV variety programs, talk shows, and sitcoms. And, he continues to entertain in person, performing via an underground railroad of dinner theatres and arenas. In working with Tim, I learned that old television performers never die: They continue to delight the public in cities and towns located, for the most part, in America's heartland. The most famous of these showbiz Valhallas is Branson, Missouri. Branson—population six thousand—has at least one hundred different showcases. In Branson, as in other hamlets spread throughout the country, classic performers—such as Tim, Carol Burnett, Pat Boone, Charo, Bill Cosby, Barbara Eden, Gladys Knight, Barbara

Mandrell, Wayne Newton, Kenny Rogers—still delight audiences hungry for pure entertainment. Tim was one of the first to recognize the potential in these golden-age venues and he easily transitioned from television to stage. The change went smoothly because, from the very beginning of his career, Tim either wrote his own material or collaborated with staff writers.

Can this septuagenarian verging on octogenarian still hold large audiences in his thrall? You bet! Not long ago, Tim performed before some four thousand people at the Nokia Theatre in Los Angeles for AARP's annual gathering. The show featured a host of familiar names including Jane Goodall, Martina Navratilova, Carol Burnett, and sportscaster James Brown. Tim was scheduled to do a bit of stand-up following the Goodall segment, after which he was to introduce Burnett. The two of them would reminisce and take questions from the audience.

Tim was in his dressing room when a young program organizer came to the door with a message from Martina Navratilova. The tennis legend asked if it would be okay for her to drop by and say hello. Tim eagerly said yes.

Another knock on the door and Navratilova was ushered in. Tim and she shook hands and began chatting. Tim thought that she was from Romania, where his mother's family originated, and said so. Navratilova quickly responded, saying, "I'm Czech!"

"Oh," said Tim, pleasantly, "Isn't that the same as Romanian?"

"No!" she said with a touch of nationalistic fervor.

"Really? I thought it was," Tim answered.

Navratilova looked at him. She grinned. Tim was playing, and she got it. They continued to converse. At one point, she told him that when she came to the United States she had a hard time because she didn't speak the language.

"I actually learned English watching your show," she confided.

They talked a little longer, and then it was time for Tim to go onstage.

In the auditorium, huge screens were scattered around so that the thousands gathered there could get a closer look. James Brown was speaking onstage.

"We all thank Jane Goodall for her wonderful work, and now we'll get on with the show as soon as the crew removes the tables and chairs."

The stagehands came out from behind the curtain and headed toward the furniture. Suddenly, screams of laughter filled the theatre when they caught sight of Tim Conway working along with the crew. He had not planned this beforehand. He simply got in line with the stagehands and did his thing. The stagehands were laughing, James Brown was laughing, everyone was laughing, except for Tim. Straight-faced, he picked up a chair, and disappeared through the curtains—a perfect example of his instinctive playful reaction to the moment.

Tim is a good man to know for many reasons, and I've saved one of the best for last. I received a call from him one afternoon, and at the end of the conversation he said, "I don't know if you're a betting woman, but the jockeys in the Breeders' Cup race are all talking about one particular horse. So, if you feel like it, put some money on number three."

I thanked him for the tip and hung up. I had never bet on a horse race before, yet there was something in the way Tim spoke that made me think this was the time to do it. I went online, got to an offtrack betting site, located the five million dollar Breeders' Cup race, and filled in the necessary information. But, when I was prompted to key in my Social Security number I balked, and clicked off the computer.

That night I turned on the evening news and was brushing my

teeth when I heard the sports announcer say, "In a thrilling race, the Breeders' Cup was won by Drosselmeyer, and here's a look at the finish."

Toothbrush in hand, I ran to the set and watched as a scrum of horses galloped toward the finish line. Drosselmeyer lurched forward and nosed out the rest. The number emblazoned on the side of his saddle was "3".

There's so much more I could say but, at this point, I'm going to turn the show over to Tim. I think you are in for a real treat, hearing him tell his story in his own words. Remember, Tim is a savvy guy in rube's clothing, so don't be fooled by his unassuming, aw-shucks manner. It's a ploy that has been used, to good advantage, by quite a few American humorists, from Mark Twain to Will Rogers to Andy Rooney.

—Jane Scovell

Dear Jane,

Without your assistance, this would have been a pamphlet.

—*Tim*

Introduction

People have often asked me, "If you weren't in show business, what would you be doing?" The truth is, I don't think there's anything else I could be doing, so the answer would have to be, nothing. Then again, there's nothing I love more than making people laugh, so I guess you could say I'm in the only business I could be in. I was born to enjoy life and I've always wanted everyone to enjoy it along with me. That's why I can't see myself any place other than standing in front of an audience with one purpose in mind—to make people feel a little bit happier than when they came in.

I didn't start out to be a comedian. I didn't want to grow up to be a policeman, or a soldier, or a fireman, either. I wanted to be a jockey and, believe it or not, I actually gave it a try. It didn't work. The truth is, I was terrified of riding real, live horses. And when I did, I had a habit of falling off them. This sort of thing wouldn't work for a jockey. You'd be amazed how angry a bettor can get when the horse he's put money on crosses the finish line without a rider.

Fifty years ago I slid head first, without a helmet, into the entertainment industry. I came of age during one of the most exciting, innovative, and influential eras in the history of television. My first big show was *McHale's Navy*, which was followed by *The Carol Burnett Show*, where I remained until it ended. That was four decades ago, and I'm still performing. Maybe not on a weekly basis, but you can catch me on shows from *SpongeBob SquarePants* to *30 Rock*, and from *Hot In Cleveland* to *Mike and Molly*. While Carol, Harvey Korman, Vicki Lawrence, and the rest of my *Burnett* buddies have a special place in my heart, working with people like Tina Fey, Melissa McCarthy, Wendie Malick, and Valerie Bertinelli is not chopped liver. I also perform, live, in theatres, and in dinner clubs from Martha's Vineyard to Los Angeles, with plenty of stops in between. In other words, I continue to ply my trade, whatever that means. And, considering that I'm approaching the big 8–0, and am still going strong. Not only do I have a classic American rags-to-riches story to tell, I'm living proof that life keeps getting better and better, if you let it. Kind of motivational, don't you agree? That's one of the reasons why I decided to write a book.

So come along and let me entertain you, this time on the printed page. And if I give you a laugh or two, great, and if I don't, keep it to yourself.

My Beginnings

At the age of eighteen, my father, Daniel Conway, left Ireland and came to this country accompanied by his seventeen-year-old sister, Madge. They were orphans when they left the old sod, and they were still orphans when they arrived in the United States. The Irish are stubborn. According to my father, he and Madge were in the elite section of steerage—there was a toilet. Odd definition of elite, but it sounds a lot like my dad. He wasn't a big talker. Wait, he wasn't a talker, period, but whatever little he said, he had the Irish gift of wit.

Back in the Emerald Isle, Daniel Conway had a profession; he was a whip. In case you don't recognize the term, whips are an essential part of the grand old sport of foxhunting. And if you're not up on that tradition, it involves a bunch of people on horseback chasing after a poor little creature that's been sniffed out by a pack of hounds. A friend of mine told me that Oscar Wilde referred to foxhunting as "the unspeakable in full pursuit of the uneatable." I couldn't have said it better myself. Whips were in charge of keeping the hounds in order. You can spot them in all those hunt paintings; they're the guys carrying whips. Apparently, my father came to this country because he thought there was a crying need for a man with his skill. As you may have noticed if you've looked out of the window on any given Saturday, not many fox hunts are taking place in America. I have no idea how long it took my dad to figure out that he might not make it big in the New World as a whip, but it must have been shortly after the boat landed.

I can picture him standing on Ellis Island holding a paper bag stuffed with clothes in one hand and an old whip in the other, wondering not only how to earn a living, but where. For some unknown reason, he chose Cleveland, Ohio. Cleveland? It's a city you make jokes about. Here's an example: What's the difference between the Titanic and Cleveland? They're both disasters, but Cleveland has a better orchestra. Want more? Back in 1969, a fire broke out on the Cuyahoga River. The flames, fueled by all the oil and sludge in the harbor, went as high as five stories. It was headline news all over the country and inspired Randy Newman to write "Burn On (Big River)." Can't you hear the Cleveland fire chief yelling, "All right, men, let's get some water on the river and put this thing out!" A river on fire, that's Cleveland—the perfect location for my dad. He went there; sister Madge stayed put. She had no desire for further travel, found work as a housekeeper, and never left New York.

Dan—if you don't mind, I'm going to call my parents by their first names—arrived in Cleveland and ultimately found his way to Hunting Valley, an exclusive suburb twenty-five miles out of Cleveland. When I say "exclusive," I mean *exclusive*. Hunting Valley is located on eight square miles containing grassy fields, rolling hills, a bona fide forest, river gorges, and elegant estates that are linked by hiking trails, polo fields, and bridle paths. A lot of prominent Cleveland families were residents of Hunting Valley as well as members of the Chagrin Valley Hunt Club. Polo was the big draw but members also participated in Saturday fox hunts. Each hunt had a chosen route, and a tried-and-true method ensured that the horses took it. Before the start of the chase, a fox was placed in a burlap bag; the minute the bag closed, the terrified critter peed. A horse dragged the bag and its contents through the woods, thereby laying the trail. The hunt began. The dogs instantly picked up the scent which they followed to the finish where, rather than a fox, a catering truck awaited. Luncheon was served. Meanwhile, the little fox had been taken back to the barn, washed off, and kept in relative comfort—until the next Saturday's hunt. Look, nothing's perfect but six days out of seven, the fox did lead a good life. Although, if you ask me, since no one gave two hoots about catching the little critter, it probably would have been just as effective to drag along a pastrami sandwich.

Dan got a job as a groom at the Chagrin Valley Hunt Club. While he did assist in the hunts, his main job was tending to the polo ponies. Basically, that meant scooping up horse manure in the stalls. I could go on describing my father's profession, but for now let's leave the pioneer pooper-scooper, rake in hand, and move on to my mother.

Bet you think she was a fair, Irish lass, or something like that. Think again. Sophia Murgoi was born to Romanian parents, in either Warren or Columbus, Ohio. When she was four, her parents whisked Sophia, her three brothers, and two sisters back to Romania, the Cleveland of Europe. Brilliant move. It meant that, in a dozen or so years, they'd have front row seats to World War II.

Fortunately, Sophia was shipped back to America before the Nazis marched in. She went to Cleveland because she knew some Romanians who lived there. As far as I know, the rest of the family remained in occupied territory. Sophia never talked about them, at least not to me. Come to think of it, except for a rare mention of his sister, Dan didn't talk about his family, either. Then again, he was an orphan. Neither Dan nor Sophia seemed to give a rap about looking up relatives, consequently I never had the luxury of aunts, uncles, and cousins. It was just the three of us, but it was enough. I do recall one time in the early '40s when Dan decided we should drive to New York City and visit Aunt Madge. We got into our trusty, rusty, second-hand, four-door Ford, headed east, slept in motels, went through the Holland Tunnel, and arrived in Manhattan. Dan drove around and around but he couldn't find a parking space. Finally, he sucked in his breath, cried out, "That does it!," and then, so help me, turned the car around and went back through the tunnel. We spent the night in New Jersey.

It wasn't until several decades later, after I moved to California, that I even came close to meeting my aunt. It happened when Charlene Beatty, the woman who would become my second wife, and I planned a visit to New York City. I called my parents to tell them of the upcoming trip.

"Look up your Aunt Madge," ordered Dan.

"Aunt Madge?"

"My sister," said Dan.

"I know she's your sister."

"She lives on East Fifty-ninth Street across from some big store," continued Dan. "She's a housekeeper for a church, and they sent me her address. She doesn't have a phone, so you'll have to go there."

He didn't say what church or why they sent him her address. I could only assume he'd asked for it, but why? I remember thinking there's no use looking for rhyme or reason at this stage of the game. Dan said to do it, so I'd do it.

Charlene and I arrived in Manhattan and after we finished doing what we'd gone there to do, we went in search of Aunt Madge. She lived in a run-down, brownstone apartment building across the street from Bloomingdale's department store. We walked up the front stoop and scanned the names listed on the directory at the side of the front door. I pressed the buzzer next to the name "Madge Conway" and waited.

"Yes?" answered a voice over the intercom.

"Aunt Madge, this is your nephew, Tim. You know, the one on television."

"I don't have a television."

"Really? Oh, I'm sorry. I'm Dan's son, and he said for me to say hello."

"Yes?"

"I'd love to see you."

"I don't go out."

"I could come up," I suggested.

"That's not necessary," she answered after a long pause. "Thanks for stopping by."

The intercom clicked off. I looked at Charlene, she looked at me, and without saying a word, we walked down the steps and ambled across the street into Bloomingdale's.

Despite her abrupt dismissal, I felt a little bad that I hadn't seen my aunt. I wanted to do something for her, but what? Maybe a gift would be appropriate. She said she didn't have a TV, so that seemed to be a good bet. We went to the electronics department, bought a small portable set, and arranged to have it delivered. When I got back to California, I received a notice from

Bloomingdale's telling me that the television had been returned and that the refund had been credited to my account. I thought maybe Aunt Madge didn't want to have anything of value around. Charlene suggested that she didn't want to know me. Whatever the reason, we didn't see each other. Matter of fact, to this day, I've never met a Conway or a Murgoi.

Speaking of the latter, let's get back to Mom.

When Sophia Murgoi arrived in America, she, like Aunt Madge, found employment as a housekeeper. Get this: Sophia, a United States citizen by birth, spoke almost no English, and what little she spoke was heavily accented. One of the few things Sophia could say was "chocolate sundae." Consequently, she spent most of her spare time watching her face break out. The language barrier didn't stop my father from courting her. How they communicated is beyond me. It had to have been some version of English since Dan never learned Romanian.

My mother, a stranger in the land of her birth, remained fiercely proud of her Eastern European heritage. I was well into my showbiz career when, out of the blue, Sophia asked, "How come when you're on those TV talking shows, you are never mentioning you are part Romanian?"

Sophia watched everything I did so she would have known I hadn't bragged about my ethnicity. Not long after her rebuke, I was on Johnny Carson's *Tonight Show* and, to please my mother, I decided to reveal my heritage.

During my conversation with Johnny, I told him, "You know I'm part Romanian."

Johnny drew his head back, lifted an eyebrow, sort of smiled, and then went right on talking. As for the audience reaction, normally people will applaud whatever you say—your favorite city, your favorite color, your favorite ice cream flavor, the name of your first grade teacher, just about any person, place, or thing will get them going. Not one pair of hands slapped together at my disclosure. Sophia never brought up the subject again. Neither did I.

Are you starting to get a picture of my parents? I have to confess, to this very day, they continue to dumbfound me. How is it that I know practically zilch about their backgrounds? They met in Cleveland, but where, how, or why, I couldn't begin to guess. If I had to take a stab, I'd say that they probably met each other through friends. Anyway, it's a good bet Irish Dan didn't attend a Romanian Singles Evening. Dan was a tall, slim, good-looking dude, a dapper dresser with a great head of hair. Sophia was short, a bit on the dumpling side, but with a round, pretty face. Her vivacious nature would have appealed to my taciturn father. I inherited my height and my round face from my mother and the ability to speak English from my father. Although I never saw a marriage license and though they never actually mentioned a wedding date, I presume they were married sometime before I was born on December 15, 1933. It's crazy that I know so little about my own parents, but it's the truth. Neither one of them ever sat me down and said, "Son, this is who we are." As I said, Orphan Dan probably didn't know and Sophia didn't seem to care—maybe because what was left of her family was thousands of miles away. (I gave up trying to discover their histories, but if there's some eager genealogist reading this, be my guest.) I've come to the conclusion that, all things considered, the only word for Mr. and Mrs. Daniel Conway is zany. You don't have to be a Sigmund Freud to figure out that if you put those two people together, you'd come up with me.

Dan and Sophia were living in Willoughby, a suburb of Cleveland, when I was introduced to the world on a second-hand sofa in their living room. I'm happy to report a doctor was present. My official birth certificate read: "Toma Conway." Eventually it was altered to read: "Thomas Daniel Conway." With Dan and Sophia in charge, I'm lucky it wasn't changed to Betty Lou. (Later, you'll find out how I became Tim.)

I was a colicky baby for the first few months of my life. During this time, Sophia kept busy looking after me; Dan found consolation by downing glass after glass of home-brewed beer, the classic Irish remedy for anything and everything. Besides upsetting my parents, my colicky state delayed my baptism. I was nearly four months old when I was hustled off to receive the baptismal sacraments in a Romanian church of Sophia's choice. Would you believe it, in Cleveland she actually had a choice.

At the beginning of the twentieth century, around two thousand Romanian immigrants lived in Cleveland, making it one of the largest Romanian enclaves in the country. Most of them were members of the Orthodox Church but some of them, the "Greek Catholics," belonged to the Catholic Church of the Byzantine Rite. The difference is, the Greek Catholics recognize the Pope. Naturally, there had to be two different churches. The Greek Catholics built St. Helena's in 1905 and the Romanian Orthodox built St. Mary's in 1908. (They each were the first Romanian churches of their respective faiths erected in America.) Sophia was Romanian Orthodox, so I was taken to St. Mary's. I'm not saying it had anything to do with me, but St. Mary's was the first American Romanian parish to have a stamp issued in its honor by the motherland, Romania.

I can't quite recall mine, but the Romanian Orthodox baptism is a beautiful ceremony, especially if you like incense. The priest, the parents, and the relatives (or, in my case, lacking relatives, a janitor who was selected as a witness) gather around a miniature manger. That's right, a manger, which is placed on a low table in front of the altar. The child is put on a pillow inside the cradle and lies there looking up at the ceiling. Those present take hold of a long prayer scarf and, with heads bowed, walk around the table repeating various prayers designed to get the child through the pearly gates when the time comes. Talk about planning ahead. At my baptism, the celebrants, deep in thought and prayer, continued to mutter and circle until the incantation ended and the participants came to a halt. Priest, parents, and janitor looked down: the manger was empty.

"He has risen," muttered my father.

"No, he has fallen," said the priest.

The priest was right. While they were marching around, I had wriggled off the pillow, over the side of the manger, and from there to the floor, all without a squawk. The celebrants were so busy pushing for my future acceptance into heaven that no one noticed my earthly disappearance. A quick search ensued. The janitor found me under the table, picked me up, and put me back on the pillow. He held onto my legs, Sophia pinned down my arms, and I was duly entered into the faith.

Following my christening, I was brought home and placed back in my crib, not a store-bought article but one that Dan had fashioned from a heavy-duty cardboard box used to ship polo balls. As an infant, the faint aroma of wood clung to me. That's because, in those days, polo balls were made of bamboo. The wooden balls made a whistling noise when they flew through the air so that polo players could hear them coming and duck out of the way. Today, 90 percent of the balls are plastic and they're noiseless. Better look out!

In 1935, we moved into a cozy cottage on the estate of Thomas H. White, an outstanding player on the Chagrin Valley Hunt Club's championship polo team. Mr. White was the founder of the White Sewing Machine Corporation, the White Motor Corporation, and the Cleveland Automatic Screw Machine Company. Need I say that polo, like foxhunting, is a rich man's sport? Dan tended to Mr. White's ponies and, in due time, was promoted. My father became head groom, my mother continued keeping house, and I was the Little Prince. Once I'd made my debut, my parents decided to have no other children. I like to think it's because they'd created something so perfect they didn't feel the need for improvement. I have pictures to prove that I was a cute tyke. Just get a load of me in my sailor suit in the photo section. I've never grown out of my baby face, and, considering my age, it's a little ridiculous.

We had a good life. The funny thing is, I always thought we were rich. Why wouldn't I? For me, life began in a fairy tale cottage surrounded by green lawns and formal gardens, and woods filled with all sorts of trees—maple, oak, spruce, poplar, cherry, dogwood, you name it. There were stables housing elegant riding horses as well as snappy little polo ponies. And we had plenty of good food to eat. The fact that nothing belonged to us completely escaped me. Our home, in fact, was full of they'll-never-miss-them items, which was Sophia's blanket excuse for her peculiar brand of petty larceny. Don't get me wrong; Sophia was honest as the day is long. She never would have thought of taking money or jewelry or furs or anything like that. However, if it came to an about-to-be-given-away garment, or extra foodstuff, that was a different kettle of fish. Bless her, she couldn't stand to see food rotting away, and lots of it did in the homes of the rich. Thus, she had no qualms about dipping into her employers' larders and refrigerators to make sure her Toma was well fed. You can't imagine the fantastic cuts of meat that wound up in my stomach. More improbable, would you believe I tasted caviar before I was six years old?

To say that I was attached to my mother's apron strings would be an understatement. I never left her side and, literally, lived in her shadow. She took me with her everywhere. She brought me along when she cleaned and would let me sit astride the mop handle as she pushed the mop back and forth over the highly waxed wooden floors of the rich folks she worked for. It was great entertainment for me, and a body builder for Sophia. A little over five feet tall in her stocking feet, she was strong and solid and had arms Popeye would have envied. Dan was about five feet ten and rail thin. I believe he weighed in at a swift 124 pounds. In deference to her memory, I'll not speculate as to Sophia's fighting weight, but she could have sent Dan to the moon with one uppercut to the jaw.

We remained in the White cottage until the winter of 1936 when we moved to Chagrin Falls, a small town on the Chagrin River.

Chagrin Falls is forty minutes or so from downtown Cleveland and was named for the waterfall that's smack in the center of town. That waterfall got its name from the Chagrin River. How did the river and waterfall get their names, you might ask, and even if you don't, I'm going to tell you. Ordinarily, when you hear the word "falls" you think of something majestic, like Niagara and its mist-covered, roaring, rushing waters. Erase that image. Think small. Chagrin Falls barely falls. Encyclopedias might tell you that the Chagrin River got its name from "Shagarin," an Erie Indian word meaning Clear Water. That's pretty dry. I prefer local lore, which goes like this:

Many moons ago, a canoe bearing a young Indian and his bride floated down the river. The boat came to the falls and lurched over. "Oh, Sha . . . garin," ("Hang on!") cried the groom. The canoe overturned, and the couple hit the water. They swam to shore, took a look around, liked what they saw, and built their tepee on the riverbank. Soon, others joined them and a town sprang up. In honor of the original couple, the town was called Chagrin Falls with Brave and Squaw in the Canoe. That mouthful was later shortened to Chagrin Falls. Sometimes, residents refer to it as just plain Chagrin.

Okay, you've got two choices, the encyclopedia account and what I like to call *The Carol Burnett Show* version. Come to think of it, the latter explanation could have been a sketch we did back then. (Can't you just picture me in the bow and Carol in the stern of a rocking canoe tipping over a fake falls?)

Chagrin Falls is about as picturesque a place as you can imagine. A lot of the homes and buildings are listed on the National Register of Historic Places. Trust me, it's a dream town, a living template of mid-nineteenth-century America. And, I haven't even gotten to the people. The population was around four thousand when I grew up there and still is. People cared about their neighbors, really cared. Not just to stick their noses into other people's business, but cared to make sure all was well with them. You simply couldn't go wrong growing up there.

Our first home in Chagrin Falls was on Franklin Street. We stayed for almost a year when—and don't ask me why—Dan moved us some sixteen miles down the road to the town of Kirtland. Kirtland was the home of the original headquarters of the Latter Day Saint movement. Led by their founder, Joseph Smith Jr., the Saints came marching into Kirtland from Upstate New York in 1831 and stayed until 1838. The Mormons, in fact, built their first temple there and it's still standing. One hundred years later, in the summer of 1938, Dan Conway moved his flock out of Kirtland and back to Chagrin Falls. That's where my folks stayed for the rest of their lives, and that's the place I call home. It hasn't changed a pebble since the day the Conways arrived, and I honestly believe that living in that wonderful village shaped my life.

Upon our return to paradise, Dan rented a house on Oak Street with a kitchen and living room on the first floor and two bedrooms upstairs. We thought it was a palace. The neighbors on either side of us more likely saw it as a remodeled garage, which indeed it was. That first night on Oak Street was memorable. Lying in my own bed, on a calm summer evening, the window open, a slight breeze carrying just the hint of a coming shower, comforted by the knowledge that my Dan and Sophia were on the other side of the wall, was heaven. Most nights I asked Sophia or Dan to turn on the hall light, but not that night; the moon was my beacon. I didn't want to fall asleep, but how could I not when I was in the house of my dreams?

Dream house or no, the Conways never lingered. In a little over a year—1940 to be exact—we moved a few doors away to another Oak Street house. Sophia, Dan, and I actually carried our big, hunter green couch up the street to the new place. In 1942, we reached our final destination, 43 Orange Street. I spent the rest of my Chagrin years in that house, and, albeit two-family, what a house it was—a beautiful one-hundred-and-forty-year-old, two-story, white-pillared mansion, one parallel street away from the river. Financially, it was a bit of a stretch. The rent was a whopping eighteen dollars a month, about twice as much as we'd been paying on Oak Street. But it was sure worth it.

No question, we moved a lot in the early years. The good thing is, each house we occupied was a bit better than the previous one and usually located a few doors down the street or around the corner. Every move consisted of the same routine. Sophia would pack into boxes what few belongings we possessed, Dan would load them in our beat-up Ford, I would jump in the rumble seat, and away we'd go. At times it would have been quicker to walk than drive. No matter how close the new house was, Sophia always made the same comment as we inched our way down the street.

"Wait, I think this is it!" she'd cry, pointing to a particular house. You'd have thought she was sighting land after a long sea voyage.

Dan would pull the car up to the curb, and we'd pile out and start to bring the boxes inside the house. As a rule, our new neighbors did not greet us, mainly because they weren't new neighbors, just people who lived a hop, skip, or jump from our last residence.

After we finished unpacking—not a lengthy process—the three of us would sit down at our blue Formica-topped kitchen table. We'd sip our respective beer, tea, and milk and assess the surroundings while the denizens of afternoon soap operas babbled over the radio. Back then, family life was centered in the kitchen. A radio set was enthroned, either on a counter or on the table itself, and the sounds from it echoed throughout the house. I grew up with Stella Dallas, Lorenzo Jones, and Mary Noble in the afternoons, and The Shadow, Lum and Abner, Jack Benny, Bob Hope, and Fred Allen in the evenings. Whichever house we were in, Sophia, Dan, and I spent our downtime sitting at the kitchen table, staring at the lighted half-moon dial on our battered Philco radio, and listening to unseen, but all-enveloping, entertainment.

Our moves had a comforting sameness and never bothered me. Each time we arrived at a new residence, Sophia had to make the place ours. She did this by providing certain touches, specifically, curtains and wallpaper. Because she had a sewing machine, curtains were easy to produce; she made them for our first house and altered them to fit the windows of our subsequent homes, adding new ones if necessary. Those curtains followed us all the way to Orange Street. My Sophia had a sewing machine she operated by pumping a foot pedal. Dan was going to get her an electric model, but finances never seemed to be in the right moon, so to speak. I'd guess that the bad knee that plagued my mother in later years might have come from all that pumping. Sophia's machine was a chain-stitch model, which means that the stitches are connected to each other. The admonition, "Don't pull that thread!" accompanied any article she sewed and since she made most of our clothes, I heard that command a lot.

One Sunday morning we were in church, and as the sermon droned on I began looking around for something to do. I spotted a thread hanging from the collar Sophia had finished making for Dan that morning. I reached over and gave it a tug. To my surprise it continued to come at me. I kept pulling on it until there was nothing left to pull. By then I had a small wad of thread in my hand, which I shoved into my pocket. The last hymn was sung and we rose to leave. As we walked up the aisle Dan's collar popped off. A lady behind us picked it up and, tapping Dan on the shoulder, handed it to him. Dan thanked her. He turned and walked up the aisle and out of the church with his tie neatly tied around his neck and his collar tucked in his pocket. I did not mention the thread in *my* pocket. (By the way, we went to a Methodist church when we went to church, which wasn't that often. I'd say Christmas and Easter might find us there for sure, the rest of the year was a crapshoot.)

As good as she was at sewing, Sophia was a similar whiz at paperhanging. The minute we settled into our first Oak Street residence, she was off to the local hardware store with me in tow. After looking at a number of samples, and after a bit of haggling, she purchased several double rolls. She had to buy the paper, but no way would Sophia pay for paste. "Paste too expansif," she informed the clerk as she picked up the rolls and dropped them in my open arms. When we arrived home, Sophia grabbed a bag of Pillsbury flour, emptied it into a bucket, and added water while I stirred. That was the way the Murgois made paste in Romania (though not with Pillsbury's), and it remained Sophia's recipe. Admittedly, the resulting glue did not have the sticking quality of a commercial product. Then again, you couldn't make pancakes with store-bought stuff.

I'll never forget the wallpaper she chose for my bedroom. Perhaps in deference to Dan, it showed a fox hunt complete with horses, riders, fences, and trees. A challenging pattern, under the best of circumstances, was made more so because our home, the converted garage, had uneven walls—very uneven walls. Armed with the paper and paste, Sophia and I began our work. She masterminded; I assisted. It was almost impossible to match the seams and the result was a helter-skelter display of horses running in one direction in one segment, and the opposite way in the next. In the corners, you'd see a horse jumping a rail fence with the nose of the horse following him jammed up his butt. One day, a friend came over to play. We went up to my room where he immediately eyeballed the wallpaper.

"Why is the black horse sniffing the rear of the brown horse while they're jumping over the fence?" he asked.

Dan overheard our conversation and called out, "They're trained to do that so they won't lose their way home."

Sophia and I did a lot of paperhanging back then, and an awful lot of rehanging. Why? In cold weather, the heat from the furnace dried out the Pillsbury paste, causing the paper to crack and loosen. You could hear the snap, crackle, and pop all through the night, and the next morning there'd be shreds dangling from the wall. I worried most about the corners; the horse with the other's nose up his behind was a valuable asset. I needn't have worried; the rehangings simply brought the horses a little closer. Eventually, the wallpaper in my room stopped cracking and stayed firmly fixed. By that time, the black horse was stuffed up to his hind legs inside the brown one, and my wallpaper had become a neighborhood phenomenon. Friends were treated to private showings of the bizarre fox hunt that graced my walls, and they were suitably floored.

Growing Up and Liking It

There were plenty of kids to play with in Chagrin, and a constant stream of us ran in and out of each other's homes gathering forces to make up teams. We carried our mitts and bats and balls over to a homemade diamond in an unoccupied field to play baseball. We nailed a bushel basket with the bottom punched out to a telephone pole and played basketball in the street. We played kickball in an empty lot. We played until it became too dark to see anything, even something as big as a basketball, and then we went to our respective homes for supper. One summer we all spent a memorable week splashing around in the Brights' pool. Well, it wasn't exactly a pool. The Brights had created a hole in their backyard to accommodate their outhouse, but before they moved the privy Mr. Bright filled the crater with water providing us with a solid week of private pool time. It was a sad day when the crapper was repositioned. But, that's progress.

My childhood consisted of all the wonderful things a small town provides, or, maybe I should say, used to provide—plenty of places to play with no fear about anything bad happening to the children, no matter how late they came home. And I always had the joy of coming home to Dan and Sophia. I loved my Dan as much as I loved my Sophia, but my father and I rarely talked to each other. It was nothing personal; he was just a nontalker. Consequently, we never had arguments. Of course Dan, being Irish, felt he was right about everything so there really was no point in arguing with him. In his own Gaelic way, my father was as off-the-wall as my mother. He considered himself a jack-of-all-trades, someone who could make, fix, or do anything. His success rate didn't quite match his estimation of his skills. To illustrate, the following stories are true and the names have not been changed because everyone was guilty.

In 1942, just after we moved to Orange Street, Dan bought and installed a doorbell, backward. Somehow he messed up the wiring, which resulted in a continuous low humming that stopped only when a visitor rang the doorbell. After two weeks of this subliminal droning, I finally spoke up.

"Dad, I think that the wires are crossed on the doorbell."

"Leave it alone," he answered.

So, we sat in the kitchen or the living room listening to the doorbell's constant purr. And on the rare occasions that it stopped buzzing, Dan would get up and head for the door saying, "I'll get it." Some time after I called the situation to Dan's attention, I got up to go to school, and, for the first time in nearly a month, everything in the house was still. No more buzzing. Whether it was a miracle or whether Dan secretly fixed it himself, the doorbell functioned normally.

Speaking of visitors, back in those days people actually visited one another. You didn't wait for a formal invitation, either; most often you dropped over to a friend's house just to say hello. As I remember, Sophia and Dan did less dropping in on folks than receiving them. People would appear at the front door and be invited in. Sophia would bring out some goodies and, depending on the time of day, she'd serve coffee or tea. Also, depending on the hour, Dan would offer up some of his home brew. We welcomed most everyone except for one particular family, a husband, wife, and their twin girls who were a couple of years younger than me. I honestly can't remember why these folks weren't welcome, but there are some people who simply aren't pleasant to be around. If we were lucky we could avoid their visit. At her command head-quarters at the kitchen window Sophia could spot anyone approaching. Whenever that particular family came around, we'd go into red alert. (I just had a thought. I have to say that Sophia Murgoi Conway spent 90 percent of her day in the kitchen. What's more, I don't think she was alone. Mothers were in kitchens when I was young. I'm not saying that's where they should be—far from it—but it's funny how you get used to something and then it all changes.) The minute Sophia caught sight of their car coming up the drive, she'd cry out, "*O, Dumnezeule, sunt aici!*" ("Oh Lord, they're here!")

That was the signal for us to dive under the kitchen table and pull the tablecloth down to the floor. We'd huddle together behind the protective cloth, whispering to each other, while they peered in through the windows to see if we were home. We wouldn't come out until at least five minutes after we heard their car leave. At that point, Sophia would lift the tablecloth and cautiously take a peek. When she was pretty sure we were out of danger, she'd crawl out and take another look through the window just to make certain they weren't doubling back. Then she'd give us the all clear.

Rubbing his bad knee, my dad would emerge and slowly get to his feet. I liked being under the table—it was cozy—so I took my time surfacing. Even after the enemy forces were long gone, we'd continue our whispering, just in case. On those rare occasions when the family slipped under Sophia's radar, they were admitted into the house and we would sit with them in the living room. Sophia didn't offer any goodies or beverages and neither did Dan. Nor did my parents initiate any conversation. The enemy didn't take the hint and hung around for what seemed like ages. It was torture. Funny, though, when I got older I actually missed those visits and the excitement of diving under the table. Sometimes I'd pretend that we were a family of French partisans hiding from the Nazis.

Like Sophia, Dan, a basically honest man, had a larcenous side that popped up now and again, especially on Christmas Eve. Although our Christmas was as normal as anyone else's, the night before was different. My father was no more likely to buy a Christmas tree than my mother was to buy wallpaper paste. Starting in December of 1938, here's how Dan got our trees.

He'd drive home on River Road till he reached the White's property, when he'd pull over and turn off the ignition. Next, he'd take a long, slow look at the evergreens growing near the roadside. When he spotted one that suited him, he'd reach in the back, grab a handsaw lying on the seat, and get out of the car. He'd walk over to the chosen tree, cut off the top, and bring it home. I know exactly how many years he did this. In the mid-'60s and early '70s, I'd bring my kids to Chagrin for a few weeks in the summer. During our visits, I'd take them for a ride down River Road and point out the topless evergreens. There were exactly fourteen. Unless some other crazy man was decapitating them, those trees were the remains of the Conways' Tannenbaums.

Dan could pull a stunt like that and Sophie could load up on caviar and shoes and it was okay, but I was never supposed to do any-thing the least bit shady. It was inevitable that I would. I was around nine when Dan took me shopping at the Sears on Mayfield Road. When we walked out of the store, I showed him a screw I'd taken from a display bin in the hardware department. Dan didn't say a word as we got into whatever rattletrap Ford he owned at the moment.

"Stay here, I forgot something," he suddenly announced. He got out and went back into Sears. Within a few minutes of his departure, a policeman came over to the car and motioned for me to open the window.

"What's your name?" he asked.

"Tom," I replied. (Oops, forgot to mention that by this time Toma had been Americanized. How did I become Tim? I'll tell you later; I'm in the middle of a story.)

"Tom what?"

"Tom Conway."

"And where do you live?" he continued. I was getting worried.

"Oak Street," I gulped.

"Step out of the car," he ordered.

Now, I was just plain terrified. I opened the door and got out. He told me to raise my arms, which I did.

"Do you know what shoplifting is, Tom?" he asked as he reached into my pocket and withdrew the screw.

I remember thinking, "These cops are well trained; they can spot shoplifters in two seconds."

He took his handcuffs off his belt and dangled them in front of me.

"Are you ever going to do anything like this again?"

"No, sir," I fairly shrieked.

"Okay, I'm going to let you go this time, but if it happens again, I'm going to take you in and lock you up."

With that, he turned and left me trembling on the pavement. I got back into the car and Dan returned.

"What did the cop want?" he asked as he got behind the wheel.

I sat there staring straight ahead, unable to speak. Dan backed out the car and looked over at me.

"Did you pee your pants?"

I didn't have to answer. I was loaded with evidence. Believe me, I learned my lesson. I never stole anything again. How could I when I assumed that the next time meant I'd get the electric chair. You gotta hand it to them, Dan and Sophia were blithe spirits, for sure, but I learned a lot of life lessons from them. Lessons I tried to pass on to my own kids.

It's hard to move away from Dan stories because I love telling them. You always could rely on him to say or to do something wacky. We were living in the larger two-story section of the two-family Orange Street house, which, as I've said, was our most elegant and permanent residence. Rex Hollis, our landlord, and his wife lived in the smaller section. Rex worked in the transportation department of the Chagrin Falls Township; he drove a snowplow in the winter, fixed potholes in the spring, and painted yellow lines on the roads in the summer and fall. No wonder Orange Street was one of the first to be plowed in winter and among the first to have the potholes filled in the spring. Our home, a real palace compared to the Oak Street garage, stood on a small knoll and had four huge white pillars in front. Like I said, the rent was a little pricey for Dan and Sophia but they paid it. As far as Sophia was concerned, the basement was the one drawback. The floor was dirt, which got very damp, and there was very little headroom. Sophia, however, got it into her head that the dirt had to be replaced with cement. At that time Dan was working for the Mitchell Coal and Cement

Company and was able to fulfill Sophia's wish. He did this by borrowing a little bit from each cement order he was assigned to fill. On his way to the designated purchaser, he'd stop at our house, back up the truck, empty a small portion of the load down our coal shoot, then hurry downstairs to smooth things out before setting off for the final destination on his delivery schedule. The process took many weeks to finish. Because he used bits and pieces from many different orders, the color and texture of the floor varied wildly. Some of it was blue, some green, some had large pieces of gravel while other portions were smooth with white stones mixed in, the kind you see around fancy swimming pools or bird baths. It was pretty psychedelic.

When the house was built back in the early 1800s, the basement was purely and simply for storage; a pot-bellied stove in the first-floor living room provided heat. Years before we moved in, a proper furnace had been installed. Periodically, Dan had to go to the cellar and stoke the thing. Dan soon learned to stoop over when he went to tend the boiler. He had to because the clearance from the dirt floor to the ceiling was about five feet four inches. Those were the dimensions before Dan laid down his three-inch, multi-textured masterpiece. You can do the math. The change affected two out of three Conways. At a little over five feet, Sophia could clear the beams except when she wore her work shoes with their raised inner soles. Then, she could count on a rap or two. I was completely in the safety zone. Dan was another story. At five feet ten inches, he was in constant jeopardy. We always knew when he banged himself, since any blow was announced by a long, dragged out cry of *"Jaanneey Maaac!"* ("Janey Mac" is an Irish euphemism for the Lord's name that dates back to the mid-nineteenth century. It's used in order not to take His name in vain. Unaware of this at the time, I thought Janey Mac might be a relative.) Sophia would go to the top of the basement stairs and call down, "You all right?" A long pause would ensue, followed by another howl.

"Get me a Band-Aid, dammmmit!"

My father had a permanent piece of plaster on his forehead until he wised up. He learned to stoop over, way over, on his way down to the cellar and never stood upright until he returned to the first floor.

Were my father and mother truly as eccentric as I remember? I think so. Almost every memory I have of them is a study in lunacy. Thanks to Dan and Sophia, I lived in a benign twilight zone. Following are a few more uncensored examples of the craziness that enveloped my growing up years, especially as they relate to my father.

Did you ever hear the one about the Irishman and the Scotsman? Well, here's the Conway version. Dan's best friend was Bill Butler, a red-faced, bowlegged Scotsman with a thick brogue. When my father and he got together, between Dan's Irish accent and Bill's Scottish one, it was anybody's guess as to what was being said. They met mucking out the stalls at the Polo Club and became instant friends. They were inseparable. Among other joint ventures, Bill assisted my father in brewing, bottling, and corking his homemade beer in our kitchen brewery. The Anheuser and Busch of Chagrin often added extra yeast which would cause the beer to cook a little too rapidly. That, in turn, caused the bottles to pop their caps long before the yeast had finished fermenting. Sometimes there'd be a big blow off in the middle of the night. I'd lie in bed and listen to the *pop-pop-pop* of the bottle caps hitting the ceiling. (No surprise, our kitchen ceiling was polka-dotted with beer spots.) At the first *pop*, Dan would rush down to the "brewery" and try to salvage at least a swig of the swill he and his pal optimistically called beer. Dan drank what little remained. Barely a drop was left for Bill.

Bill was lucky to miss out on a lot of the brewed product, but that's where his luck ran out. The poor man barely survived being Dan Conway's best friend. Seriously, my father inflicted a lot of physical damage on his buddy. One of the closest calls happened when they were ratting out the stables.

Rodents burrowed tunnels under the clay floors of the stalls, and every so often they had to be exterminated. Usually Dan would stick a garden hose down a rat hole and turn on the water. Bill waited at another hole with a raised baseball bat. When Mickey Mouse's distant relatives came up for air, they'd get a bonk on the noggin that finished them off. This was the established procedure but, of course, Dan Conway had to build a better rattrap. Drawing on his Irish wisdom, he came up with an alternate plan. I happened to be with him on the day that he put the plan into play. The three of us drove over to the barn where the horses were kept. Dan backed up the truck as close to the barn as possible, connected the garden hose to the exhaust pipe, and ran the hose into a hole in the stall floor. Bat in hand Bill went into the barn. Dan thought he should be at the ready in case any dazed rat managed to make it to the surface. Do you see the flaw, here? If so, you qualify as far brighter than either Bill Butler or Dan Conway. I sat in the front of the truck with my father and watched as he pumped the gas pedal. After a short spell, Dan and I got out of the truck and went into the barn to see what was up.

"Aye, Bill!" cried my father.

No answer.

"Where are ye, Billy?"

Still no response. We followed the hose to the end to see how many rats Bill had stacked up. The only thing on the ground was

Bill, still clutching the bat in his hands but barely conscious. No wonder. Along with the rats, he'd been inhaling the exhaust fumes. Dan got behind him, grabbed him under the arms, and pulled him out of the barn. He propped Bill up against the barn wall and began slapping his face. At first, Bill didn't seem to notice, then he shook his head, looked blearily at my dad and cried, "Stop yerrr slappin'!"

Once Bill revived, I waited with him while Dan went to the truck where he turned off the ignition, and then removed the hose from the exhaust pipe. We helped Bill into the truck and took off for home. The Pied Pipers ended the evening guzzling their beer in our kitchen. If my father was looking for a better way to kill the rats, he should have considered pouring his brew into the rat holes. It would have wiped out Chagrin's entire rodent population.

Another of Bill's misadventures with Dan took place during the second chukker of a polo match on Mr. White's field. A horse fell and broke his right front leg. Sad to say such accidents do happen in racing as well as in polo matches. The galloping horses kick up the turf creating gaps in the ground. If a clump of dirt is over a ground hog's tunnel then a really large hole can result. And, if a horse steps into it he'll likely snap his leg and crash to the ground. More often than not, there's no hope of repairing the injury and the horse has to be euthanized. Today, a track vet will give the beast a lethal injection. In those days wounded animals didn't get shots, they got shot. It was a horrible scene. A couple of guys would hold up a blanket to hide the poor beast while another pair of men went behind the blanket, one to keep the horse on the ground and the other to shoot him. Once the shot was fired, the blanket holders would let it drop over the dead horse. Then all four guys would drag the covered carcass onto a sled and take it off the field. It didn't happen that often, but when it did, it was terrible.

That afternoon at Mr. White's, the minute the polo pony dropped, Dan and Bill jumped into the pickup truck, drove over the field, and pulled up near the fallen animal. They got out and assessed the damage. Unfortunately, it was the worst-case scenario; the polo pony had to be destroyed. Two guys held up the blanket while Dan took a .22 rifle from the truck. Meanwhile, Bill took the horse's head between his hands and held it down to keep the horse from trying to get up on his feet. Dan and Bill were behind the blanket, and all that the spectators in the bleachers could see was the raised blanket and the horse's legs sticking out. Bill finally got the horse's head secured and gave Dan the signal. Dan placed the rifle on the beast's forehead and fired. There was a moment of silence and then came a howl in the distinct brogue of a certain Scotsman.

"Ya crazy *bampot*, you've shot me! (In case you're wondering, *bampot* is a Scottish word for "idiot.")

In the same instant that the animal was put out of his misery, Bill Butler was put into his. The bullet went right through the horse's head and Bill's foot. With one shot, Dan euthanized the horse and blew off his friend's little toe. From that day on Bill walked favoring his right leg.

One December 31st, Dan and I, and Bill and his son, Billy— my best friend—were on our way down River Road to Gates Mills and the Chagrin Valley Hunt Club to feed and water the horses. Dan and Big Bill sat in the front of the old Ford, and Little Bill and I were in the back nestled against a dozen bottles of Dan's home brew. The number of bottles in the back decreased as two were passed along into the front seat and emptied by Dan and Big Bill. We arrived at the stable, and the two of them, fortified by beers, continued their early celebration of New Year's Eve. While they began mucking the stalls and pitching hay to the twenty or so horses, Billy and I went out to the polo field and tossed a ball back and forth. We returned to the barn and found Dan looking for Big Bill. We joined the search and soon found Little Bill's dad passed out in one of the stalls. Dan, Little Bill, and I got him to the car and shoved him into the front seat. Billy and I jumped in the back as Dan slammed the passenger door and went around to the driver's seat. We started the journey home and had traveled a few miles when Big Bill started moaning something that sounded like, "Brakeihhairin."

He said it over and over, and each time he moaned, Dan would call out, "Shut up."

We reached Bill's house, and Dan got out and went around to help his friend out of the car. When he opened the door, he discovered that he'd closed it on Bill's hand. From then on, four of Bill's five fingers went in different directions. It didn't seem to hinder his work, but he did have trouble pointing.

Several years passed before Bill received his next body-altering blow.

It happened in the Orange Street house. All the kitchen appliances were plugged into one extension cord, and if too many appliances were turned on the fuses blew. It happened a lot of times until Dan put a penny in the fuse box, which seemed to handle the overload. (Please, don't ask me any technical questions about this. I saw him do it and I saw the result, and that's all I know.) One fine day Sophia wanted an electrical extension in their upstairs bedroom. Dan consulted with Bill, and the Edison and Tesla of Chagrin set about granting Sophia's wish. They bought twenty feet of electrical wire, a four-way plug, and electrical tape. The plan was to tap into the already overloaded kitchen outlet, run the wire through the polka-dotted ceiling, and connect it to the newly installed four-way plug in the upstairs hallway. Dan drilled a hole through the kitchen ceiling and then needed to figure out where it was going to emerge in the hallway. Big Bill said he'd go upstairs and find the exact spot, and off he went. Meanwhile, Dan got a broom to stick up through the hole so Bill could easily find it. I assume the pending calamity is making itself clear. Bill saw traces of sawdust and the edges of a circle. He cupped his hands over the soon-to-be hole, and lowered his head onto the top of his hands. His eye was right over the hole. At that moment, Dan pushed the broom handle through the ceiling and into Bill's eye. Bill was an amateur boxer and capable of taking some pretty big blows, but the old broom in the eye floored him.

The last time I saw Bill Butler was a few months after my Dad's funeral. Charlene and I were in Chagrin and ran into Bill at Dinks, a local restaurant. He spotted us with his good eye, limped over to our table, stuck out his hand with the fingers pointing in different directions, and as I took his crippled hand in mine, said with loving sincerity, "Ah, Tommy lad, how I miss yer Dad."

Me, too, Big Bill. Me, too.

Few of Dan's acquaintances escaped unscathed. Poor Rex Hollis was another victim. One January morning, my Dad got in the old Ford, gave the key a turn, and the engine sputtered to a slow, wintry start. He tried to back out the car, but it wouldn't budge. Rex saw what was happening through a window and, being a neighborly type of fellow, came out and asked if he could help.

"If ye'd get in front and give the car some pushes whilst I press on the accelerator, I think I'd be able to back out," answered Dan.

So, Rex got in front and with his hands gripping the bumper began to rock the car as Dan gently pressed the gas pedal while shifting from forward to reverse.

"Now, gun it in reverse," Rex called out.

My dad floored the pedal and Rex, his hands firmly on the

bumper, gave a huge push. The car moved back. Oh, I should mention that a tree stump under the car was sticking up high enough to catch the bumper as the car scraped over it. Well, the final push did it, and my Dad backed out, waved to Rex, and drove on to work. Had he glanced in the rearview mirror, he would have seen Rex waving good-bye with all three fingers of his right hand. That's right, three. You see when the car scraped over the stump Rex's hand went with it, and that little maneuver amputated the tips of two fingers on his hand. Miracle of miracles, they remained friends.

Perhaps because Dan and I were related by blood, I only suffered minor indignities, not physical harm.

The next case in the Daniel Conway dossier.

Rex offered Dan a can of yellow paint left over from his spring roadwork chores. Why he assumed that my father would have any use for it is beyond me. But, as usual, Dan came up with something.

"C'mon down, Tommy," he called up to my room. "We've got some work to do. We're going to surprise Sophia." I came down and found Dan standing with the paint can in one hand and two brushes in the other.

"Here, take this," he said, handing me one of the brushes. "You know how your mother's been after me about how bad the car looks? Well, we're going to spruce it up with a coat of paint."

So saying, he marched out the front door with me close behind. And that's how it happened that my father and I set about painting our broken-down Ford a lurid yellow. The color would have been weird enough on its own, but there's more. The car was parked in front of the house, and Dan and I got right to work. We moved fast. We had to because the paint had a quick-drying element that made it difficult to apply. Remember, it was meant for painting lines on asphalt not for sprucing up automobiles. We finished and went into the house for a spot of ice tea. That's the good part of the story. The bad part—it was summer and Canadian soldiers had inundated our town.

For those who don't know what I'm talking about, let me explain. Canadian soldiers are mayflies, huge bugs that resemble the praying mantis. They have really large wings and travel in large swarms that come down from Canada by way of Lake Erie in late spring. They're a force to be reckoned with, and that force had already arrived in Chagrin, which Dan and I discovered when we returned to the car. What a sight. Maybe it was the smell of the paint that attracted them, but whatever the reason, the result was hundreds, possibly thousands of those bugs stuck to the Ford. Their transparent wings were fluttering like crazy, but their bodies weren't going anywhere. (I think if one more swarm had landed, those insects could have picked up the car and carried it off.) Dan rubbed the back of his head and said, "Your mother's got to see this."

I didn't know why Sophia had to see it, but I wasn't going to argue.

At this point, Sophia was making slipcovers to order, a business that involved two visits to a customer's home. The first was to take the measurements, and the second was to drape the finished product over the chair or sofa and collect the fee. Sophia was on one of her slipcover gigs when, bug wings flapping in the breeze, Dan and I drove over to get her. We pulled up to the curb, got out, and stood beside the lemon-colored Bugmobile. Sophia came out of the house, took one look, and cried, *"Ce s-a întâmplat?"* ("What happened?")

Dan explained. Her face contorted with disgust, Sophia got into the car and grumbled in Romanian as we drove back home.

On the way she drew a dollar from her purse and handed the money to Dan saying, "Stop at hardware store and buy black paint."

That same day, Dan and I scraped away the bugs and applied two coats of black paint. The result was lumpy but at least it was black and not bright yellow.

Here's another example of my father's idiosyncratic thinking. Dan had his own particular logic that rarely, okay, *never* resulted in a simple one-plus-one-equals-two formula. Late one afternoon on Orange Street, Dan and I were sitting at the kitchen table, Sophia was at the sink, and Lum and Abner were chattering on the radio. (Lum and Abner were radio, movie, and TV stars for twenty-five years. They also were a major influence on country shows like *The Beverly Hillbillies, Green Acres, The Andy Griffith Show,* and *Hee Haw.* Today they're almost totally forgotten.) All of a sudden you could see the sky turning an eerie reddish color through the window. At the same moment, a *whoosh*ing sound filled the air. The next second, the sky went dark and we heard what sounded like a train thundering up the street. Then, everything was silent.

Dan got up slowly from the table and went to the front door. I was right behind him. He opened the door and stepped out onto the porch with me on his heels. The first thing I noticed was the house across the street no longer had a roof. I saw that trees, not only in our yard but all up and down the street, had either been uprooted or had broken branches dangling from them. Telephone poles, some split down the middle, were a jumble of loose wires. Debris was scattered everywhere. A tornado had torn a path along the river, and Orange Street was one of the hardest hit areas. It was chaos. Dan stood there, hands on his hips, taking in the scene. He looked up the street, then down, then back up again, and shaking his head muttered, "Those damn kids."

My parents' quirks were complementary, and they enjoyed each other's company. They liked to do things together, like dancing. One time they decided to take dancing lessons at a local studio. At the first lesson they were given a strip of paper with two sets of footprints on it, one for the man and the other for the woman. It was a basic dance pattern. The idea was to take the sheet home, put it on the floor, put a record on the phonograph, and step on the appropriate footprints in time with the music. Simple, right? Not for my parents. When I came home from school, I found them standing in the middle of the living room with the music blaring from the phonograph. They looked at me sheepishly and asked if I could help them. Help them? How could I help them when what they'd done was cut out the footprints from the paper and pasted them on the bottom of their shoes? I guess they figured that would make the shoes magically do the steps. When it didn't happen they were stopped in their glued-on tracks.

Chagrin Falls

We were living the good life in Chagrin Falls when the day came, and I knew it would, because Sophia kept saying it was coming: I was to start school. I was afraid that it might not be the easiest of transitions and I was right. At home I was numero uno and firmly attached to my mother. Forgive me, but I can't resist saying I learned more at Sophia's knee than at any other joint. You already know about my wallpapering skill. What you don't know is that my mother also taught me how to clean, how to cook, and how to sew. Nobody cleans a house better than I do, and I cook very well, too. I was at Sophia's side when she prepared meals and I watched everything she did. I also honed my cooking skills at the Chagrin Valley Hunt Club. On weekends and during summer vacations, I worked in the club restaurant and on the fox hunt catering truck. My chores at the restaurant consisted of buffing floors, washing and drying pots and pans, emptying garbage, sharpening knives, and peeling and washing whatever needed peeling and washing. Except for the floor buffing, I did the exact same chores at the catering truck. The chef was a good guy. I learned a lot by watching him. After a while, he let me assist him. I made simple dishes and salads. My pièce de résistance (chef talk for "specialty") was hardboiled eggs. One cooking task I hated was throwing lobsters into boiling water. "They don't feel a thing," the chef assured me. Still, I had nightmares about it. I'd wake up in a cold sweat after dreaming about lobsters scratching at the side of a pot desperately trying to get out. Lobster phobia aside, I still can turn out pretty good chow, old-fashioned food with—thank you, Sophia—a slight bow to Romania. Don't scoff, Romanian cooking blends Turkish, Hungarian, Greek, Slavic, and French styles into a lot of great dishes. You want recipes? Just ask.

In 1940, I was enrolled in Chagrin Falls Exempted School, a big, red-brick building with no distinguishing architecture; it was just a square, red-brick building. The school housed grades one through twelve. When I graduated there were fifty-two students in my class and, although a new high school has been built since then, I'm pretty sure no more than sixty-five or seventy students graduate today. Hey, it's a small town. The Exempted contained a really big gym, a good-size auditorium, and a large shop with all the tools necessary to make a little shelf to hang at home. When I took Shop in eighth grade, I didn't make a shelf, I made a bar, the first and only one ever created in the Chagrin Falls Exempted School. Norman Frye, a great guy, taught Shop. Though he questioned why I wanted to make a bar and not a shelf, he let me do it. I set it up in my bedroom and invited my friends over for drinks. I'd get behind my bar and serve Cokes.

My first day at school was challenging. First, in terms of

distance—it was a good two-mile walk from our house. Because Dan had to leave at 7:00 A.M. to feed and exercise Mr. White's horses, I had no ride. My transportation was my two-sizes-too-big, brown-and-white saddle shoes that Sophia "borrowed" from Thomas White's son, Timmy. She gave them to me saying, *"Timmy a abundentei de pantofi. El nu vrea sa la pierdet."* ("Timmy has plenty of shoes. He won't miss these.")

Besides the long trek, another hurdle loomed. Up until that first school day, I had never been beyond shouting distance of my mom or dad. Now I was about to spend an entire day out of their decibel range. I was a bit downcast at the prospect. Sophia wasn't exactly jumping for joy, either. In fact, she walked over to the school and spent hours sitting on the schoolhouse steps waiting for me to appear. Stella Dallas had nothing on Sophia Murgoi Conway. Not surprisingly, my biggest problem that first day was directly attributable to my dear mother who, as I've mentioned, had been speaking to me in her native tongue since the day I was born. Romanian was practically my primary language, a fact which Mrs. Palmer, the first grade teacher, couldn't quite grasp. When she asked me a question in English, I responded in my finest Romanian. She continued in English. Smiling broadly, I replied in, you guessed it, Romanian. My seventeen classmates kept looking back and forth between the teacher and the pupil trying to figure out who was on the right page. At last, very slowly and very deliberately, Mrs. Palmer asked, "Do . . . you . . . speak . . . English?"

"Da, îmi face," I exclaimed, which translates as "Yes, I do."

Mrs. Palmer sighed and spoke once again in that slow, deliberate way people speak when the listener seems not to understand. Don't get me wrong, I understood and could speak English, but somehow I equated "teacher" with "mother" and thought it was more respectful to speak Romanian to her.

"Toma . . . where . . . is . . . your . . . mother?"

I responded just as slowly and just as deliberately, *"Ea . . . este . . . lucru."* ("She is working.")

Mrs. Palmer gave up.

The day went quickly. By the time the teacher passed out paper cups, poured the milk, and handed out Fig Newtons, my assimilation process had picked up speed. Somewhere between *cookie-uri și lapte* ("cookies and milk") and dismissal time, I decided to file Romanian under What to Speak When I Visit Bucharest and joined my American classmates in using English exclusively. I only talked the old country language with Sophia and I completely stopped doing that around the time I entered the third grade.

"English, Ma, say it in English," I'd tell her.

Good old Sophia could never say no to Crown Prince Toma, and from that time on gamely struggled to speak like an American. Today, I couldn't hold a conversation in Romanian if my life depended on it. However, I did put my mother's mangled English to good use at least twice in my career.

The first practitioner of the Sophia Murgoi speaking style, Mr. Tudball, an ongoing character I portrayed on *The Carol Burnett Show*, had a funny way of talking that people loved to imitate. What I actually did was put the word "huh" in front of other words, like "huh-what are you huh-doing?" Most people thought my accent was Swedish but it wasn't, it was Sophia-ish, something I pulled from my memories of listening to her. In the many sketches that were aired, Tudball's dizzy secretary, Wanda Wiggins, aka Mrs. huh-Wiggins, played brilliantly by Carol, drove him to distraction. Their battles were as much fun for Carol and me to do as they apparently were for audiences to watch.

The second character to benefit from my mother's eccentric English was Dorf, the stunted fellow in the bad toupee who spoke a similar mishmash of my mother's tongue. More on him later; I've got to get back to school days before I'm arrested for truancy.

Another school-associated trauma, one that was not solved as quickly as the language gap, concerned my clothing, specifically, my pants. What was once a mortifying experience for boys of my generation has been almost completely forgotten. I'm talking about the squeaky pants syndrome that plagued all of us who wore corduroy knickers, and we were legion. You couldn't take two steps without announcing your approach because the friction of two corduroy-wrapped legs rubbing together made a distinct *squeak-squeak* sound. The individual squeak was bad enough but an orchestra of squeaks was earsplitting. Try to imagine a school hallway filled with lads racing to class with all those cords rubbing together. If you were wearing corduroy knickers, you could not hope to go undetected. Did you ever hear of a bank robber, CIA agent, or hired assassin outfitted in cords? Mothers loved them; they probably invented them to keep track of their sons. Forget about sneaking past your parents' bedroom when you came home late from a school-night movie. You could walk as bowlegged as an old cowpoke, but that corduroy couldn't be shushed. Sophia always knew when I came in the front door because she could hear me coming from four blocks away. She kept me in cords well into the eighth grade until, one glorious day—I must have been fourteen years old—she ditched them and I moved into some silent material. What a joy to walk down the street without people making cracks. For a while, though, I missed it; there was something comforting in being accompanied by the sound of your own pants.

Grades one through six at Chagrin Falls Exempted School were relatively uneventful, but there were bright spots here and there. One of them came first thing in the morning when you arrived at the crossing of Washington and Franklin Streets. Officer Smith, the cop who stood guard there, was a big, friendly guy known to one and all as "Smitty." Every kid who crossed that intersection had a daily treat. You'd stand poised on the sidewalk and then, at the signal change, rush halfway across into Smitty's outstretched arms. He'd give you a wide swing in the air, turn you around, put you down, and you'd race to the other side. Sometimes the line of kids waiting to get their swing would be so long, you had to wait for two light changes before it was your turn. Even so, no one was ever late for school because of Officer Smith. Smitty was one of a kind.

There was another Chagrin Falls' citizen who had a big impact on our lives. His name was Ken Shutts, and he established, owned, and ran Chagrin Hardware. Ken's store was one of the great destinations of my early life. The shelves were jam-packed with every possible article that came under the heading of hardware, and the store itself was a gathering place. You didn't just come in for a washer or a lightbulb or a screwdriver; you came to while away the time chatting with your neighbors and the proprietor. Ken was always present; I'm not so sure that he wasn't born in that store. The only problem with shopping there was that Ken ordered so many things that he lost track of his merchandise. Legend has it that a guy from the IRS once turned up and confronted him.

"I'm from the Internal Revenue Service, and we noticed that you haven't filed an inventory accounting for Chagrin Hardware. Is there a reason for this, sir?"

"Yes," answered Ken. "There's too much stuff to waste time counting it."

Besides his hardware store duties, Ken Shutts was the town's unofficial psychiatrist. You got a problem? Step into his office over by the bird feeders. No kidding, if a kid got in trouble, his parents were likely to bring him (*him*, girls didn't get into trouble in those days) to Dr. Shutts. Ken would have a serious talk with the wrongdoer and pass sentence. No matter what the crime, the punishment remained the same, two weeks of hard labor in the hardware store. He'd set the offender to counting screws, rubber washers, mouse traps, etc., and apparently never shared the results of their labor with the IRS. I served my time in the Hardware counting drawer knobs. Long after I left Chagrin Falls, Ken Shutts remained a very important part of my life.

When I was in the third year of *McHale's Navy*, I received a phone call from my mother, supposedly to discuss her grandchildren. She had an ulterior motive and soon got to the point.

"Tommy, I'm hearing that Ken Shutts is going to hire another person to help in hardware store."

"So?"

"Well, I'm thinking you know Ken pretty well. Why don't you see if he would consider taking you on."

I looked into space for a moment and then, with superhuman control, said into the receiver, "Ma, have you been watching TV for the last three years? I've been doing a television series."

"I know, I know. I saw it, but that crap isn't going to last. You got chance to get good steady job. You should take it."

Ken Shutts has gone to the big Hardware in the sky where he's most likely ordering halos in assorted colors. But the family is still running the store. Please, if you're anywhere near Chagrin Falls I urge you, drop in. It's like walking into history.

Throughout my school years, I was an average student—rather, a little below average. Although I wasn't diagnosed with it until many years later, dyslexia was a big contributor to my less-than-impressive grades. Even though it wasn't easy to live with, especially because I didn't realize I was living with it, being dyslexic probably was a key contributor to my comic outlook on life. Being funny was a defensive ploy. I was always the smallest kid in the class; humor kept me from getting smacked around. Whenever I was called on to read aloud in school, I'd mess up words or put things into sentences that were nowhere to be found on the page. Everybody thought I was kidding and my efforts usually ended with my classmates laughing their heads off. One time I did a book report on *They Were Expendable*, a popular novel about World War II. I read it as *They Were Expandable*. The class went wild.

"Expandable? What are you talking about, rubber people?"

Their laughter poured over me. I thought, gee, I must be funny. I got a taste of performing the hard way and I liked the results. Of course, I can't discount the original influential comedic source, Dan and Sophia, my in-house George Burns and Gracie Allen.

Going into the seventh grade was somewhat different. I still had the same classmates, but the classes were held in another section of the school where we had almost no contact with the younger kids. My best friend, Marty Hawthorne, and I moved on up together. Marty was a bit skinnier and taller than I—then again, who wasn't—and our combined IQ probably wouldn't have added up to a hundred and ten. No wonder we enjoyed each other's company. We liked the same radio shows, sports, movies, and all the stuff that bonds kids. We had another chum, Dean Imars, who was a bit more serious. Dean was taller than I, of course, and stocky. I'm sorry to say that Marty and I often took advantage of Dean, mostly because he was not quite as nutty as we were. Dean had a weekly paper route and was paid on Friday afternoon. Marty and I would meet him and suggest a visit to Bright's Drugstore. Mr. Bright, of pool/outhouse fame, ran the local pharmacy, a real old-fashioned drugstore complete with soda fountain. We would convince Dean to join us at the fountain, and once the root beer floats we ordered were finished, Marty and I would run off, leaving Dean to pay. After all, he was the wage earner.

The number of stupid things kids did in those days was some-thing. Our hijinks may have been dumb but they weren't mean, just silly stunts that made us laugh. Generally speaking, no one got hurt, physically or otherwise. For example, after trips to the movie theatre, Marty and I would stop in front of the A&P for a bit of fun. The A&P had a cat that roamed the store at night to keep the rodent population from exploding. The cat's name was Oscar. The store had a big window in front where cereal boxes were displayed. We'd stand at the window and try to catch Oscar's attention. He'd almost always come around. When he did appear, we waited till he got close and then we'd start yelling and banging on the window. Poor Oscar would turn tail and run through the stacked boxes of cereal. Down they'd tumble. The idea was to see how many boxes we could get Oscar to knock over. One magical evening, Marty really frightened Oscar, who promptly upended an unbelievable twenty-six boxes of Wheaties. We wrote to General Mills, gave them the count, and asked if they would put a picture of Marty on their box cover. They actually wrote back and said that a kid from Michigan named Howard held the record of thirty-one boxes. We had no way of checking, but I'm sure they were brushing us off. I know I never saw a box of Wheaties with a "Howard" on it.

I yearned to have a proper pet like Oscar the cat, but we watched our pennies pretty closely so I had to make do with other kinds of animals. Over the years I had some rats, a rabbit, a lizard, and a bird. It wasn't a fancy bird like a canary, but a regular bird, probably a sparrow. I also remember a chicken I named Clucky. I considered him a pet, but he went missing one day and that night we had fried chicken for dinner. *Hmmm.* There was a dog that strayed into our yard once and stuck around because no one claimed him. I named him Frisky. One day Frisky made a terrible mistake; he bit Dan. Dan immediately whisked Frisky off to live on a farm, assuring me that the dog would be happier there. Dan said we could go visit him from time to time, but we never did. *Hmmmm.*

Before I forget, I've got to discuss a major part of life in the late 1930s and the 1940s: the movies. You really can't talk about small towns in those days without mentioning the local movie houses. Ours was The Falls Theatre, a typical Art Deco building, about a mile from our house. Outside stood a freestanding box office beneath a triangular-shaped marquee. You'd get a child's ticket for a dime (adults paid a whopping twenty-three cents) and go inside. You'd pause at the brightly lit candy counter, get your refreshments (for five or ten cents), show your ticket, and proceed into the dimly lit, red, plush-seat interior that reeked deliriously of freshly popped corn, not nachos or chicken fingers. Television, as we now know it, has obscured the fact that movies were the entertainment lifeline for my generation, and for the previous one, too. I'm here to tell you that nothing has ever matched the thrill of slipping into a darkened theatre, reveling in a newsreel, a selected short, a cartoon, and then, a double feature. It was entertainment with a capital *E.* I'd sit there laughing and applauding, never imagining that I'd grow up to meet and actually work with some of those bigger-than-life people on the screen. In 1964, I returned to Chagrin for the opening of the movie version of *McHale's Navy.* When I arrived at my beloved Falls Theatre, I looked up to see my name above the title on the marquee. Ernie Borgnine was the star, but in my hometown, I got top billing—one of the biggest thrills in my life!

I loved almost all movies, especially the comedies. Come to think of it, I can remember only one film that I didn't enjoy watching. I saw it on a Saturday afternoon at The Falls. I met Marty at the box office, and the two of us went in for a matinee featuring a re-release of Boris Karloff in *Frankenstein.* We bought a nickel box of popcorn to share and took our seats in the first row. There'd been a lot of hype about *Frankenstein*. We knew that it was about a doctor who rips off body parts, takes them back to his lab, and sews them together to make a monster. Big deal. Did they actually think this was going to scare people?

Marty and I began nibbling the popcorn as the story unfolded on the screen. It got a bit interesting when Dr. Frankenstein was in the lab putting The Monster together. Marty and I, seasoned moviegoers, took little notice when the music started and then began to build. Who were they kidding? They always used mood music to get you going, to prepare you for the shock of seeing something really terrible. Marty and I were totally prepared for that moment. The music became more and more frenzied, and the scene shifted to a dimly lit cobblestone street. From afar, I could hear the metallic sound of the monster's hobnail boots dragging on the stones. The rest of the folks in the theatre stopped eating their popcorn. A hushed silence filled the auditorium as everyone around us strained toward the screen.

"It's only a movie; people are so *gullible*," I thought, although that exact word might not have been in my mind.

Just then, accompanied by a deafening blast of music, The Monster came around the corner and lurched toward us. I took one look at his huge scar-seamed head held on by bolts on either side of his neck and, popcorn flying, I was up and out of my seat before you could say Jack Robinson. Marty was still sitting and chewing when I bolted, but by the time I reached the last row, he had passed me. We ripped through the doors and hit the sidewalk. Without stopping, Marty continued on his way up the hill to his house, and I was in full flight toward mine. The gray and foreboding sky matched the sky's color on the screen and, certain that The Monster had burst through that screen and was in hot pursuit, I threw a glance backward. Nothing was there, yet. I raced down Cedar Street, across Maple, cut through the Maraglia's backyard, jumped over Fram's Creek, ran up the stairs to our front porch, charged through the door, and, totally exhausted, threw myself on the three-cushioned green couch. Sophia was in the kitchen preparing supper.

"You back?" she called out. "How was movie?"

"Good," I squeaked.

"Was scary?" asked Sophia as she emerged from the kitchen.

I took a look over at the front door, made sure it was closed tight, and replied, "Not really."

I honestly don't know what I would have done without those Saturday matinees; they were an essential part of my life. So essential I still remember the shock when the price of a ticket went up from ten to fourteen cents. Even though Sophia and Dan were convinced that the price hike meant people would stop going to movies, I knew better. I was beside myself. How could I live without Roy Rogers, Hopalong Cassidy, and Flash Gordon? I wouldn't let those movie theatre owners deprive me of my beloved movies. I needed dough.

I'm sure kids today still take odd jobs to get pin money, but in my day it was a way of life. Both of my parents worked hard to make ends meet. Dan had his horses and then various other jobs while Sophia eventually dropped housekeeping and went full-time into making slipcovers. Slipcovers were all the rage, and it had to do with the economy. Maybe you couldn't buy new furniture, but there was a better chance you could scrape together enough to buy a fresh shroud for a dead chair or sofa. Sophia brought her wages home and then combined them with Dan's, and don't for a minute think that anything was deposited in a bank.

Sophia kept a cardboard box in the kitchen, which contained a bunch of envelopes marked Rent, Water, Phone, Food, Insurance, and Gas. Another envelope, marked Savings, never had anything in it. (Even if a few bucks managed to get tucked away, they'd never make it to the end of the month. Something always came up forcing my mother to rob Savings to pay Emergencies.) Sophia put the monies into their respective envelopes and, at the end of the month, would ceremoniously take out the contents of each one and pay the bills. Our lives were financed out of that cardboard box. If I wanted something that didn't fall into an envelope category, I had to provide for it.

I had two sources of income, pocket money from Sophia and Dan, which didn't amount to much, and what I earned mowing lawns and delivering newspapers, which didn't amount to much, either. Together they added up to a small something; still, it barely covered the cost of movie tickets. I couldn't hit up my parents for extras when the ticket price hike came, so I decided to add more lawns. I would have done more paper deliveries, too, but the route and the routine were prescribed. I'd cram the newspapers into a shoulder bag, get on my bike, and shoot up and down the streets, slinging the papers over the lawns and onto the front steps or porches of the subscribers. The delivery drill was always the same except on rainy days. Then, either Dan or Sophia would drive me around the block and wait in the car while, my jacket held over my head, I ran up to the front doors and dropped the news. As far as mowing, I usually could do from four to six (average) lawns in half a day. That is, until people began requesting that I cut the grass into patterns. I was a mower, not a sculptor, and this fussy stuff really slowed me down. Fortunately, another job came along; this one was a pip.

Answering an ad in the local paper, Marty and I applied for employment with a "government agency." We were interviewed, immediately hired, and went to work Friday and Saturday evenings in a small factory over a furniture store. What did the factory produce? I still have no idea. The product was "top secret" and rumored to have something to do with the military. We sat at a long table and, with our eyes covered by clear protective glasses, we drilled holes no thicker than a human hair into small pieces of plastic. We had to be very, very careful not to press too hard or we'd break the bit. The first night Marty broke at least two dozen and was quickly moved to packaging. I busted some myself, but nowhere near Marty's total so I remained a driller. Driller or packager, we each earned twenty-five cents an hour, big bread in those days.

The factory had a cloak-and-dagger atmosphere, and everything was very hush-hush. It was rumored that the plastic with the tiny holes had something to do with periscopes on submarines. Whatever their use, we were warned not to talk to anyone about what we were doing. That didn't stop Marty. He believed the story about the periscopes and the subs and went around telling everyone that we were doing top-secret work and then gave a blow-by-blow description of our top-secret work. I didn't get too upset with him for spilling the beans because I didn't buy the periscope story. Besides, the war was over so his loose lips weren't going to sink any ships. I realized one thing about my pal, though. If we really were at war, with blabbermouth Marty on my side, my life wouldn't be worth a nickel.

After a few months, I left the hole-in-the-plastic factory and found weekend work in one of the local bakeries. I still got twenty-five cents an hour but I got a "raise" in my new job, pun intended. At the end of my workday, I could take home a dozen assorted donuts and two loaves of bread, either white or rye. I opted for two white; rye bread was sticky and got in Dan's false teeth. The pay and the perks were good, but my working hours weren't. Again, I worked only Friday and Saturday nights but I had to be at the back door of the bakery at 2:30 A.M., which meant I had to walk through town even earlier. (I can just see some readers shaking their heads and saying to themselves, "a kid out on the streets at that hour?" Don't forget, this happened a long time ago in a small town. In those days, you were safe 24/7.) Many a frosty winter night found me racing through the streets, and not just because it was cold. The truth is, that old Frankenstein Monster had a habit of popping into my head, and the mere thought of him was enough to send me streaking to the bakery door. Once safely inside, I went about my appointed task, frying donuts. I discovered that, like drilling holes in plastic, it required a bit of dexterity.

I learned my new trade from a guy named Joe who owned the bakery. The first day, I stood by and watched as Joe put an extra large pan, filled with oil, on the stove. Next, he dropped a large mesh screen, with handles on either side, into the liquid. Finally, he turned on the burner. The prep over, we waited in silence for the oil to reach the proper degree of heat. If the temperature was too low, the donuts absorbed the oil and turned soggy; if it was too high, the donuts burned before they cooked through. The right temperature set the oil to bubbling, and, soon after, the bubbles to popping. If you didn't watch out, your arms would be peppered with burn spots. Joe took a tray of prepared donuts and, as the bubbles began bursting in air, quickly placed six rows of six donuts into the hot oil. So far, so simple, but now, enter skill. The top and bottom of the finished donut have to be the same color, which means you've got to know exactly when to turn over those suckers. Here's the secret. By the time he dropped number thirty-six into the bubbling oil, number one was ready to be turned. Once he finished dropping, Joe started back at number one and began tapping one edge on each of the fried donuts with a foot-long, pencil-thin stick.

The tap sent it into the air where it flipped over and fell back into the boiling grease. He went right down the line, conducting with that skinny baton while the donuts did their somersaults. When the last donut had been turned, Joe whirled around and shouted, "*Out* of the way!"

Pushing me aside, he grabbed a couple of beat-up oven mitts from a wooden table, slipped them over his hands, rushed back to the stovetop, and grasped the handles of the mesh liner. In one swift motion, he drew the screen up and out of the oil-filled pan and brought forth three dozen perfect donuts. I burst into applause. The man was a frying genius. I have to say I became pretty good at it myself. I often thought that if the showbiz thing collapsed, I could join the donut-flipping circuit.

My eighth grade year in school was marked by two significant occurrences. The first happened when we took a class trip to the Cleveland Museum of Art, and someone cut the cheese in the back of the bus. Everyone, including me, blamed it on Joey G. (not his real name) who, despite a history of such incidents, firmly denied that he was the cutter. Joey G., if you're still alive, forgive me. Okay, I've got that off my chest.

Here's the other experience.

I had just begun to notice girls. They were a little scary, and it took me a while to get comfortable with them. Did I say a while? I was twenty-seven years old when I got married the first time, and in those days that was pretty old for a guy to tie the knot. I'll get to that subject in a later chapter.

I had never thought about girls, maybe because nobody bothered to tell me the facts of life. Wait, my dad gave it a shot when I was about twelve. We were riding home through the countryside in one of Dan's fifth-hand Fords. It was fall and the grass was fading, but the trees were alive with changing colors. I looked out the window and noticed a bull and a cow out in a field. Evidently there'd been a strong wind because the bull had been blown up onto the back of the cow. I thought it looked funny and believed that the cow saw the humor in it, too, because she was smiling, or so it seemed.

"What are they doing?" I asked my father.

"They're making cookies," replied Dr. Kinsey.

This explanation confused me a bit. When I finally started dating, a girl called up one day and asked me if I wanted to come to her house and make some brownies.

"Gee, I'd love to," I said, "but I don't think it's windy enough."

With one exception, I had a pretty good time in my growing up years. My biggest disappointment was not realizing my childhood dream of becoming a jockey. I've loved horses all my life. Why wouldn't I? I was surrounded by them when I was a kid. One thing I learned is that you shouldn't have one as a pet. They're not bright. And even if they were bright, what can you do with them? You can't teach them to fetch the evening paper. You can't put them on your lap and watch TV with them. And you can't just put a bowl of food on the kitchen floor to feed them. Nope, horses are swell to ride, period.

When I grew too big to accompany Sophia on her housekeeping rounds, Dan brought me to Mr. White's stables to help him. Basically my job was to clean the polo ponies' stalls. Not very exciting work but there was a plus side. Besides his polo ponies, Mr. White owned a couple of racehorses that he ran at Randall Park in Cleveland. My father trained them. Well, he didn't fully train them because he didn't have the knowledge, but what he did have was his whip. Just a snap of his wrist and the resounding crack was enough to keep the horses in line. On weekends Dan would take me to Randall Park and let me ride with him while he exercised the horses. I'd be seated on some docile old mare following my father down the track but in my mind, I was up on Man o' War getting ready for the big race. I'd ridden my pillow and the back of the green sofa to victory after victory; now I was on the real McCoy. Well, more McNag than McCoy, but that didn't stop me from daydreaming. From time to time, I was allowed to climb on a horse and run him around the training track. What a thrill. Honestly, there's nothing like it. It's hard to put the feeling into words. It's like you own the world. I wanted nothing more than to become a jockey, but a few things stood in the way. First of all, I didn't have a clue as to what being a jockey meant. I thought you just put on your silks, pulled on your boots, grabbed the crop, hopped on your steed, got in the starting gate, and, *bingo*, you were off like a shot. Of course, you crossed the finish line first, and then you and your horse were brought to the winner's circle and the roses were draped over the horse's neck. Ha.

The truth is thoroughbred racing jockeys are among the best-trained athletes in the world. They put their lives on the line every time they get a leg up. It's an unimaginably difficult life. Their days are spent exercising, dieting, lifting weights, running several miles, as well as rising at 4 A.M. to work out the horses. In general, a jockey starts his career at around fourteen or fifteen years old, a very early age because they're restricted to a one-hundred-and-ten-pound limit. Imagine being that age, that weight, and climbing aboard a totally unpredictable one-thousand-pound animal that is not exactly a rocket scientist. A racehorse knows how to run fast and turn left or—if he's running in Europe—right; the rider supplies everything else. And, he has to do this from the most precarious position imaginable.

When you're atop a racehorse, you're not comfortably seated in an enveloping saddle. You've got a thin strip of leather between you and the hard body of your steed. Your butt is in the air and only the toes of your boots are in the stirrup, the soles and the heels are hanging out there just like your rear end. The only thing you have to hold on to is a slender rein. Real jockeys will tell you that you have to be fearless when racing. Your mind has to be dead set on doing your job. The moment your thoughts wander—*What am I doing here? How fast is this thing going?*—it's over. I have to confess those were my exact thoughts every time I got on a horse. Even so, I might have stumbled along as a jockey had I not grown too tall (for a jockey). The final blow to my racing career came about by accident.

I was riding one of Mr. White's horses at a blistering walk on the outer edge of the training track. In my mind, I was about to win the Kentucky Derby when the starter yelled, "Kid, get that horse in here!"

He pointed to the starting gate. I knew right away that he wanted me to break the horse from the gate. Horses had to do that three times before they were eligible to race so that they'd behave and break when the actual starting bell rang. I'm sure you've seen horses having difficulty at the gate. Sometimes a horse can get so skittish he's taken out of the running. Anyway, this was one of those opportunities for me to speak the truth, which was that the horse already had his gate work with his regular exercise rider. If I put him in the starting gate, the only one who'd be learning anything would be me. I'd never been in the starting gate. I simply couldn't pass up the opportunity.

I waved to the starter, gave a slight tug on the rein, turned the horse I'd been leisurely walking, and headed toward the iron monster. An assistant grabbed the reins and led us into starting gate number four. I knew this was a good day to advance my riding career because four is my lucky number. God was talking to me, and this was his way of saying, "You are going to be a jockey, my son."

The starter stood in the viewing stand. He looked down and cried out, "Kid, are you ready?"

Ready? Was he kidding? I'd been ready for years. I leaned forward on the horse's neck, grabbed a little hunk of mane, raised my rear end ever so slightly off the tiny racing saddle, looked straight ahead, steadied the horse, and called out, "Let him go!"

I should explain that when the starting gate opens, in an instant the horses break and go from a standing position to forty miles an hour. The second I cried "Let him go," the starting bell rang, the gates flew open, and my horse leaped forward. I didn't. The next thing I knew I was sitting on the ground looking at the rear end of the horse speeding down the track. I remember thinking, *"God, I wish I were on that horse."*

Thus ended my racing career. I never lost my love for horseracing, though.

Aside from my failure to ride in the Kentucky Derby, my childhood proceeded without undue stress. Long before the Boomer Babies came along I was a card-carrying member of the Depression Babies. My early years were spent like any other kid whose parents were scrambling to make ends meet. Even as they struggled, and as screwy as they were, Sophia and Dan somehow managed to give me a sense of security, which has stood me in good stead all these years. All the more remarkable when you consider that I lived through the Depression, World War II, and Major Bowes' Amateur Hour. I'm not so foolish as to believe that everything in my childhood could have been as rosy as I remember, or as I choose to remember. It's my nature to see the glass half full; I think that might have been Sophia's nature, too. Dan, I'm sure, saw the glass full in order for him to down the contents.

Thinking back, maybe the most significant and terrifying event of my early years was the death of President Roosevelt on

April 12, 1945. Sophia and I were listening to the radio when a voice broke into the regular broadcast to announce that he had died. We both jumped out of our chairs. Sophia put her hands up to her face and rocked her head to and fro. My mouth fell open and stayed that way while the announcer gave the particulars. I was dumbstruck. How could Franklin Delano Roosevelt die? He was the only president I had lived under, and for millions of kids like me, and a lot of grown-ups, too, he was right up there with the Good Lord Himself. It's not like today where presidents come and go and everything they do, and I mean everything, is in the news. FDR had had polio and couldn't walk, but who knew? They never showed him on crutches. Of course, we only had newsreels then, not television. Still, photographers and filmmakers were respectful; pictures showed him from the waist up. He had broad shoulders and when you saw his big face with the great smile, he looked more like Charles Atlas than a polio victim. For Pete's sake, FDR was immortal. If he could die then Dan could, and Sophia, and, maybe *me*. What was happening?

Sophia and I stood still while the radio droned on. Neither of us said a word. Then, from the depths of the cellar, came the familiar bellow, *"Jaanneey Maaac!"* Dan had bonked his head on a cellar beam and his accustomed howl was a sure sign that, despite the immediate tragedy, life would go on.

School Days: Part Deux

I continued my climb up the educational ladder, squeaking through the first eight years with below-average grades that were just good enough to get me promoted. Then, before you could say Horatio Alger I entered ninth grade. What really impressed me about freshman year in high school wasn't my teachers or my studies; I couldn't get over the fact that I didn't stay in one room all day. I actually had to get up and change rooms for different classes. I'm being a little flippant about the teachers; I had some special ones. Foremost among them were Elsa Jane Carroll, who taught English; and Ralph "Quiz" Quesinberry, head of the physical education department. These two wonderful people eventually became personal friends and remained so until the day they passed.

English had always frightened me. Maybe it had something to do with Sophia and her struggles, but I think it had more to do with my dyslexia. Throughout my elementary school years, I agonized over my homework and often cowered when I had to read aloud in class. I got laughs, for sure, but it took me a while to get comfortable and to realize the kids were laughing with, not at, me. However, getting words down on paper, as well as reading the words that already were there, were chores that Elsa Jane Carroll wouldn't let me dodge. In later years, she informed me that she spotted something that told her there was more to this little runt than just being funny and she was determined to bring it out. Bless her, she stood over me and made me write, and read, and recite, and, in so doing, saved me from total humiliation and ensured my future success. Elsa gave me the courage to express myself but she's got to take responsibility for my spelling.

Ralph Quesinberry had been recruited as athletic coach from Bowling Green State University when I began seventh grade. Quiz recognized my athletic ability, and under his guidance I flourished in baseball, track, boxing, and, don't laugh, football and basketball. I devoted myself to sports in high school and, because of my academic record, this required a bit of finagling. I needed Sophia's signature on my report cards. (Forget Dan, he never even looked at my report cards let alone signed them.) So I spent a lot of time altering those Ds to look like Bs. Before giving the card to my mother, I would a draw a horizontal pencil line joining any Ds midsection that was dark enough to look genuine but light enough to erase with no trace. Once Sophia signed off, I would rub out the line and return the card to the teacher. On some occasions, I eliminated the middleman (Sophia) and signed the report card myself. With hindsight, it would have been a lot smarter if I'd put the energy that I devoted to changing my grades into working for them. The one grade I didn't have to mess with was for Physical

Education. Quiz gave me all As. Most of the time I earned them, although sometimes I didn't.

I remember a track meet when one of the guys on the mile relay team twisted his ankle right before the race. In his infinite wisdom, Quiz chose me to sub. I questioned his choice; I wasn't a runner, I was a pole-vaulter. My running consisted of zipping down the forty-foot approach to the bar where I'd plant the pole and hoist myself up and over. I could clear seven feet, which wasn't all that bad for a high school kid, but that was the extent of my participation in track-and-field. Nevertheless, when Quiz pointed the finger at me that day, I jumped off the bench and got ready for the relay. If he thought I could do it, by golly, I could do it. I lined up for the second leg of the mile. A guy named Don Evans ran the first leg and led all the way. I had a clear track ahead of me when I took the baton from Don. Grasping it in my fist, I put my head down and took off like The Flash, one of my DC Comics heroes. I was blazing along and continued to lead the others as we reached the turn. I soared into the back straightaway. Boy, was I full of myself. Then, it happened, I hit the wall. It felt more like I'd smashed into one. In a split second, my legs and arms left my body and were replaced with rubber. Gasping for breath, my eyes rolling in my head, my limbs flailing, I teeter-tottered forward. The Flash was flushed. Here's the thing: I didn't have a clue how to run a quarter mile, and Quiz didn't have time to tell me. Who knew you were supposed to conserve some energy. I expended it all in the first few seconds. *Whoosh!* I felt a refreshing breeze as the rest of the field stampeded by. My slow-motion jog soon became a foot-dragging stroll. I had about another fifty yards to go and, though my vision was too blurred to see them, I could hear my teammates urging me on. At last I reached the baton-exchange area. The guy running third leg started moving with his arm outstretched behind him, expecting to receive the baton from yours truly. Unfortunately, I only had *reached* the exchange area when, overcome with nausea, I stepped to the side of the track and began puking. Mr. Third Leg, realizing his hand was empty, turned, saw Mr. Second Leg bent over the field spilling his guts out, and ran over. He pulled the baton out of my hand, and flew down the track in a futile effort to catch up. We lost by a quarter of a mile, and I puked all the way home. My running career was over.

Among other innovations, Quiz introduced boxing to the athletic agenda. I signed up and was immediately put into the fleaweight division, one rung below flyweight. Any lower and I'd be fighting leprechauns. Billy Butler was a fleaweight, too. In fact, the two of us fought each other in the first championship bout. Sophia had made my powder-blue trunks on her sewing machine and embroidered LITTLE BUTCHER on the side. Could it get any better? Billy and I were about the same weight, but he was a good foot taller than I. We must have looked like Mutt and Jeff in the ring. The bout, itself, was very professional. We wore sixteen-ounce gloves and fought for three one-minute rounds. The bell sounded. Billy and I came rushing out of our corners and started punching. As befitted our respective statures, Billy kept hitting me in the head while I attacked his midsection. All three rounds followed the same pattern. And so it went for the entire match with only one divergence. At the start of the third round, my Little Butcher powder-blue trunks began slipping downward. I grabbed them with one gloved hand and held on for dear life while I kept on punching with the other hand. I didn't hear the crowd roaring (with laughter), but apparently people found it hysterically funny. In the end, although Billy and I were pretty evenly matched, I won. I'm sure it was because I provided a comic interlude. Billy and I really were the best of friends, and I felt bad taking the trophy. Our dads were so close, and I knew that Big Bill, an amateur boxer, had trained his son for the fight. When we got to the locker room, I offered Billy the trophy, but he wouldn't hear of it. I'm happy to report that a variation of a happy ending came for Billy in the next year's tournament. I lost in one of the early rounds, but Billy went on to another title bout. I said "variation" because Billy didn't win but he had participated in two championship fights. I only got to one.

Football provided the next sporting highlight for Chagrin Falls's own Jim Thorpe. I went out for the team in my freshman year, all ninety-seven pounds of me. Thanks to a steady intake of milkshakes, I managed to push my weight up to a hundred and three pounds over the summer but, by the time school started, the milkshakes were over, and, I'd lost all the added poundage. I weighed ninety-seven pounds again with my socks on. (My socks probably weighed ten pounds.) Coach Quesinberry wanted to make me the water boy, but I insisted that I wanted to be on the field. Miraculously, perhaps foolhardily, Quiz put me in as a starting guard. I had to earn my spot, though. You weren't just given a uniform and sent on the field, you had to prove you were a "Tiger." I cemented my position on the team the day we had tackle practice.

The squad formed two lines facing each other; on one line were the runners, on the other line stood the tacklers. At the signal, the runners would run ten yards and try to avoid the tacklers. The first thing I did when I got in line was count down the other line to see whom I'd be tackling. I was ninth in the tacklers' row. I'm counting six, seven, eight, nine, holy smoke. It couldn't have been any worse; my corresponding number nine was Ralph Tinge, the senior first-string tackle who weighed two hundred and forty pounds without his socks. The Titanic and the iceberg were on a collision course. Quiz must have counted the lines, too.

When the nines stepped forward, the coach took a look at the two of us and said, "Hold on a minute."

I brushed him off, saying, "I've got it."

I put my head down and hurled forward, straight into Ralph Tinge. At the impact, I felt that I'd gone to another place. My body seemed to accordion and my head settled into my lap. As I lay there, I could hear the faint sound of my teammate's applauding.

"All right, Conway," Quiz called out, "you've got a uniform."

I was pleased to know that I made the squad and relieved to be alive. At least I wouldn't have to tackle Tinge again; he was my teammate, now. The first thing I did when I got my uniform was to have Sophia sew a tuck in the pants so they wouldn't fall off during a game. I was never so proud as when I put on the Tiger orange and black. It's funny what you consider important when you're young.

Quiz had the same faith in my athletic abilities as Elsa Jane had in my scholastic ones; the difference was his belief could have killed me. The guys I faced were giants, but that was the secret of my success. While they lumbered forward, I scooted down the field like a little rat, slipping in and out of the opposing line. By the time anyone got a bead on me, it was too late to throw a block; I was already in their backfield. That's not to say that the Artful Dodger escaped unscathed. Ironically, it was a fellow teammate who wiped me out. During the big game with our archrival, Orange High School, our own fullback ran his helmeted head, full force, into the middle of my back. I hit the ground and lay there. Nobody rushed out to see how I was doing and I just kept on lying there. Finally, Quiz and a few other guys came on the field to check things out; after all there was a game to play. Quiz leaned over and whispered, "C'mon, kid, get up and show them you can walk it off."

Walk? I couldn't even talk; I couldn't feel anything below my neck let alone move. I managed a weak smile. Quiz and the others got me to my feet, let me go, and down I went again. EMS this wasn't. Obviously, I wasn't going anywhere on my own. The guys took hold of my arms and legs, lifted me up, and carried me off the field—no stretchers in those days. I was taken to the locker room and placed on a training table. At this point I wasn't so certain who I was, let alone where I was. I simply couldn't talk. For the next half hour, I lay on the table staring at people who were staring back at me. Gradually, I came to. I recovered my ability to speak and to (tentatively) walk. I was pretty shaken up, though. A wise man might have gone home to bed. We are not talking about a wise man, however. Undeterred by my condition, I elected to go to the postgame party.

At the party, I was a bit woozy but okay enough to chat with friends and teammates. We strolled over to a serving table piled high with all kinds of hot dogs. I picked up a chilidog, took two bites, and passed out. For the third time that day, I hit the ground. Someone removed the dog from my hand and took me to the local hospital where I was examined and questioned by the doctor. The chilidog was exonerated; it happened too fast to be food poisoning. The doctor took an X-ray and found everything in order. So what's the problem? Nothing, except that I was really sore, and I couldn't move too easily. The good doctor taped me up, put me in a neck brace, and sent me home. I stayed in my brace/tape cocoon for about three weeks. Most of that time I had to move at a painfully slow pace. Barely able to lift my feet off the floor, I shuffled around the house and up and down the school corridors. After the third week, I went back to playing football. Ah, youth. The story doesn't end here, though. There's a follow-up—two follow-ups, in fact.

Follow-up #1. I'd been living in California for many years when I began having back problems. I went to a doctor, was X-rayed, and was dumbstruck when I was told that my spasms were a residual effect probably stemming from a broken vertebra.

"Broken vertebra?" I said. "I never broke my vertebra."

"Think back," replied the doctor, "you must have experienced some sort of trauma. It could have been a while ago, when you were young. Did you ever have a sports injury?"

I thought about it—a sports injury—and the lightbulb went on! I told him about the football field smashup and what happened after I ate the chilidog.

"You may not realize it," the doctor answered, "but you are one lucky man. Here's what I think. Your vertebra probably was broken when you were hit, but when they picked you up and carried you to the locker room, your back got stretched out. I'd guess that the vertebra went back into place. The X-ray may not have shown anything at the time but, I assure you, you came very, very close to being permanently disabled. If they hadn't moved you, it might have been a different story."

Follow-up #2. Do you remember my saying that I had to move at an excruciatingly slow pace after the accident? I never forgot that experience. Later, I took those shuffling steps and gave them to one of my most popular characters on *The Carol Burnett Show*, The Oldest Man. It took The Oldest Man an eternity to get from point A to point B, and two eternities to get from point B to point C. (Again, if you want to see what I'm talking about, go to You-Tube. Or, better yet, buy one of those DVD sets of the show.) Oh, one other thing before I move on. Ever since that incident on the football field, which might have altered the course of my life, Jesus and I have stayed in constant touch. I never stop saying thank you.

No question about it, except for Elsa Jane Carroll's high school English classes, I was totally focused on sports. I always had been. Every summer, from grade school through adulthood, I went to the Chagrin Falls Recreation Center. It cost five dollars to get a pass for the entire summer, seven days a week. The pass entitled you to use the baseball diamond, the basketball and volleyball courts, and the pools. You could also attend any of the craft classes and loop leather lariats to your heart's content. My heart was more content being on the diamond and in the pools. I started in the little pool and stayed with the swimming program right through college. It was a great way to spend the summers. I couldn't wait to get to the Chagrin Falls Recreation Center in the mornings and to spend the day with my pals. We all looked the same, blue jeans, T-shirt, tennis shoes, a baseball hat with a Cleveland Indian patch on the front, and, of course, a well-oiled baseball glove enveloping our catching hand.

The Rec Center was my playground and learning ground. And, it was my introduction to sex. Not sex-sex, but an introduction to the difference between boys and girls and the answer to the question why it was necessary to have two separate areas for bathers to change. I found out thanks to a hole behind the towel rack that had been poked through the cement wall dividing the dressing areas. The older guys had drilled it for the benefit of all the boys to use but only after they'd had their fill of peeking. For a long while, I couldn't figure out why anyone would come to the Rec to swim and spend so much time lined up at the wall. One day I finally got on the line myself. As I moved forward, I noticed that the person at the head of the line would crouch down and press his face to the wall. Suddenly, I was that person. The next thing I knew my knees bent beneath me and I was peering through the hole. All I saw were benches lined up beneath hooks on the wall where clothes were hanging. What the heck was this? Guys were spending valuable sports time looking through a hole to see . . . *Hold it*, what was that? Oh, no! I couldn't believe my eye. A girl! I strained my eye against the hole to get a better view when someone called out, "That's it for today. We're closing the pool. Get dressed and clear out."

This was the one and only time I was able to use the peephole.

That very afternoon, Coach Gurney found out what was going on, and the hole was filled.

Like I said, I loved sports and enjoyed all of them, but it bugged me that I wasn't able to become a jockey. Lots of kids don't get to do what they aspire to, and not just little twerps from Ohio. You take a guy like Dwight Eisenhower, the thirty-fourth president of the United States. I read this quote of his:

> When I was a small boy in Kansas a friend of mine and I went fishing, and as we sat there in the warmth of the summer afternoon on a river bank, we talked about what we wanted to do when we grew up. I told him that I wanted to be a real major league baseball player, a genuine professional like Honus Wagner. My friend said that he'd like to be president of the United States. Neither of us got our wish.

To the end of his days, Eisenhower swore that not making the baseball team at West Point was one of the greatest disappointments of his life, maybe the greatest. Dwight David Eisenhower and Tim Conway, both thwarted in their childhood quests.

I may have been thwarted but I still had a great time in high school. The guys: Marty, Fitz, Jim, Bob, Billy, Tom. And the girls: Rhea, Barb, Sue, Betty, Alice, Rosalyn, Carolyn, and Carol. Just saying their names brings back such wonderful memories. I can't turn a page of the Class of '52 yearbook without a smile and a grateful look back. The kids, the teachers, the wonderful people, and that cozy little town where you could embrace life and know it was going to hug you back.

A Little Higher Learning

$\mathcal{I}$ *chose to attend* $\mathcal{B}owling$ $\mathcal{G}reen$ State University, Ralph Quesinberry's alma mater and one of the few schools that would accept me with the grades I sported. (Do I think that Quiz put in a good word for me? You bet I do.) In the fall of 1952, along with my friends Marty Hawthorne, Don Britton, Dick Kenney, and Jim Fitzpatrick I entered BGSU. The first semester, our Chagrin Falls ranks thinned out. Marty brought a trunk full of 45 rpm records, spent most of his time listening to them in his room, and was the first to hit the road back to Chagrin. I hung on, but barely. I had to for my parents' sake if nothing else. I wasn't your scholarship kind of guy. Sophia and Dan worked their butts off to put the money together to finance my college years. I swore it would all come back to them; it pleases me that, eventually, I was able to keep my word. When I went off to BGSU, Sophia and Dan gave me fifty dollars in spending money . . . for the entire school year. I never told them that it was gone within days. Money was a big problem. I always needed it. Consequently, I took just about any work that came my way. I had some odd jobs and some even odder ones. And now is about as good a place as any to tell you about a few of them.

My first job was in the dining hall at the fraternity I joined, Phi Delta Theta. I waited on tables and washed dishes. Nothing odd about that, but then I moved things up a notch. Broadly hinting that I was sous-chef at the Chagrin Falls Hunt Club, I told the fraternity's chef that I had experience in preparing food. Before you could say voilà, I was Phi Delta Theta's assistant chef. I pulled off this stunt for a good reason; I needed round-the-clock access to the kitchen to carry out a little plan to make extra money. Late at night, I'd go down to the kitchen and hard boil eggs, a lot of eggs. Then I'd make egg salad sandwiches, which I'd take over to nearby sorority houses to sell. Not only did I make money, my social life vastly improved. I was king of the lunch run until my fraternity received a whopping egg bill and fingered me the errant egg man. Back to the tables and the dishes for ex-Chef Conway.

One of the more unusual means of making a buck that I was involved in was a scheme cooked up by my frat brother, Bill Bradshaw. I don't know how much you know about golf, but there's usually body of water somewhere on the course. The public golf course in Toledo had a pretty large lake in front of one of the holes. Bill suspected that an awful lot of golf balls wound up in that lake rather than on the green. We got ourselves to Toledo, rented Aqua-Lungs, and went over to the course. We stripped down to our bathing trunks, put on the Aqua-Lungs, and dove in—to golf ball heaven. There were so many of those little buggers they actually formed a solid floor on the lake bottom. We filled up burlap bags with our loot, brought them over to the local driving range, and sold them for a dime apiece. Including transportation and Aqua-Lung rental, we made a profit. I should have stuck close to Bill; he had a real head for business. On the other hand, my pal Dick Moss had a head that should have been examined.

One Christmas, Moss suggested that we rent a truck, buy some fir trees, put them in the back of the truck, and drive around to houses where we would sell them. We were bringing the trees to the customers instead of their having to go out and buy them. Slight hitch. We'd ring the doorbell, and when the homeowner appeared, we'd ask if they wanted to save time and buy a tree from the back of our truck. Every single time the potential customer would ask us to unload the merchandise so they could take a look. Thirty trees had to be unloaded and reloaded. After a dozen or more attempts we hadn't made a sale. We decided to cut up the trees and make Christmas wreaths which were a lot easier to unload. We sold most of them but still came up short, thirty bucks' worth of short. When it came to commerce, I never listened to Moss again.

I was so eager to make money I never turned down a job, and, believe me, there were many times I should have. One, in particular, was a bummer. Cecil Collier, the father of my high school friend Rhea, needed four guys to join him in driving five bus chassis from Detroit to Pittsburgh, a nearly twenty-hour trip. I was home from college and was one of those chosen to make the run. The four of us gathered at Cecil's garage at five in the morning and found him waiting. Our quintet piled into his Oldsmobile and, with Cecil at the wheel, took off. We drove for five hours in driving rain. Two coffee stops and three toilet breaks later, we arrived at the Detroit garage and found five chassis inside. May I remind you that a chassis is the bare frame of a vehicle? And that's exactly what awaited us in Detroit, five steel frames each with a steering wheel, a gas pedal, and a brake, but without a cab, a seat, or a windshield. We were each given an orange crate that was placed behind the steering wheel and wired to the chassis. Those crates would be our seats for the next two-hundred-fifty-plus miles. Mercifully, we also were given plastic blow-up pillows to place between our butts and the wooden cases. So, the Lafayette Escadrille mounted their respective chassis, blew up their cushions, put them in the appropriate places, and took off. Did I forget to mention that I was the only member of the team who did not have a driver's license? I was taking a Driver's Ed course, but I had very little road time under my belt, or should I say, butt. Speaking of butts, my cushion hit a nail on the crate, sprang a leak, and was as flat as a pancake before we hit the outskirts of Detroit. I took off my jacket, folded it, and slipped it between my crate and me. It wasn't much of a cushion and it left me wearing a T-shirt in weather that did not improve.

The trip was a nightmare. The rain never stopped and the noise from the rattletraps we were delivering was deafening. By the time we pulled into the receiving yard, I was soaked through, my ears were ringing, and my backside was all but petrified. I crawled out of the chassis, got into a car and, along with the other three guys—Cecil stayed in Pittsburgh—was driven to the Greyhound station. We caught a bus to Cleveland where I transferred to the Rapid Transit in Warrensville Center to take me to yet another station to catch the bus to Chagrin. At a little past 2 A.M., I sat on my bed at home, holding two lousy twenty-dollar bills in my hand and wondering, "What was I thinking of?" I still shudder, recalling that painful misadventure. There's something else here, though. All these wacky adventures I experienced stayed with me and later, I incorporated them into comedy sketches I wrote. Come to think of it, I began messing around with comedy in earnest at Bowling Green.

When I joined Phi Delta Theta freshman year, I did some minor entertaining for my fraternity brothers. By "entertaining," I mean that I took about fifteen jokes from a joke book, put them in order, memorized them, and became the master of ceremonies at the frat house and the Newman Club. The Newman Club, a Catholic social organization, was a second home to me. I often performed there with my friend Dick Moss (of the Christmas tree sales fiasco). I questioned Dick's business acumen but his comedy sense was attuned to mine. We told the same jokes every Friday night at the Newman Club pizza parties. We also dined on the leftover pizza for the next week. Moss and I branched out from the campus to the local fifty-watt radio station. We did comedy sketches with the morning disc jockey and, from time to time, read the morning news. My dyslexia kicked in from time to time, too, and the results were often funnier than the sketches. On one occasion, I reported a story about President Eisenhower's recent hospitalization. Instead of announcing, "The president has been speaking with a nurse," I said, "President Eisenhower has been sleeping with a nurse."

I had one misadventure after another while I was at BGSU. Some were thrust upon me and others were of my own devising, but in each case, the Devil would get my tongue. I got into situations that I easily could have gotten out of if I'd only given a simple honest answer. Suddenly, however, I was Pinocchio. Stories just poured out, and once I was into them, I refused to yield. Here's an example:

During the hunting season, you had to be very careful when you were out walking on the campus. Hunters flushed out pheasants from the woods onto the open fields, and when pheasants were flying about four feet off the ground the hunters took aim and fired. On any given day in the season, a lot of shot could come a passerby's way. One fall afternoon, I was walking to class and thrust my hand into my pocket not realizing that an upside down pencil was already there. The lead point went right into my palm and broke off. It hurt like a son of a gun and was buried too deep for me to get out myself. I took a detour to the infirmary where I showed my hand to a nurse.

"What's this?" she asked, thus innocently creating one of those charged moments when, and I can't explain it, I can't help myself. The answer should have been it's lead from a pencil, but I found myself saying, "It's a bullet."

"A bullet?"

"Yep, a bullet. I was walking across the field and evidently someone took a shot at me and hit my hand." The words tumbled out of my mouth.

"Well, with a bullet involved," said the nurse, "I have to report this to the police."

This is the exact moment when I should have said, "Ah, I'm kidding. It's lead from a pencil." What did I say?

"Well, you gotta do what you gotta do."

So the nurse called the cops. A couple of them showed up and she filled them in. Then they turned to question me. I heard myself getting deeper and deeper in the hole.

"Did you get a look at the guy who shot you?" asked one of the cops.

"Nope, too far away."

"What kind of gun do you think it was?"

"Ahh, don't know."

Now, I was really in the soup but I just couldn't end it. I was elaborating on my tale when the doctor entered the room. He took my hand, took a look, took out the lead, and held it up.

"I understand you said you had a bullet in your hand."

"Right," I answered.

"Well, this is pencil lead," declared the doctor.

"Yes," I confirmed, "the guy shot me with a Dixon Ticonderoga 2."

Why I wasn't immediately put into an observation ward, I'll never know. I was beginning to learn that if I looked totally sincere and didn't back down, I could say almost anything and get away with it. By the way, I still have a tiny piece of that lead in my hand. I refer to it as a war wound.

What was my college social life like I hear you ask? *Fine,* I hear me answer, adding defensively, *I had girlfriends.* Some were a little more serious than others, but that's true for all college kids. There was one I liked a lot, enough to pursue her to the full extent of my ability. Let's call her Sue. One weekend, I decided to drop in on Sue unannounced, probably not a smart move since Sue went to another college some one hundred and twenty miles from BGSU. I hitchhiked my way over and phoned her when I reached my destination.

"Hi Sue, it's Tom. I'm here."

"Where?"

"I'm on your campus and I wondered if you'd like to have lunch with me."

"Oh dear, well, you see my mother's here and we're leaving right now for the country club. Some friends are joining us."

"Oh," I answered.

"Well, um, you're welcome to join us, too," replied Sue hesitantly.

"Gee, that'd be swell," I said enthusiastically. I asked for and received the address and told Sue I'd be right over.

I wasn't exactly dressed for country club dining but I didn't exactly know that. Oddly enough Sophia and Dan had never belonged to a club, which left me in total ignorance of behavior and dress codes. I went to the address Sue gave me and was confronted with a slightly smaller version of the Taj Mahal. I walked in and immediately was stopped by a guy in uniform. I explained that I was joining Sue for lunch; he said I needed a jacket and tie. And when I explained that I didn't have either, he grimaced, disappeared, and returned carrying a jacket and tie, a much better jacket and much nicer tie than I had ever owned. I put them on and entered the dining room. Sue was seated at a table, her mother on one side of her, a nice-looking guy on the other, and an older couple seated opposite them. I said hello and slipped into an empty chair at the end of the table. Unbeknownst to me, Sue and her mother were having lunch with Sue's "boyfriend" and his parents. Could've fooled me, I thought I was her boyfriend. I'd met Sue's mother and got the feeling that she went to bed every night praying that her daughter would meet a nice boy. Her dreams had come true in the other guy, and here was her nightmare crashing the party. Like I said, Sue was a good person and obviously invited me because she felt bad that (1) She was dumping me, and (2) I'd hitchhiked all that way to see her.

I was totally out of my element, which became very evident as the meal progressed. Unfamiliar with some of the advanced tableware, I proceeded to make gaffe after gaffe. Forget the old one about picking up the finger bowl and drinking the water, they didn't have finger bowls. What they did have was a gravy boat, a piece of crockery I'd never before come across. It's a small ceramic pitcher attached to a plate underneath. The plate's there just in case you spill some of the gravy when you are ladling it out of the pitcher. The ladle sits in the bowl and when the boat is passed, you hold on to the handle and scoop out the gravy. Then you put the ladle back in the bowl and, with a broad smile that says I do this every day of the week, you put the bowl down. That day, a waiter put the gravy boat on the table next to me. I didn't know what it was or what it contained but I had to do something with it. I thought about it and then took a wild guess that I had been served soup. I picked up the bowl and was surprised when the bottom plate came along. I tried to separate the two pieces. I gave up when it became obvious they were inseparable. I remember thinking, *Okay, I'll just put the whole piece in front of me while I eat.* I moved the gravy boat, picked up the ladle, and proceeded to eat the "soup." (Do you eat soup or drink soup?) All eyes were on me. I looked up, smiled, drew my napkin across my mouth, and said, "Very good, a little salty, but really very good."

After lunch, I said good-bye to Sue. I should have said farewell because I never saw her again. I assume she married the nice boy, who didn't say one word to me during the meal (actually, no one spoke to me but Sue), and that they lived happily ever after. I hitchhiked back to Bowling Green sadder, wiser, and a little sick to my stomach from the gravy.

You're in the Army Now

Right after I graduated from BGSU in 1956, I volunteered for a two-year hitch in the United States Army. (Why is it when I tell people I was in the army they always ask, "Ours?") It was peacetime, and my thinking was why should I wait until I was gainfully employed for the draft to get me? This was quite an assumption on my part since I wasn't anywhere near being employed. It's possible I enlisted because I didn't want to go back to the bosom of my loving, loony family, or maybe I enlisted because I just didn't know what else to do. A lot of my friends did the same thing. I enlisted and after that leap I had to pass a physical. At one point during the exam, a doctor put his fingers on my private parts and said, "Cough."

"Please, I hardly know you," I protested, slapping his hand. The expression on the doctor's face was priceless. Lucky for me, he had a sense of humor. I like to imagine that he might still be telling that story and getting a laugh. That's all I ask of life, residual laughter.

The night before I was to leave for basic training at Fort Chaffee in Arkansas, Sophia and Dan had a small gathering of friends and neighbors at our Orange Street mansion. Everyone wished me well, and we all enjoyed Sophia's canapés—that is, her Romanian version of them, which were bigger and spicier than any canapés you ever ate. After the party, I went to bed and was up the next morning at 6:30 A.M. Sophia got up, too. She fed me, and gave me the classic, tearful take-care-of-yourself good-bye that mothers have given to their soldier boys for generations. It was peacetime, but my Sophia carried on as though I was headed for the Normandy Invasion.

I took a bus to Cleveland and arrived at the train station at 8 A.M. From there I was to board a train for St. Louis where I'd connect with another train for Fort Smith, Arkansas. (Fort Chaffee was in the town of Fort Smith, a bit confusing but I was in the army and "confusing" was the operative word.) I showed my ticket to an official who informed me that I was a day early. So I got on a bus and was back home in Chagrin by 10:15 A.M. I walked in the door and found Sophia in the kitchen. She looked at me and said, sharply, "You crazy? What you doing home?" This from the woman, who, a few short hours ago, was sobbing at my departure.

"I'm on leave," I told her, but she didn't get it.

The next morning I was up and out and on my way to a two-year stint with Uncle Sam.

I arrived at Fort Chaffee and immediately was given another physical. Thanks to the eye-test portion of this exam I learned that I had a birth defect in my left eye. The vision was slightly blurred in that eye, but not in the other. That meant I could draw a bead on targets with the right eye. Naturally, birth defect and all, I was cleared for front-line duty. The doctor wrote a prescription and sent me off to be fitted for frames. The technician was all business. He put a few frames on my face and without asking my opinion, chose a pair, put them in a carrying case, and handed them to me.

"Take these. They'll notify you when the lenses are ready, and you can bring the frames back to have them put in."

I thanked him and then, remembering my last physical, asked if he wanted to check "my private parts." He didn't say a word. I headed for the exit. The sergeant at the front desk looked up as I walked by and said, "You got glasses?"

"Yes," I answered and took out the case with the frames in it. I was about to explain that there were no lenses, but the sergeant didn't wait to hear what I had to say.

"Put those things on!" he ordered.

I opened the case and slipped on the frames.

"And don't let me catch you without them," the sergeant warned. "You got that, soldier."

"I got it," I said.

"You got it, *what*?" he said.

"What what?" I replied in all sincerity. I looked at him with complete ignorance written on my face. He was fuming. Then I realized what he wanted me to say.

"I got it, *Sergeant*," I blurted out, at the same time saluting him.

That threw him off guard. You're really only supposed to salute high-ranking officers. He returned my salute, realized what he was doing, made a fist, shook it at me, and screamed, "Get out of here!" I obliged. There was no sense of humor in the army, but that never stopped me from trying.

About a month after I arrived at Fort Chaffee, I pulled guard duty. It's a pretty standard routine. You walked your post with your rifle in hand, for what seemed like twenty-four hours but probably was more like eight. Guard duty in peacetime is extraneous. For one thing, I was guarding a service club, and for another, there were no bullets in the rifle I carried. Part of the ritual called for a lieutenant to appear every two hours to make sure you were doing your duty. When he approached, you pointed your rifle at him and said, "Halt. Advance and be recognized." The lieutenant then gave you his name and serial number, and you'd respond, "Carry on." He'd go off, and you wouldn't see another officer for two hours. You did this all night. It wears you down especially when you're only guarding a service club full of Ping-Pong tables and not NATO headquarters.

Around 2 A.M., just after a lieutenant had been halted, been seen, been recognized, and had gone, I decided I needed a little break. I went into the parking lot, got into the backseat of a car, and grabbed some shut-eye. I awoke with a start, checked my watch, saw that it was 3:55 A.M., and realized that another officer was due. I jumped out of the car and raced back to my post. I got there only to discover that I'd left my rifle in the car. There was no time to go back and get it. I needed a substitute fast. I found one in the Dumpster next to the service club—a three-foot fluorescent tube. I grabbed it and hustled back to my post just as the lieutenant came around the corner.

"Halt," I cried, pointing the tube at the officer. "Advance and be recognized."

He gave his name and started to rattle off his serial number when he caught sight of the weapon in my hands.

"What's that?" he demanded.

"It's a lightbulb, sir, and if you come any closer, I'll turn it on."

Didn't get away with that one, folks. For two weeks, I had to pick rocks out of a pile, paint them white, and place them along the drive to the officers' mess.

Following the guard duty debacle I was put on fire duty. Instead of a rifle, I was armed with a shovel. My duty consisted of shoveling coal into a furnace thus heating the building, in this instance the infirmary. One evening, duty called and I began shoveling—6 P.M., 8 P.M., 10 P.M., you get the picture. By midnight, I'd had enough of this every-two-hours business. I figured if I just shoveled all the coal into the furnace, it would pretty much take care of the job for the rest of the evening. So I loaded every lump into the furnace and went back to the barracks to get some sleep. Around 4 A.M. I heard a fire engine. From the siren's sound I figured the engine was heading toward the hospital. By golly, I was right. I threw on my clothes and raced over. When I arrived, the infirmary's occupants had been evacuated and were lounging around on the lawn. The hospital wasn't on fire; it was just full of smoke. The next day, I found myself in front of my superiors, the you-can't-handle-the-truth gang. They had a bunch of unkind things to say to me and then asked if I had anything to say in my own defense. I should have kept my mouth shut but no, I spoke.

"In a way, you could look at what I did as a kind of miracle."

"Miracle?" the lieutenant in charge boomed. "What are you talking about?"

"Well, you know that a lot of guys in the hospital were faking illness to get out of duties on the base. Some of them were even carried in on stretchers."

"What's your point, soldier?" demanded the lieutenant.

"Well, those guys may have been carried in on stretchers, but when that smoke hit them, they came running out. I think that qualifies as a miracle."

It didn't matter what I thought, I was back at the rock pile. Like I said, with a few scattered exceptions, there was no humor in the army.

After basic training, I was sent to Fort Lewis near Seattle, Washington. What a cushy assignment that was. I was part of a small team based in the States; our command unit was in Japan. The main job was to send out replacement troops to our bases in the Far East. Guess which private was in put in charge of the books? Keeping track of the men sounds easy, but a lot of my GIs got lost in the shuffle. Sooner or later, they'd show up but no thanks to Private Conway. One time a unit in Korea sent a request for two cooks. I don't know how it happened, but they got fifty of them.

It may have been chaotic for my comrades in the Orient, but I was living the life of Riley at Fort Lewis. The officers lived off base with their families, so we enlisted men had the barracks all to ourselves. We had a TV room, a pool table, a Ping-Pong table, couches, and easy chairs. We also had very little to do. I usually could be found at my desk tapping my pencil on a note pad. All I did was tap; I don't think I ever took a note. The warrant officer was a good egg and let us take turns taking afternoons off to watch TV or to hit the service club for a sandwich and soft drink. The command unit would call once a week and ask how things were going. We'd say, "It's going good," hang up the phone, and go back to doing nothing. And that's the way it went for the rest of my army years.

For decades after my discharge (honorable), I suffered from what I called the soldier's nightmare, a variation of the actor's nightmare. The latter goes like this: You're onstage and suddenly, you can't remember your lines. It's happened to me. I dream that I'm doing a play or a show and I go completely dry. I run around looking for somebody to lend me a script. The audience starts booing, and I start shaking in my boots. I wake up screaming "Curtain! Curtain!" In my soldier's nightmare, I'm dragged, kicking and screaming, to the enlistment office for a physical. I keep trying to explain that I'm too old and that I've already served, but they won't listen. I wake up holding my crotch, screaming "4-F! 4-F!"

I can kid all I want about my years in the military, but, bottom line, the army did me a service. While I was defending our country, I initiated and participated in the kinds of misadventures that were later integrated into my television role as Ensign Parker on *McHale's Navy*. One sketch took place in a military hospital, and a bunch of soldiers in wheelchairs jumped up and ran off just like those guys in the Fort Chaffee infirmary. Most important, while I was serving my country the idea of going into show business really took root. I'd been kicking it around for a long time, now, after two years away, I decided that I was going to become a professional comedian. Thanks, Uncle Sam.

Let the Laughs Begin

Dick Moss, my college chum and erstwhile business partner, got out of the army a little while before I did and came to Fort Lewis to visit me. Like I said, I wasn't exactly tied down with work, so Moss and I had plenty of time to sit around and schmooze. Our thoughts drifted back to college days. We'd had a great time doing our cut-rate Martin and Lewis comedy skits at the frat house and the Newman Club, and, at the time, had toyed with the idea of going professional. Any such thoughts were put on hold when we both enlisted. During the two years we served our country, Moss had come to the same conclusion as I had regarding the future. We really wanted to give showbiz at least a try. And that's exactly what we did right after I got my discharge.

First, we moved into the local YMCA and then we did what all comics did in those days, we bought used tuxedos. (I wonder if there's a young comic today who even owns a suit let alone a tux.) Next, we arranged an audition with the manager of The Country Club, a Seattle comedy nightspot. Ah, Seattle. Remember Noah and the forty days and forty nights of rain? Well, Seattle had eighty-one days of rain in a row that year, and our audition took place around the seventy-first day. Moss and I set out in a downpour to make our debuts. We didn't have raincoats and wore our army overcoats to protect the tuxedos. Army overcoats are made of wool and when they get wet they reek like a herd of billy goats. That's exactly what Dick and I smelled like when we turned up for our audition. We were taken to the owner/manager's office and, after removing our stinking coats, stood before him, resplendent in our tattered tuxedos. The manager, an Edward G. Robinson type, sat behind his desk puffing on a cigar, which, by the way, smelled worse than our coats. Moss and I went through our snappy seventeen-minute routine while Eddie G. chomped on his cigar, staring at us. At the end of the audition he was still staring at us. He hadn't said a word. I figured we didn't have a cat-in-hell's chance of working for him. After an interminable amount of time, Mr. Robinson took the cigar from between his teeth, leaned forward, and said, "I'm going to give you boys a try. I need you to do four shows an evening, five thirty, seven thirty, nine, eleven, and if things go well, you can do the twelve-thirty spot, too. You'll start tonight."

Moss and I were absolutely floored, four spots, and a possible fifth. This was unreal. It did cross my mind that we never mentioned we had only one routine for those four-possibly-five spots. I didn't dwell on it. Because of the weather, we decided to hang out at the club rather than go back to the Y. The overcoats already were moisture laden; another couple of trips would have made the smell, and the weight, lethal. We settled in at the club for the day. Eddie G. was kind enough to send out a couple of soggy sandwiches and some tepid coffee from the kitchen to fuel us. I munched on a sandwich and sipped the coffee. All I could think was, I'm going to be in show business.

At the 5:30 show, a grand total of twelve people sat at tables that were placed around the apron of a small stage. At one table sat a mother and three young children. She was in the process of cutting up a toasted cheese sandwich and handing it to the kids. Moss and I leaped onto the stage. Recorded music blared forth and so startled the mom, the sandwich flew out of her hand and onto the lip of the stage. We performed our entire act with it lying there. I guess she was too embarrassed to retrieve it, and neither of us was savvy enough to kick it off, or, better still, to pick it up, take a bite, and then, give it back to her. (Later in my career, I'd have done twenty minutes with that toasted cheese sandwich.) I started the act with my version of a comedy monologue I'd seen on (stolen from) *The Ed Sullivan Show* on TV. At the end of my turn, Moss came onstage and did his imitations of musical instruments. Then I joined him for our closing comedy bits plus a couple of duets. Nobody clapped when I finished my monologue, nobody clapped when Moss finished his imitations, and nobody clapped when we finished the duets. Nevertheless, we took our bows, waved our arms, and enthusiastically shouted, "Thank you! Thank you!" to the silent horde. We jogged off the stage à la Martin and Lewis and turned around to go out for our final bows as the stage lights went off and the room lights went on. The audience members already were on their way to the exit.

Despite the lack of applause, Moss and I thought that things had gone pretty well. At 7:30, we again strutted our stuff. The fifteen people in the audience didn't even look at us. We finished, and the silence was deafening. As we stood at the side of the stage, Eddie G. came over.

"Fellas," he said, "I think that'll be it for the act. But, since you've got those tuxes on I want you"—he pointed to me—"to cover the front of the house and seat the guests. And you," he said to Moss, "grab a water pitcher and fill up the glasses on the tables. I'll settle with you after the last show."

Our first gig and we had gone from feature act to maître d' and water boy.

The next morning, Moss and I took inventory of our assets, discovered that we didn't have any, and decided to go home. We packed up our belongings and put them in the trunk of the used 1948 Pontiac that I'd purchased a few short weeks earlier. I got into the driver's seat and Moss slid in beside me. I put the key in the ignition and turned it. Nothing happened. I tried it again, same result. I must have tried a half dozen times when Moss said, "Call the automobile club." I got out of the car, went to the phone booth inside the Y, and dialed the auto club. They sent a guy over in a truck. He got into the Pontiac and tried the key. When nothing happened (I could have told him) he muttered under his breath, got out, and took a look under the hood.

"Look," he said, "I can't see anything wrong. I think if you start the car up and I get behind you and give you a little push forward, the engine will click in."

I got back into the car, and the guy brought his truck up against the Pontiac's back bumper. He started nudging us forward, I turned the key, and, bingo, the engine came to life. We took off, followed by the truck. Our rescuer was beeping his horn; I looked in the rearview mirror and saw him motioning for us to pull over. I didn't want to test the Pontiac's ability to start again so I waved back and zoomed away. The last thing I saw in my rearview mirror was our rescuer throwing us the bird. We probably should have paid him before we got in the car.

The ride home was uneventful. For three days and three nights we ate peanut butter and mayonnaise sandwiches and drank Coke after Coke. For a while we talked about maybe trying to get our act into a couple of nightspots in Cleveland or Akron, but Moss's enthusiasm petered out.

"I've had it, Tom," he said with a sigh, "It's time for me to retire. I want to get married, get a job, and settle down."

"How can you leave show business?" I asked.

"I think I can handle it," he replied.

He did. Moss left show business, married his girlfriend, moved to Florida, and became an insurance salesman. He led a good normal life, and yet I'll bet you anything that ratty old tuxedo is still hanging in his closet.

Be It Ever So Humbling
(and It Was)

There I was in 1958, out of uniform, out of Seattle, out of work, and, frankly, out of ideas about what to do with my life. Naturally, I went home. There's a line of poetry that's stuck with me over the years. It goes, "Home is the place where, when you have to go there, they have to take you in." I was welcomed with open arms by Sophia and Dan. But even their unconditional love wasn't going to solve my problem. What was I going to do with myself? I'd been working since I was ten years old. Now, my obligations were out of the way, and I was expected to start my life's journey. The problem was I didn't have a clue as to where that journey was going. My situation wasn't unique. Every young person comes to the point where he or she has to ask, "What am I going to do with the rest of my life?" And the answer usually comes back, "How should I know?" I knew what I didn't want to do. I didn't want to be a whip.

I didn't want to deliver newspapers, or mow lawns, or drill holes in plastic, or make donuts. I could get a job as a night watchman at one of the Cleveland plants down in the flats, but that wasn't going to lead to anything. I wasn't trained to do anything that I wanted to do. *Screw it,* I thought, *I'll just lie in bed until spring.* Which is what I tried to do.

Early one afternoon, Sophia called from the kitchen.

"Tommy!'

"Yes, Ma."

"What you are doing?"

"Yelling back at you."

"Don't be smarty pants. I need bread."

"So do I!"

"What?"

"Nothing, nothing," I called down, "I'll get it."

I dragged myself off the bed, put on my shoes, went downstairs and out the front door; the most exercise I'd had for the past day. I got into the Pontiac and headed for the A&P. Before I got there I dropped into Bright's Drugstore where I bumped into Marty Hawthorne.

"What's up?" he asked.

"Not me," I replied. "Things are looking pretty grim. I haven't worked since I got out of the army."

"Hey, cheer up, buddy," he answered. "Things weren't looking so good for me when I left the service, either. Then I got a job at KYW-TV. I'm selling time and I'm making a lot of money. Come to think of it, there could be an opening for you at the station."

"Really, what?"

"A guy named Jack Riley who works for Big Wilson, the radio disc jockey, just got called up by the draft. Biggie hosts the morning radio show. He plays records, he has guests, he tells jokes, and he plays the piano. He's got this canary in a cage on top of the piano, and the bird sings when Biggie plays."

"So what does Jack do?" I asked.

"Well, he picks out the records to play, he answers the fan mail, and he writes jokes for Biggie."

"I don't write comedy," I said.

"Trust me, neither does Jack," laughed Marty. "He just pulls jokes from a joke book."

"And that's all he does?"

"Well, he's cleans out the birdcage, every day."

"You know," I said, "I think I'm qualified."

I hopped into my Pontiac, zipped into Cleveland, went to the KYW station, and, using Marty's name, asked to see Jack. (Protocol was different in those days, especially in Cleveland. You could just drop by and talk to anybody. Today, you'd have to book an appointment months in advance, even in Cleveland.) We had a chat and Jack thought I'd be a perfect replacement. We never mentioned salary—probably because, as I later learned, it was thirty-five dollars a week. Hey, it wasn't bad considering that I didn't have to pay room and board. I was hired on the spot. When I arrived home later that afternoon, Sophia was in the kitchen.

"Where's the bread you supposed to get?" she demanded.

"I just got a job, Ma," I cried.

"*Multumesc, Isus!*" ("Thank you, Jesus!"), shrieked Sophia.

She gave me a big hug, and after she let me go, I told her what had happened.

"This wonderful news. Your father will be pleased. Now, go get bread."

A couple of weeks later, Jack left for the armed services, and I began doing my life's work, making people laugh.

Acting as Big Wilson's assistant was a breeze. Monday through

Friday, I'd pick out the records, give Biggie a sheet of jokes that I'd copied from various joke books, answer his fan mail, and clean the birdcage, the bottom of which usually was lined with the previous day's jokes. And there was a bonus, an unofficial service attached to my job that Jack hadn't mentioned. On weekends, Biggie hosted record hops at various high schools in the area, and, as part of my workload, I helped him. I'd arrive at the appointed time, play the records for the first hour, and then Biggie showed up for maybe forty minutes. He'd do some snappy patter, spin a record or two, and split, leaving me to spin the platters for another couple of hours. I did most of the work but Biggie paid me twenty-five dollars in cold, hard, beautiful cash. You don't have to be Einstein to figure out the formula: Thirty-five dollars plus twenty-five dollars equals Easy Street. I bought a three-piece suit, a sports jacket, a new pair of shoes, a new battery for the Pontiac, and a book, *1,000 Jokes for All Occasions*. Plus, I got to entertain the record-hop crowd with the material I gleaned from any comedian appearing on *Ed Sullivan's*. I was in show business. I was in hog heaven.

Around this time, I moved out of my ancestral home in Chagrin and rented a studio apartment in Cleveland. Thus, I was able to celebrate my twenty-fifth birthday in my very own place. I decided to make it a surprise party. I sent out invitations informing the guests that someone was going to take me bowling and that I wouldn't be home until 8:00. Then I gave instructions: The guests were to come to my apartment around 7:00 and set up the food and drinks, which they were assigned to bring. The key would be left on the sill over the door so people could let themselves in. I also suggested that everyone bring a small gift that didn't exceed ten dollars.

The fifteenth of December came and everything went smoothly. Nobody had trouble finding the place because I included a map in the invitation. So everyone was there waiting for the birthday boy to make his appearance. Eight o'clock came and went, as did nine o'clock, but the birthday boy never showed up. Finally, at around 10 P.M., the guests left, convinced that I'd given the wrong date. I hadn't, and when they called the next day to see what had happened, I told them quite simply, "I never got an invitation."

It was one of the best birthdays I ever had. I didn't have to listen to a lot of small talk and party into the wee hours of the night, which is what usually happens at birthday celebrations. I really enjoyed bowling (by myself) and I took in a movie, a western called *Apache Territory*, which was pretty good. Best of all, when I got home I had a whole bunch of presents waiting.

A lot of recording artists came through Cleveland and once it became known that I was the person who selected the records that Biggie played, many of those artists requested that I include their latest efforts on my list. I had no objections and was happy to do so. They, in kind, were so happy that they'd often bring me little gifts to show their appreciation. I didn't think anything of it because the gifts were nothing more than tokens. I did notice that the visiting artists gave envelopes to some of the other guys who selected the DJ music for the afternoon and evening broadcasts. I assumed the envelopes contained thank-you notes. They didn't. Something else was afoot.

It all started in 1951 when a disc jockey named Alan Freed began playing rhythm and blues recordings on WJW in Cleveland. In those days, Cleveland was a pop music breakout city, a place where national trends first appeared in a regional market. Freed was the city's most popular DJ and had a huge following. He pioneered rock and roll and brought it front and center. He also was one of the organizers of a show on March 21, 1952, at the Cleveland Arena, an event now recognized as the first rock and roll concert. (The concert had to be shut down because there was a near riot when too many people crowded inside.) Freed went on to New York City and national fame. Then, in the early '60s he was named in the notorious payola scandal that rocked the music world. Recording companies and artists were paying disc jockeys to play their records, proof that those envelopes contained a lot more than thank-you notes. Fortunately, I never got any kickback, just knickknacks. Freed's career was ruined. Mine wasn't.

I picked up another source of income at the station by working Friday nights during the high school football and basketball seasons. After 10 P.M. people would call in to ask the final scores of the local high school games, and I'd rattle them off. Now, if that were all I did it would have been boring. To keep myself amused I'd vary the results. A typical conversation went something like:

Caller: "I want the Euclid and Independence score."

Me: "The final score of the Euclid and Independence game was Euclid eighteen."

Caller: "Yeh, but what was the Independence score?"

Me: "I don't know."

Caller: "Whaddya mean you don't know?"

Me: "I mean I don't know."

(Pause.)

Caller: "Is there anybody there that does know?"

Me: "I don't know. I'm a recording."

(Long pause.)

Caller: "Is there anybody there who isn't a recording?"

Me: "Just Tony"

Caller: "Let me talk to Tony."

Me: "Tony's off tonight. Do you want me to put you on hold till Monday?"

(Longer pause.)

Me: "Sir?"

Caller: "Never mind. I'll get a newspaper."

As he hung up I heard him say to someone with him, "Can you believe how stupid these people are?"

I had another routine that worked pretty well, too. Someone would call for the score, and I'd say, "The final score of the Rocky River and Parma game was twenty-one to seven."

Caller: "Who won?"

Me: "Twenty-one."

Didn't last too long on the Friday Night Scoreboard. But, it sure provided good material for the future.

After three months at the radio station, a job in promotion opened up in the television division of KYW. I jumped at it. On paper my new work was pretty simple. Throughout the day a slide showing a scene from an upcoming program, usually a movie, would flash on the screen while an offscreen announcer read the copy written by me. If, say, a Humphrey Bogart movie were scheduled, I'd write something like "Bogie at his best in the Warner Bros. action-packed drama *To Have and Have Not* based on the Ernest Hemingway novel. Directed by Howard Hawks and featuring sultry Lauren Bacall and gravelly voiced Walter Brennan." When the three stars were shown on the TV screen, my script was read. So what could go wrong? Well, supposing a Three Stooges movie also was scheduled that day and a mix-up occurred. The result? The Bogie, Bacall, and Brennan slide might appear onscreen as the announcer read, "Curley, Moe, and Larry wreak havoc in *Boobs in Arms,* a slapstick romp in which the three nitwits are inducted into military service." Or, vice versa. The slide for *Boobs in Arms* might be shown as Curley, Moe, and Larry were identified as Bogie, Bacall, and Brennan. You get the picture. Whenever a glitch like this happened the station manager would call in and scream, "Who screwed up!" Invariably, the blame would be placed on the innocent copywriter. I used to watch TV at night in total fear whenever my promos came up. Sometimes the picture and text matched but the slide was in upside down. Whatever. You always could count on a mess.

Quirky little incidents like these rarely happen today because everything is so high-tech. Consequently, spontaneity is hard to come by, and a lot of the fun in broadcasting has gone by the boards. Looking back, but not as far back as those Cleveland days, I know that's one of the reasons *The Carol Burnett Show* was so enjoyable. We made mistakes, and if those mistakes got a laugh, they were kept in. That wasn't the case at KYW-TV. Basically, my job in promotion was to keep numbers and slides in order, not exactly a dream job for a dyslexic.

The Importance of
Being Ernest Anderson

$\mathcal{E}$*rnie Anderson, a well-known entertainer* in early television, was also one of the greatest guys you could ever hope to meet. He'd been a disc jockey in Providence, Rhode Island, when WHK in Cleveland brought him out to be their morning man. This was a big deal. His face was plastered on billboards all over town. Everyone at KYW was worried that he'd put a big cut in our morning radio shows. Among the most worried were Biggie Wilson and, of course, me. We spent weeks trying to think of ways to compete with the new voice in town that threatened our very being. Not to worry, Ernie took care of our problem.

WHK held a big party the night before he was to start broadcasting, and Ernie was asked to say a few words to the audience of sponsors, station employees, and guests. He went up to the microphone and started telling a series of jokes. Whenever he got near the end, a guy in the crowd would yell out the punch line. Ernie let it go for about four jokes. Then he asked the guy, who, unbeknownst to Ernie, happened to be the owner of the station, "How do you know all the punch lines, sir?"

"I can anticipate them."

"Really," said Ernie, "well anticipate this . . ." At which point he suggested that the gentleman go do something—which is quite personal and physically difficult if not impossible to do—to himself. Those were the last words Ernie Anderson ever uttered into a WHK mike. He was immediately relieved of active duty, and the regular disc jockey returned to the morning show the very next day.

Purely by happenstance, I officially met Ernie a few nights later as I was driving down Euclid in my used Volkswagen Bug that had replaced my late Pontiac. I was doing about thirty-five miles an hour in first gear because it was the only working gear at the time. I figured if I could get to the automobile shop I could leave the car to be fixed. I lurched along accompanied by the high-pitched roar caused by driving that fast in first. A 747 taking off didn't make as much of a racket as my little VW. I'd stopped at a red light and was gunning the motor to keep the car from stalling when another car pulled up beside me. The driver rolled down the window, and I recognized Ernie Anderson. He didn't know me from Adam but that didn't stop him from calling out, "Hey, schmuck, are ya charging your battery?"

We started talking and bonded immediately. Ernie followed me to the auto shop, and after I dropped off the Bug, he drove me to my apartment. That was the beginning of a forty-five-year friendship.

In the early days of our relationship, I spent most of my spare time with Ernie listening to tales of his screwups. They were legion. His immediate problem was his lack of work. I suggested that he get a job as a booth announcer at KYW until something better opened up. He did, and we did a lot of on-air bantering together; we really thought we were hot stuff. We began doing live promotions for the station, and not long after, Westinghouse, our parent company, sent someone out from New York to check out the two guys on the morning show. When we heard that a man was coming from the home office to see us, Ernie and I were sure it was to discuss terms for a new show. We had it made.

The Westinghouse executive arrived and met us in the conference room. He sat across the table from Ernie and me and glanced through some of the promotional copy, which the station manager had given him. He dropped the papers on the table and looked up.

"Who's responsible for this crap?"

I pointed to Ernie and he pointed to me. The guy dismissed us and we went back to our booth. Later that day, the program manager called.

"I want you and Anderson in my office at three o'clock on Friday." This was Wednesday. We knew we were going to be fired. They never fire you on a Wednesday; they always wait till Friday.

On Friday, Ernie and I went to the program manager's office. He was seated behind his desk and the second we walked in the door, before he could say anything, we both said together, "We quit."

The guy's mouth fell open as the two of us turned and left the room.

Our firing/quitting wasn't such a disaster. Ernie and I already had decided that we had more to offer than chitchat and had made an appointment to see the station manager at WJW-TV. We were going to pitch a morning show with Ernie as the talent and yours truly as the director. Ernie's talent was still in question and there was no question that I had never directed anything. The crazy thing is the station manager hired us. We had one week to prepare *Ernie's Place,* a two-hour morning show on which a movie would be shown. During the intermission, Ernie would chat with a guest. Our first week on the air was an unequivocal mishmash, two hours of confusion, which I aided and abetted from the director's booth. Did I mention that I'd never directed a TV show and that I didn't have a clue how to do so? I couldn't even get the show on or off the air at the appointed times. I had no idea how to "back time" a movie, which means timing it so that the film ends at an exact moment. That first week whether or not the movie had ended, it was cut off at 10:00 in order for the station to go to network programming. If you saw *Citizen Kane* on *Ernie's Place,* you'd never know what "Rosebud" was.

Some of the experienced staff members realized that I was useless, and we got a few of them like Chuck Schowdoski to do the actual directing. The alleged director (me) sat in the booth twiddling his thumbs while Chuck and the others ran the show. As far as guests, nobody knew who Ernie was, therefore nobody wanted to appear with him. I came up with a plan to fill the guest slots. I'd lock the camera on, come out of the booth, and join Ernie as the guest. I played a whole bunch of people. Ernie would introduce me by saying things like, "Today we're delighted to welcome Chef Luigi Schumaci." I'd come out in the guise of an Italian chef, and we'd do an extemporaneous interview about making "veal ears à la Diavolo."

One time I sat down in front of the camera and talked with what I called a pseudo-Romanian accent.

"Hello, I'm huh-Dag Herferd," the name popped into my head.

"I understand you're a bullfighter," shot back Ernie.

"That's huh-right," I answered not bothering to change my Sophia-inspired accent to a Spanish one. I spent the next seven minutes talking bull(s).

During these interviews, I was all over the place uttering non sequitur after non sequitur while Ernie played it straight. This was great training. Gradually I began writing comedy sketches for the "guests." Ernie and I had a ball with these bogus conversations and taped a few for our own amusement. Meanwhile, our show became such a joke that people actually started watching. The reviews were scathing and went along the lines of, "Want to see stink? Don't miss *Ernie's Place.*" Soon, we became the talk of the town, partly because the town was Cleveland. People expected so little, and we were able to provide it. And then, in the fall of 1960, lightning struck in the form of Rose Marie. A former child star and now a featured member of one of the most popular sitcoms of the day, *The Dick Van Dyke Show*, Rose Marie was in Cleveland on a promotional tour and scheduled to appear on Mike Douglas's talk show on KYW-TV. Her visit literally launched my career.

She arrived at the station and, while awaiting her call to the Douglas show, she watched *Ernie's Place* on a monitor. She thought we were hilarious. She dropped into our studio, introduced herself, and asked if we had tapes of our show. We screened a few for her. She really liked them and asked if she could take a few back to Hollywood to show to her friend Steve Allen. We gave her a couple of reels and off she went. Steve Allen was one of the kings of television, and neither of us ever expected anything to come of it. Surprise, a couple of weeks later someone from *The Steve Allen Plymouth Show* called and asked if I would come out to Hollywood and appear on the program. They didn't mention Ernie. I'd be on my own. I told Ernie, and he was happy for me. I told him I wasn't sure I wanted to do it but I'd think about it. He told me I was nuts. It wasn't an easy decision for me to make, though. It meant leaving Cleveland for three weeks and more important, I'd be breaking up the team. I made up my mind and told Ernie I wasn't going to Hollywood. He told me I was. And to make sure of it, he got the station manager to say that he'd fire me if I didn't. There was nothing I could do but go. I promised Ernie that if it worked out, I'd find a way to get him out there, too. The truth is my departure was the beginning of the end of our WJW partnership but not our friendship. And, I'm happy to say that Ernie Anderson went on to achieve considerable fame in television.

Ernie's rise began in the mid-1950s when Universal Pictures released their library of classic horror films, *Dracula, Frankenstein, The Wolfman,* etc., from the 1930s and 1940s. The horror TV shows became an instant national phenomenon as television stations around the country eagerly licensed the package for their local "shock theatre" programs. John Zacherle at Philadelphia's WCAU-TV may have been the country's first "shock" host. He called himself Roland, wore ghoulish makeup, dressed in black, and introduced the films with quips. Later, he went to New York where, as Zacherley, he hosted *Shock Theatre* on Channel 7, the ABC affiliate. WJW got the films, and the station manager assigned Ernie to air them friday evenings on *Shock Theater*. Ernie, calling himself Ghoulardi, wore a fright wig, a moustache and Van Dyke beard, and a butcher's white coat. Ghoulardi presented the films, commented on them, inserted himself into them, and discussed a wide range of subjects such as the benefits of smoking pot. He claimed to be a Polish worker at the Two Mile Crib. (That's the place where all the sewage from Cleveland was released into Lake Erie.) He also claimed to live in Parma, the Polish section of Cleveland. Every time Ghoulardi said Parma, a polka would play and he'd break into a dance. The real Parma residents were not amused and petitioned to get Ernie off the air. Naturally, this only increased his show's popularity. At one Cleveland Orchestra performance in Severance Hall, the guest conductor gave a little speech in which he told the audience he was from Parma, Italy. Immediately, the audience burst out singing Ghoulardi's polka theme. The conductor didn't know what was going on, but the folks from Parma who were at the concert sure did. Another petition was filed. Try as they might they could never get enough signatures to stop Ernie.

Ghoulardi also hosted Saturday afternoon's *Masterpiece Theatre; Laurel, Ghoulardi and Hardy*, a weekday children's program; and *Parma Place*, a parody of the popular soap opera, *Peyton Place*, which was yet another shot at Cleveland's Polish community. The funny thing is Ernie was about as unprejudiced a person as you can get. He liked everybody unless they proved to be unlikeable but it had nothing to do with ethnicity or race. Ernie was simply outspoken and about as un-PC as you could get. He didn't pull his punches; he socked it to his audience and, as a result, had plenty of detractors. Fortunately, he had more supporters. After I permanently settled in Los Angeles, I'd return periodically to Cleveland and appear on Ernie's show. We'd revive some of our old sketches and had a swell time doing it. I even duked it out with Ghoulardi on a few occasions.

In 1966, I urged Ernie join me in Los Angeles and he finally did. I was appearing on *The Carol Burnett Show* and arranged for him to get some television exposure. Carol always began her show with an unrehearsed exchange with members of the audience. She'd take questions and then, before the first sketch, she'd introduce any celebrities who happened to be there. I had a chat with my darling Carol and she agreed to go along with a little plan I'd hatched. If you watch *The Carol Burnett Show* DVDs, you'll notice there are a number of episodes where, during her opening appearance, she calls out, "And, look who's here with us tonight, Ernie Anderson!" At that, Ernie would leap to his feet and wave. Nobody knew who he was, but the applause was deafening. I don't know if it had a direct bearing on these appearances, but when Lyle Waggoner, the announcer, left the show, Ernie replaced him.

One of Ernie's first legitimate acting jobs was on a TV show of mine called *Rango*. He appeared on the first two episodes. Wait, maybe there only were two episodes. We also worked up a comedy act that we performed on a television variety show and we released two comedy albums. Did I say we didn't work together professionally after I moved to California? I stand corrected.

In time, Ernie dropped all the front-of-camera work and went behind the scenes. He was the ultimate in announcing, and eventually became one of the most renowned voices in broadcasting. He was called the Voice of ABC and introduced the phrase *"Eyewitness News . . . starts . . . now."* And it was Ernie who gave the particular spin to the middle word when announcing *The Looove Boat.* His voice was all over TV, and you know what, it still is. He passed away in 1997, but to this very day radio stations still license his voice for promotions and pronouncements. Think of it, when you hear, *"Eyewitness News . . . starts . . . now."* You're listening to Ernie Anderson.

Forgive the detour but I really wanted you to know a little something about my pal, a true friend, and a genuinely funny man. Okay, back to my future. In September of 1960, Tom Conway was on his way to Hollywood . . .

Hi Ho Steverino

$\mathcal{S}ometimes\ \mathcal{I}\ get\ a\ little$ sad when I think about people like Ernie Anderson who were important in the early days of television and are now just about forgotten. Actually, most performers suffer a similar fate. Heck, I'm going to suffer it, too. (Right now I'm holding on by my thumbs thanks to YouTube. *Wait.* And thanks to Carol Burnett, whose timely DVD re-releases of her shows keep us participants before the public eye.) Still, it gets to me that, except when Public Television has a tribute of some sort, icons like Steve Allen barely rate a blip on the radar screen of today's viewers.

What a career Steve had. For starters, he was the original host of *The Tonight Show,* which began on NBC in 1954 and is still going with Jay Leno at the helm. Steve pioneered the format for talk shows in general—things like the opening monologue, audience participation, comedy sketches, celebrity guests, and the resident band.

If you watch late-night talk shows you'll notice nothing much has changed from his original format. Steve Allen was my kind of guy. I stayed up five nights a week for the hour-and-forty-five-minute *Tonight Show*. I loved the talent he showcased, people like Don Knotts, Louie Nye, Tom Poston, Jonathan Winters, Steve Lawrence and Eydie Gormé, Bill Dana, and Pat Harrington. Steve himself was a true renaissance man, a comedian, a writer, a musician, a composer, and an actor. No kidding, he was the brightest man I ever met. I told him that, adding also that I was proud of being the dumbest person in show business. He agreed. By the time I got to appear on Steve's show, he'd already been through a landmark battle in the television ratings wars. His *Tonight Show* was such a success NBC decided to use him to bring down one of the most popular TV shows of the day. *The Ed Sullivan Show* on CBS had locked in its 8 to 9 P.M. Sunday evening time period for eight years. *The Steve Allen Show* premiered on June 24, 1956, directly opposite Sullivan. Steve continued to do both his shows till 1957 when NBC took him off *The Tonight Show* so he could put all his efforts into Sunday night. While Steve did better than the rest, Sullivan remained invincible. In 1958, *The Steve Allen Plymouth Show* was moved to Wednesday, then cancelled in 1960. In 1961, he went over to ABC but *The New Steve Allen Show* was dropped after fourteen weeks. His big hosting days were over, but Steve continued to appear on television in various other shows. My first national television appearances were on *The Steve Allen Plymouth Show.*

I arrived in Hollywood armed with a portfolio of my material and, thanks to Rose Marie, met with Steve and his writers in a conference room just like the one at WJW, only this room was the size of a football field. We sat around a table that a Piper Cub could have landed on. A staff of muckety-muck writers surrounded me. One of them handed me a piece of paper.

"We think this sketch will work for you," he said, disdainfully.

I read it, thought about it, and said, "This is okay, but why don't I do something that I've written."

The look on their faces was something to see.

"You want to do something you've written?" one of them said to me, drawing out each word with special emphasis on "you" and "you've."

I knew what he really wanted to say, and he probably would have said it, too, but Steve stepped in.

"Wait a minute, let's see what Tom has to show us before we make any decisions."

I fished around in my briefcase (a shopping bag), found a routine that I thought would do the trick, and handed it to Steve. He took a look and liked it, and that was that, I would do my own material on his show. I know I infuriated the writers. Writers can be very territorial; I am when it comes to what I'm going to perform. It's not that I'm snotty or think that I know more than anybody else. Far from it. But I sure know what works for me better than anybody else. Eventually, the writers calmed down.

It was Steve Allen who did away with "Tom" Conway. We were going over a sketch when Steve asked if I'd ever considered changing my name. A little puzzled as to what he was getting at, I told him that I'd already done that when I was a kid. Steve absorbed that information, agreed that Tom was a better choice than Toma, but still thought it was time for another change.

"The reason I'm bringing it up is there's an actor out here named Tom Conway," Steve explained. "He's George Sanders's brother and has been playing The Falcon in movies. I honestly think he's well known enough for it to interfere with your career. It's confusing to have two performers with the same name."

"To tell you the truth," I said, "I've never liked the name Tom that much. I don't mind changing it, but what should I call myself?"

"Why don't you just dot the *o*, and be Tim," said Steve.

His suggestion was music to my ears. "Tim" was my favorite name, no kidding. As for the confusion, Steve was referring to the possibility of residual checks getting sent to the wrong person. When I went to AFTRA to register as Tim Conway, I told the union official that I'd consider holding on to the Tom if Sanders's brother Tom Conway were doing better than Tim Conway. Funny, he didn't buy it. So, I became Tim Conway. I never legally changed my name and nobody (except a few old Ohio friends) calls me Tom anymore.

The first night I was on with Steve he introduced two other acts, The Smothers Brothers and Jim Nabors. I was in very good company. For my debut, I brought along one of the characters I'd created on *Ernie's Place*.

"Please welcome Dag Herferd," announced Steve as I walked out looking ill at ease. I took a seat next to Steve's desk.

"Now, what exactly do you do, Mr. Herferd?" asked Steve.

"Right now I'm in charge of transportation for the Cleveland Indians for the away games."

"Oh," replied Steve," that's a pretty big responsibility. How many men are involved?"

"Well," I explained, "it can vary, and that's what makes it tricky. For example there were forty-one players going to a Detroit game last week, and the bus only seats forty so I had to hire two buses."

"Yes," said Steve, "I can understand that."

"Yep," I continued, "I had forty guys in one bus and one guy in the other."

You have to understand I'm saying this nonsense with absolute sincerity. My answer got to Steve. He doubled over laughing. He had this high-pitched squeal that was infectious. Soon everybody was laughing, except Dag. I pride myself on my ability to stay in control and, for the most part, I do. Occasionally, I've broken. Anyway, that night was one of those magic times, everything went right. We got great reviews. I did two other shows and they were equally successful. Who knows what might have happened if *The Steve Allen Plymouth Show* had not been cancelled. Probably the same thing would have happened as happened. And here's what happened.

I returned to Cleveland and not long after received a call from someone with *The New Steve Allen Show* asking me if I wanted to become a regular cast member. I was flabbergasted and honored but I couldn't commute from Cleveland, which meant I had to think about moving to Los Angeles. However, it wasn't just a question of *my* leaving Cleveland, there was someone else to be considered. I guess it's about as good a time as any to inform you that I was now a married man. Not only that, my wife was baking our first cookie.

Allow me to backtrack.

Married with Children

When I was in college, I had a core group of friends that included a few girls and a few guys. We kids did everything together—we skied, we went boating, we took trips, we went to movies, and participated in a lot of activities. I dated a few girls and by senior year I was serious about one of them. She was in our little group, and to protect the innocent let's call her Angie. Around this time, I got really interested in religion, especially Catholicism. Angie was a practicing Catholic and influenced me to the point where I decided to convert from sort-of Greek Orthodoxy to the Roman stuff. (After falling out of my baptismal manger, I hadn't been too involved with organized religion. In that respect I hadn't fallen too far from the tree, either. Dan was the most lapsed Catholic you can imagine; Sophia wasn't that interested in Orthodoxy, either. The most she did was get us to church on a rare

Sunday and for the Big Two: Christmas and Easter. Yet, despite their seeming indifference, both my parents lived by The Golden Rule. That's the way I was raised. And, that's the way I tried to raise my children.) Angie took me around to her church and introduced me to the priest. I liked the guy and was delighted to have him as a counselor and guide.

When the time came for the big switch, I went to the church with Angie and Mary Anne Dalton, another member of the Bowling Green gang. We needed a witness and Mary Anne volunteered. The priest got ready to perform the rites but before he began, he asked me a number of questions. I gave all the right answers until he posed one that threw me.

"Who will be godmother to you?"

Godmother? Apparently I had overlooked a necessary component of the ceremony. At a loss to name someone I blurted out, "How about Angie?"

"'I don't think that's a good idea," replied the priest.

"Why?" I protested, "I'd love to have her as my godmother, she's a wonderful person. And by the way, she had a lot to do with my converting."

"Yes, Tom, but there's a concern here," said the priest. "You and Angie are dating and it's entirely possible that some time in the future you might want to get married. In which case, you'd be marrying your godmother."

"But, who am I going to get to stand in for me at the last minute?" I asked.

The priest looked at me, then at Angie, and finally, at Mary Anne.

"Would you stand in for Tom?" he asked her.

"Sure," she answered. And that's how Mary Anne Dalton became my godmother.

Like I said, Mary Anne was part of our little group in college, and, while we spent time together, I'm not sure that we exactly dated. Anyway, I always enjoyed being with her and I do remember that we laughed a lot, and, don't forget, by the time we graduated, she was my godmother. Meanwhile my romance with Angie petered out, and more and more, I was hanging out with Mary Anne. After graduation, both of us went into the military. While I was defending Seattle (did a good job of it, too, no invasions to speak of), Mary Anne joined the Army Special Services and was stationed in Germany. We lost track of each other. We found each other again after our military service was over. By then Mary Anne was living in Windsor, Canada, right across the river from Detroit where her family lived. She was teaching Phys Ed classes. We got together a few times on ski weekends and talked on the phone quite a bit. Meanwhile, I was taking a lot of heat from friends and colleagues. Everyone got on the Tom Conway-needs-a-wife bandwagon. I was frightened; people kept pushing me to get married like it was a compulsory course you had to take. I was desperate. One day I picked up the phone and called Mary Anne.

"Hello," I said, "it's Tom. Wanna get married?"

"Let me think about it," she told me.

"Hey, we ski together, it's practically the same thing as being married. And," I crowed, "look what I have to offer. Nothing."

I should mention that Mary Anne was seeing another guy, and I think she was doing a lot of assessing in her mind whether or not I would be the chosen one. I wouldn't let her off the hook. I wore her down until she finally said yes. Actually, she may have said okay, which is a little less positive than a good old-fashioned yes. Whatever.

And so, on May 27, 1961, I did exactly what the priest had

feared, I wed my godmother. We were married in Detroit where her father was an undertaker. (I used to wonder why she put a little lip-stick and rouge on me at night; it must have been her upbringing.) We had a lot of fun together for a while, and during our seventeen-year marriage we made a lot of cookies—six to be exact.

The Family Guy

It's time I talked about my children. I'm a little scared because I want you to know something about them, but I have to be careful. First of all, if they don't like what I say, they're old enough to let me have it, and I taught them boxing. Second, we're private people. I can tell you about myself, no holds barred (oh, maybe a couple of them), but I couldn't and wouldn't expose my family. That being said, I'm one proud papa and grandpa. So here's an overview of the family Conway.

As far as parenting, I did have something going for me. I was Sophia and Dan's child and I tried to pass on to my children the ideals and values that they instilled in me. It may have been easier for my parents as they only had one kid and everything was focused on that darling little fellow. Furthermore, because Dan and Sophia were (comfortably) poor, I wasn't indulged. They couldn't afford to buy me things like toys, so I made my own. And that was a good thing. Frankly, I don't think any toy company ever made anything as wonderful as a large cardboard box. You can turn it into a house and crawl inside with a flashlight. You can paint pictures on the sides or cut out windows. You can attach one box to another and make a neighborhood with houses full of your chums. Or you can attach one box to a three-wheeler and make it a cab. Okay, I couldn't make a tricycle but you get the idea. I rarely bought manufactured toys for my children, and the same holds true for my grandchildren. I create things for them. Tim the tailor has sewn little outfits for his granddaughters, Courtney and Sophia, and Tim the carpenter has made them little tables and chairs. So far, there've been no complaints. There's another thing about Dan and Sophia: They weren't in the public eye; they were just my mom and dad. I'm out there and known. Being in show business, you get to do a lot of things you wouldn't normally get to do. There are definite celebrity perks. Some people in the biz get the idea that they don't have to follow the rules. You might get a little leeway in a parking ticket, or you might get to go to the front of the line, or get a pass for an off comment you may have made in public. In general, I found that I slept a little better at night by *not* taking advantage of the perks. Nonetheless, I'm aware that my job as a performer has put my kids in the spotlight at times. I honestly tried to keep them out of it; even so, I'm sure they found themselves in situations where they probably wished I had taken that job at Chagrin Hardware.

My daughter, Kelly, who was in the oven when Mary Anne and I moved, was born in California. After Kelly arrived, life changed, shockingly. Most parents find that the first child is a thunderbolt. You walk out the door and go on your merry way when, bingo, you realize you've left something behind. You are no longer free to do what you want; you have to do what's good for your child. Guilt becomes one of your vital signs; the fear that you are not doing right by your children becomes a constant. It started with Kelly and then, in a crescendo of cookie baking, five boys: Timmy, Patrick, Jamie, Corey, and Seann, joined us. For a while, I spent more time in the delivery room than I did on the *Burnett* show.

I don't remember exactly when my marriage to Mary Anne started to unravel but it did, and we decided to call it quits in 1978 right after *The Carol Burnett Show* ended. Then, when Charlene and I married, her daughter, Jackie, came into my home and into my heart as well. Despite our divorce, Mary Anne and I remained united in our love for the children, and Charlene, bless her, was just as committed to them as well. I was a happy guy. You know who was even happier? The diaper deliveryman. We kept that guy busy for eleven years.

Having children made me think a lot more about protecting my home and its contents. I've always been leery about someone breaking in and I've always kept a low profile. I wouldn't live in a fancy mansion because to me that's like having a neon sign flashing: "COME AND GET IT, ROBBERS!" Still, mansion or not, I felt safer with an alarm system. Rather than buying an expensive one, I installed a homemade one. It was a simple system from a simple guy, and quite worthy of the son of that famous Irish inventor, Dan Conway. Here's how it worked. I put a large metal coal bucket at one end of the sliding glass door that was the logical point of entry for a thief. Next I tied a cord around a brick and ran the cord up the side of the door, along the top of the sill, and down the other side to the door handle. I pulled up the brick so it was suspended over the bucket and taped the end to the door handle when the cord was taut enough. Get it? If somebody opened the door, the taped cord would be pulled away from the handle, and the brick would drop into the bucket. The resulting noise of the brick hitting the metal bucket bottom would alert us. It was foolproof. I set that alarm every night before we went to bed.

One December evening, I got the brick in place and retired to the bedroom. Mary Anne stayed up to finish wrapping presents. She was sending a package to her parents in Detroit. Rather than wake me to ask if I'd mail the present in the morning, she tucked it in behind the alarm cord along with instructions telling me exactly what to do. She went to bed. During the night the weight of the package pulled the tape and the cord away from the handle. The brick fell into the bucket, and the resulting *bang* woke Mary Anne and me with a start and, in the same second, proved the brilliance of my invention. Naturally, the kids slept through the whole business.

"Was that the brick?" Mary Anne whispered.

I couldn't move; I was scared.

"Tom, go see what's happening."

I still didn't move. I was rigid with fear. Here was the basic flaw with my Rube Goldberg alarm system. In order for it to work, you had to have someone brave enough to respond to it. Fortunately, Mary Anne was that person. She got out of bed and went to see what had happened. When she returned she explained that the package had fallen and pulled the tape away, triggering the alarm. She got back into bed and rolled over. Before she dozed off, I said, "Did you remember to turn the alarm back on?"

She said, "(Unprintable), you idiot. Go to sleep."

I'm flooded with memories thinking of all the ups and downs of being a parent. I've been through the bruises, the cuts, the minor surgeries, and a few serious ones. All those times spent in the emergency room at Encino Hospital Medical Center, sometimes tending to the kids, other times tending to injuries the kids gave me. Most of my battle scars were the result of the search for lost retainers in places as different as a Dumpster outside a sporting goods store, and a salad bar in a local restaurant. I ripped my hand on the jagged end of the former and banged my head on the cover of the latter. Speaking of accidents, one scene is forever etched in my head. Three little Conways lying in hospital beds after a car accident that happened with son Tim, newly licensed, at the wheel. The doctor was surprised that I wasn't angry. How could I be angry? My children had emerged relatively unscathed from a collision. I was just thankful they were alive.

Aside from illnesses and accidents, the next great hurdle was getting the kids through the school years. All those years, and what I remember are the almost daily phone calls from their teachers. The message always began, "Do you realize what your child did today, Mr. Conway?" I may not have realized exactly, but I always knew the teachers weren't calling to tell me something wonderful. I don't want to go into the many incidents; every parent is familiar with them. I'll share just one scholastic episode that falls in the it-could-only-happen-to-me category.

I learned arithmetic placing bets in the exacta box at the Thistledown track outside of Cleveland. Naturally, I figured it would be a good way for my kids to learn math. So when Tim Junior was in the third grade at Encino Elementary School, I took him with me to the Turf Club at Santa Anita. My darling boy learned all about betting, including the exacta and the exacta box. (In the former, the bettor must pick the horses that finish first and second in the exact order chosen. The exacta box is a way to guarantee the outcome of the first two finishers no matter which horse wins.) How did I know that Timmy would return to school and during Show and Tell instruct his classmates on how to box an exacta. I got a call from the principal who told me that teaching a kid to gamble was borderline child abuse. To which I answered, "Let me tell you what child abuse is. The kid picks horse three and five and it comes in five-three and he loses because he doesn't have it boxed. That's child abuse." The principal didn't have to agree with me, but he had to laugh.

While they were being educated, my kids participated in sports. Occasionally I joined in, most often to coach their Little League ball games. One season, Timmy, Patrick, and Jamie were on the same team. Corey, Seann, and Kelly were in the stands cheering them on, and I was umpiring at first base. Going into the final inning, we were behind by a couple of runs. Two outs later, Timmy came to the plate and hit a clean single. Patrick was up next and either walked or got a hit, both valid ways to get on base. Now two of my boys were on base. Little Jamie came to the plate. He hit the first pitch, a slow roller back to the pitcher. Timmy was on his way to third, Patrick was on his way to second, and both were pretty sure to land safely on their respective bases. All Jamie had to do was get to first base and the infield would be loaded with Conways. Jamie's head was down and his little legs were churning away. Meanwhile the pitcher had scooped up the ball and tossed it to the first baseman. He had it in his glove before Jamie stepped on to the base. My dream of having Conway-loaded bases was about to end. I couldn't let it go. As Jamie crossed the bag, I spread my arms wide and yelled, "Safe!"

The word was barely out of my mouth when the stands erupted with shouts. Have you ever seen those movies about little league teams and how parents go nuts when they disagree with a close call? When I yelled, "Safe," I found myself in one of those movies. I was wrong and wasn't going to get away with it. Immediately, I jerked up my right arm at the elbow and cried, "You were also *out!*"

That's the call I should have made, but I guess I was a papa first and an umpire second.

When the kids were little, I was always thinking of ways to entertain them. I'd bring home costumes from the shows and dress up in them. I didn't hold on to the chicken costume I occasionally used, so they were spared that. Still, they were just as likely to come home and find a lion in the house as they were to find a conventionally dressed dad. I had as much fun playing roles for them as they did watching.

Physical activity was a biggie for the Conways. We were a gung-ho bunch when it came to athletics. Our house had a nice stretch of backyard with a pool and a pool house. One day it dawned on me that it was a perfect setup for a zip line. I think we were the first "zippers" in Encino. The cable ran from the top of the pool house to a telephone pole on the other side of the pool. It was a pretty long ride and you could build up speed. I wrapped a mattress around the telephone pole to make sure the landing was cushioned. The ideal ride began at the pool house, where you'd grab on to the handle and ride the line, not to the pole, but to the point where you were over the deep end of the pool. Then, bombs away! You'd let go of the handle and plunge into the water. Naturally, I took the maiden voyage to iron out any kinks. I climbed onto the roof and, with the kids looking on, I set off. I grabbed the handle and leaped off the edge. I let go at the designated spot and splashed into the pool. I could hear the kids applauding as I hit the water. By the time I returned the handle to the top of the pool house, the kids were lined up and ready to soar. Kelly, Timmy, Pat, Jamie, and Corey took off and plunged. Then it was Seann's turn. He took hold of the handle and, with all of us cheering him on, took off. I knew as I watched the early stages of his flight that something was amiss. He was going too fast. As he reached the deep end of the pool, we all shouted, "Let go, Seann!" But, he didn't. He was heading for the pole at full speed and he hit it. The rest of the kids and I scrambled down the ladder and raced over to Seann, who was lying in a heap at the bottom of the pole. I was shaking with fear; Seann was shaking with laughter. The mattress had safely cushioned his landing, but there was that agonizing moment when I thought he'd been injured and I was responsible.

A big plus of parenting is making your parents grandparents. Nutty as they were, Sophia and Dan filled those roles beautifully. Maybe the nuttiness helped. The kids really looked forward to summer holidays in Chagrin where they were welcomed with open arms. Those visits were an important part of their lives; they got a touch of Chagrin, and Sophia and Dan had a chance to revel in a big family. My parents also visited us in California, but not as often as we went east. Dan and Sophia preferred Ohio, and, much as I tried to pry them loose and bring them west, they wouldn't budge. They wouldn't let me buy them a fancy house, either.

Unlike me, my kids had the chance to know and love their grandparents. They knew their Maji and Papa were special. To show his affection, Timmy bought a cuckoo clock kit and put it together as a present for them. The clock consisted of a Swiss chalet from which hung the winding mechanism, two chains with pinecones at their ends, and a little door at the top of the chalet behind which the mechanical cuckoo resided and from which he emerged to announce the hour. Sophia was thrilled with the gift and had Dan hang the clock in the upstairs hallway. For the first week or so, the cuckoo made his hourly appearances with the appropriate number of cuckoos. It was too much for Sophia. She announced that the cuckoo was driving her cuckoo, especially at night. She asked Dan to keep the bird from squawking. Instead of simply tying the chains together to stop the clock, Dan took a few strips of Scotch tape and plastered them over the door to the bird's room. It seemed to work. The clock still told the time but the cuckoo couldn't get out. All went well, for a while.

Later that year, *Good Morning America* sent a crew to Chagrin Falls to film a local-boy-makes-good feature they were doing about me. While we were in my parents' home, I told the *GMA* guys the story of the imprisoned cuckoo in the clock. Sophia, who was sitting in the living room, heard my remarks and cried out, "You lying. You say that stuff to be funny."

"Really?" I countered. "C'mon," I said to the *GMA* cameraman. "Follow me."

I led him to the clock in the hall and told him to point the camera at the top of the chalet.

"Watch this," I said with a smirk.

I took hold of the Scotch tape, pulled it off, and opened the tiny door. The cameraman came in for a close-up. There, hunched over, his head scrunched between his wings, stood the poor little cuckoo. His beak was a stump. He'd battered it down trying to get out. Lucky that bird was mechanical or Dan might have had to answer to the ASPCA, or the ASPCC.

My kids are grown up now and doing their own thing. Kelly tried acting for a while but found her niche on the other side of the camera; she's now a wardrobe designer very much in demand. Tim Junior is an important contributor to radio entertainment in Los Angeles. He started broadcasting from a station in an old garage and is now Los Angeles' most familiar voice in comedy radio. Pat is the freethinker of the group. He's a delightful person because he doesn't get involved in world problems; you can sit and talk with him for hours without hearing a complaint or a disparaging word. Jamie is the worker bee. If he's only holding two jobs, he considers it downtime. For years, he volunteered his services in a drug re-habilitation program. Many a young adult owes his sobriety to the good advice received from one Jamie Conway. You want a deal? Corey is your man. There is very little that he doesn't have a hand in. The nice thing is whatever he's doing, he's always willing to give you a hand. Seann grew up as the live-in punching bag for the rest of the gang; consequently he gets along in any situation. Right now he assists in the operation of a country club golf course and restau-rant in Steamboat Springs, Colorado. Seann and his wife, Monica, blessed us with Courtney, a delightful little girl who's become a teenage wonder. I believe she's headed for the stage since she has been performing ever since she learned the words "show business." Monica and Seann have parted ways, but we're one big family when it comes to Courtney's welfare. Nearly seven years ago, Tim and Jennifer presented us with Sophia. Sophia is a quiet thinker. She has all the answers. Quiet thinkers think and then they act, and that's what my youngest grandchild excels at. She certainly didn't get that from her grandfather. I think she'd make a great studio head. Jackie was glued to Charlene's hip when I married her mother and has remained so. She got the showbiz bug and was my road manager for many years. Occasionally, she'll slip into her com-mercial threads, do a spot that runs for nine years, and then make more money than I do.

There you have it. Those are my jewels, and they've brought so much happiness into my life. Of all the memories I've stockpiled over the years, one of the sweetest is the children's hour. Going up to their rooms, reading or telling a story, and getting good-night kisses. Then turning to go and being stopped by pleas for another story. And so I'd spin a few more tales until it was time for the posi-tively last good-night kiss. Bliss.

Did I do a good job raising them? I'm not the one to answer that question; you'd have to ask them. I can only say that I tried my best. You always wonder if your kids will know what you did for them. Maybe, but what they might not know is what a treat it was. I've received more satisfaction from being their father than I can ever put into words. I hope they enjoyed the journey as much as I did.

Back to Business

Now that you know about my family, let's get back to Steve Allen and me. In a nutshell, and I do mean nut, here was the situation. I'd gone back to Cleveland after my first stint with Steve. When I told Ernie that the new *Allen* show contacted me again and wanted me as a regular, he got all excited. Then I told him I wasn't so sure I wanted to do it. I was happy in Cleveland; I loved working with Ernie, I liked being near Chagrin Falls. Ernie listened to all my excuses and said, "You've got to go for it, kid. It's a big opportunity and you never know when, or if, the next one will come along." Once again Ernie gave me his blessing and once again I went west.

I had a blast doing *The New Steve Allen Show.* Why wouldn't I, I was in great company. How could you go wrong working with people like Steve, Louis Nye, Tom Poston, Pat Harrington, Bill

Dana, the Smothers Brothers, and, most especially, Don Knotts, the sweetest, funniest man in the world. I'd watched him do his "Man in the Street Interviews" with Steve, and he had me doubled over with laughter. Don would come out as this quivering bundle of nerves, his head jerking, his hands trembling, and Steve would stop him and ask him questions. He'd ask his name, and then say, "What is your occupation?" His voice shaky, Don would answer, "I'm a ne-ne-neurosurgeon," or "I make d-d-d-dynamite." It wasn't just the material, it was the way he portrayed these people; you'd be laughing before he said a word. And it was all so gentle. Don Knotts and I got to be good friends and later worked together in movies. I did a bunch of films with him for Disney beginning with *The Apple Dumpling Gang* (1975).

My introduction to Disney, aka The Mouse Factory, was *The World's Greatest Athlete* in 1973. There's nothing as pleasant as working at the Disney Studios. When you've grown up with Mickey, Donald, and the rest of the gang and then get the chance to work in the buildings where they were born, well, it just doesn't get any better. They say that when you do a picture at Disney you get a script and then you meet your animal. Nine times out of ten that's correct. If you're doing a comedy you can rest assured that you'll be working with a variety of creatures from dogs and cats to horses and mules. In *The World's Greatest Athlete*, John Amos and I shared quite a few scenes with Ben, a man-eating Bengal tiger. Although Ben was trained, those words, "man-eating," were not very reassuring. Ben did one particular trick that we all loved. On command, our man-eating tiger would chase after anyone who was moving rapidly, reach out with his paw, knock the person to the ground, and pretend to attack him by nuzzling the person's throat. Whaddya know I was the person assigned to play opposite Ben in his signature hit-and-nuzzle scene. After the trainer demonstrated

Ben's acting ability by letting Ben chase and "attack" him, he called to me and said, "Okay, it's your turn."

I was told to run across the set. When I'm being paid, I do what I'm told, so I ran. Suddenly Ben was beside me pushing me over with his paw. The next thing I knew I was on the floor with Ben practically on top of me, his huge head nestled in my neck. I have never come so close to loading my drawers as I did at that moment.

Besides animals, Disney also had a reputation as *the* studio for pie throwing, which I discovered when I did *The Shaggy D.A.* (1976). I read and enjoyed the script they sent me until I came across the words, "pie fight." I hate to see those two words together because I know what's going to happen: My face and a pie are going to meet. Cherry is the pie of choice because of the color and its stick-to-itiveness. I learned that you try to keep your face from being directly hit for as long as you can because once they film you getting hit, you'll be wearing that pie until the scene is completed. (To counteract your dodging, Disney actually hired professional pie-throwers.) The pie throwing can go on for days or even weeks. If you go into a second day's shooting that means that at 6 A.M., somebody in the makeup department will hit you in the face with a pie in order to match the previous day's shot. You wear that pie until someone says, "That's a wrap for today." Ah, but don't think that ends it. What you want to hear them say is, "That's a wrap." Period. "For today" translates into: You're going to get a pie in the face the next morning. I wore a pie for three days. On the fourth day, the script called for me to drive a convertible with the top down through a pillow factory. I was covered in feathers that I had to wear for two more days. On the seventh day, I drove through an auto body shop and got sprayed with orange paint. Naturally, I had to get made up in pie, feathers, and orange paint the next day. The assorted goo was piled on me in the morning, and we shot through the wee hours of the next day. Then, I heard the most beautiful words in the English language: "That's a wrap."

Nothing as terrifying as tigers or cherry pies confronted Don Knotts and me when we did *The Apple Dumpling Gang*. But we did share some extraordinary moments. During the filming we were on location in Stockton, California, some three hundred miles from Los Angeles. For one scene in the movie, Don and I were disguised as two dance hall girls working in a western saloon. We wore low-cut frilly, black dresses, black stockings, high heels, and wigs. My wig was in an upsweep; Don's was a mass of flowing locks with a big feather sticking up in the back. We made a pair of pretty hot chicks if I do say so myself. We stayed at a nearby motel and every morning we'd get in my rented car and I'd drive us to the train station where we were filming. During the week or so that we worked on the dance hall sequence, Don, who never bellyached, constantly complained that he was freezing to death during his costume change. The wardrobe trailer was unheated; really it was like being inside a refrigerator. I wasn't bothered by the cold but I sympathized with him.

"Look," I said, "Just get the wardrobe guy to give you the clothes. Get dressed in the motel in the morning then you won't have to change in the trailer."

"Y'know, you got a good idea there, buddy," said Don.

That day when we got to the set we arranged for Don to bring his costume back to the motel. He was a happy man. The next morning, he emerged from his motel room in all his feminine finery and got in the car. I'll admit he did look a little strange sitting there next to me, but it was what it was. As we drove along, Don couldn't resist grabbing the opportunity to have some fun. He kept preening in his seat and giving friendly little waves to other drivers when we stopped at traffic lights. A day later the scene became even weirder.

We were shooting the dance hall sequence when the director called a halt and announced that we'd finish the next day. I got into my regular clothes, but Don stayed in his costume. He kept on his makeup, too. Dance hall girls tend to pile it on a little thick, and his face glowed with pancake powder. Not to mention the bright red lipstick, the false eyelashes, and the wig with the plume in it. I drove back to the motel and dropped Don off at his room to change. I told him I was going to get a beer at the bar across the street before we went for dinner. He said he'd change into his civvies and join me.

I went into the saloon, got my beer, and sat at the bar. Did I mention that this bar was rather a rough place to spend time? The locals didn't much care for Hollywood types. I passed because I didn't look like a movie person; ordinarily Don passed, too. I was sipping my beer and looking into the big mirror on the wall behind the bar when I saw Don enter. He was still in his dance hall outfit, the black stockings, the high heels, and the wig with a plume in it, the whole works. Everyone stopped talking, and all eyes were on him as he crossed the room and came over to me. He put his hand on my shoulder and said, loud enough for all to hear, "Have you got the keys to that room, big boy?"

Every cowboy in that bar was looking at us. I pulled my head back, slowly looked Don up and down, and then drawled, "Well ma'am, don't you think we ought to talk price first?"

I can still hear the sound of Don's laughter. We were just plain lucky that the cowboys found it amusing, too.

The Apple Dumpling Gang did well enough for Don and me to appear in a sequel, The Apple Dumpling Gang Rides Again. After that, the Gang headed into the corral, but we continued to do films together, many of which I wrote. I did the screenplay for The Private Eyes, a take-off on the Sherlock Holmes adventures.

Don played the Holmes character, Inspector Winship, and I was his sidekick, Doctor Tart. We had as much fun behind the scenes, maybe even more, than in front of the camera. The thing is, though I knew all my lines and exactly what I was supposed to do, I was always susceptible to throwing in a little something extra. For example, we were shooting a scene in *The Private Eyes* with Don and myself standing in front of a large window. I was supposed to send a message to Scotland Yard via a carrier pigeon with a little note attached to his leg. Don was to hand me the pigeon then tell me to throw the bird out the window. During the shoot, I took the pigeon but, instead of opening the window and flinging him out, I threw the bird at the pane. The pigeon smashed through the glass, adjusted a few feathers, and went sailing off. (*Wait,* don't call the ASPCA—the glass in the window was the breakaway kind.) Now if Don had laughed we'd have lost the whole scene. He didn't, though, he just gave one of his "sniff" takes, a quick drawing of air up into his nostrils, and a couple of head bobs, and walked away. Thanks to him, we were able to keep the bit in the film.

I learned a lot just watching Don Knotts at work. There wasn't a phony motion in him, everything was character driven, and, oh, what characters he created! I think Barney Fife from *The Andy Griffith Show* is one of the greatest, funniest, and truest personalities ever seen on the screen. When you watched his antics as Andy Griffith's deputy, you were watching Don Knotts. He *was* Barney Fife, a kind, gentle, fun-loving person who dedicated his life to making people smile. I'm so thankful I had the opportunity to know and to work with Don.

All of the regulars on Steve's show were given the opportunity to create characters that suited our particular comedy style. What's more, Steve was the perfect foil for each of us. My routines usually involved Dag Herferd in multiple roles. For instance, I'd be introduced as "Dag Herferd, The World's Greatest ____" and Steve would fill in the space. One time it would be "Detective," the next "Jockey," or "Cotton Picker," or "Ocarina Soloist," and so forth. Whatever occupation he announced, I'd fall right into it. I'd totter or saunter (depending on my character) out from the wings, take my seat, and answer the questions Steve threw at me. Some of it was written down, but that didn't stop me from tossing in a few lines from left field. Whenever I did this, Steve would look up with this bemused expression on his face, which gradually worked its way into a grin, then a smile, then a laugh. I loved getting Steve to cackle. I didn't realize it at the time but I was in training for Harvey Korman.

Sadly, *The New Steve Allen Show* was cancelled after fourteen episodes, but the good thing was I'd made a splash, a small one, on national television. I returned to Cleveland and to the welcoming arms of Ernie and the rest of the gang.

The Importance of
Being Ernest Borgnine

Of the many wonderful things that came out of being on the *Allen* show, right near the top would be my gaining not only an agent but a friend. Phil Weltman of the William Morris Agency saw my first appearance and immediately called the studio to get my number. The next thing I knew, he was on the phone telling me that he wanted to represent me.

"As what?" I asked.

"As your agent," he replied.

"Oh," said I, "what does that mean?"

"My agency will handle you."

"Why?"

"You're a very funny man. I think you're going places, and we can help you get there. We'll find you work and negotiate your fees, things like that."

"Gee, that sounds nice, but why would you want to do it?"

"Well, we take a percentage of your fees."

"Oh, you want money, too?"

I was half kidding. I knew nothing about agents or managers. I knew nothing about the business end of the business, which, I think, is why I had whatever success I did. I've always had a loose approach to work, whatever I was doing was fine, and wherever I was going was fine. If things didn't work out and I got fired, that was fine, too. I'd go on to the next gig. It wasn't arrogance, it's just that I did what I thought was funny and, fortunately, most of the time I was right. One thing's for sure, I was absolutely right when I signed with Phil Weltman.

In a business that was often just that, Phil was a guy who truly cared about the people he represented. He was my one and only agent until the day he died. He was a marvelous, gentle guy and also a Mr. Malaprop. He tended to relate things inside out. One time we were talking about pro football and an underdog team that, surprisingly, had won a game. Phil meant to say, "Any team can win on any given Sunday." Which makes sense. But, what he said was, "If it's Sunday, a team can win any time they want to." Which doesn't make sense. Phil had been a high-ranking army officer during World War II and had a real soft spot for England. We were talking about Anglo-American relations when Phil commented, "You know, when I was stationed in France we saw quite a bit of Wimpy."

I knew he meant to say "Winnie," the nickname of Winston Churchill, but he'd mixed up Popeye's hamburger-loving pal with Britain's prime minister. I thought I'd help him out and responded, jokingly, "You know, whenever I saw Wimpy, he always had a hamburger."

Phil corrected me, "I don't think that Wimpy had a hamburger. I'm pretty sure it was a derby."

Phil was one-of-a-kind and is the person most responsible for whatever success has come my way. He got me my first major television role soon after *The New Steve Allen Show* was cancelled. In 1962, a producer named Ed Montagne was putting together a comedy television series based on a TV drama, *Seven Against the Sea*. (Montagne already had scored big with *The Phil Silvers Show,* a military comedy set on an army base.) The upcoming series, renamed, *McHale's Navy,* took place on a Pacific island during World War II. The story centered on the commanding officer of a PT boat. Ernest Borgnine had been cast as the CO, Lieutenant Commander Quinton McHale. They were looking for someone to play the role of Ensign Charles Parker, a sweet, not too bright, inept kind of guy who was second in command to McHale and who got into some sort of trouble in every episode. (Does the description sound like someone you know?) Montagne had seen me on Steve's show and called Phil to tell him that they wanted me for the part. Then Phil called me in Cleveland and told me about the offer. I said no.

"Are you nuts?" Phil demanded.

I explained that I was having a good time doing my lousy show in Cleveland and I wasn't so sure I wanted to go back out to Hollywood. I was comfortable and happy where I was. Phil urged me to give it some more thought; I said I'd get back to him. I told a few people at the station about the offer and when I said I didn't want to take it, they questioned my sanity. Eventually, the station manager found out and this time, instead of threatening to fire me as he did when *The New Steve Allen Show* was offered, he actually did fire me. I had no choice but to go.

I went home and informed my wife that we were moving to Los Angeles. She was fine with it. As I've mentioned, our first little cookie was in the oven, and daughter Kelly would be born in

California. In fact, all my kids are Californians. When I told Sophia and Dan we were moving to L.A., Dan shrugged his shoulders and Sophia let loose a torrent of Romanian during which I heard the word *nebun* at least a dozen times. (I'll save you the trouble of looking it up; it means "crazy.") With Sophia's word(s) ringing in my ear, I took my wife and myself way out west.

Our first apartment was in Van Nuys in the San Fernando Valley. Later, we bought a house in Encino. Matter of fact, I've never left the Valley. I became a Californian, but every summer we went back to Ohio to visit with my parents and my pals. As I've said, Sophia and Dan really enjoyed being grandparents and we gave them plenty of opportunity by providing so many grandkids.

I was overwhelmed by Hollywood. I couldn't believe it. Here was a hick from Chagrin Falls breathing the same air and walking on the same sound stages as the biggest stars in the business. It blew my mind. The first day of rehearsal for *McHale's Navy*, I walked into yet another enormous conference room and sat down at a long table. Seated opposite me was Ernest Borgnine, one of those superstars I'd idolized. I saw him in *Bad Day at Black Rock*, *From Here to Eternity, Marty*, and so many other movies. He was terrific in every film he made and, while he didn't fit the description of leading man, he managed to win the Best Actor Oscar for his performance in *Marty*. The minute I sat down, Ernie reached across the table, stuck out his hand, and said, "I'm Ernie Borgnine, and you're Tim Conway, right?"

"I have absolutely no idea who I am," was what I started to say. I was so taken aback that he knew my name, or at least, what sounded like my name that all I could do was take his outstretched hand in mine and hold on to it. I wanted to freeze this moment in my memory bank; Oscar winner shakes hands with Ghoulardi stooge.

"I, ah, I," were the only words that came out of my mouth.

Ernie grinned.

"You're from Cleveland, right?" He smiled his big gap-toothed smile and offered me another chance to speak.

"I, ah, I. . . ."

Honestly, I couldn't get past the second "I." I didn't know what to say. I was starstruck. Sure I'd been exposed to a lot of talented people, but they were television performers. Ernest Borgnine was a *movie star*, like the ones I'd seen on the screen at the Falls Theatre. For Pete's sake, he *was* one of the ones I worshipped. Today, movie and television stars are interchangeable, not to mention those so-called stars from those reality shows. For me a star is a John Wayne or a Ginger Rogers.

Meanwhile, I'm still holding hands with Ernest Borgnine and my tongue is tied. Ernie, bless his big heart, realized that I was dumbstruck. Slowly and gently, he removed his hand and sat back down. I followed his lead, although I more collapsed in my chair rather than sat. Right then and there, Ernest Borgnine took me under his wing. He mentored me for the next three years and became another one of those guys with whom I had a lifelong friendship—and it all began with *McHale's*. We were buddies right up until his death at the age of ninety-five in July of 2012.

In nearly a century of life, Ernie never lost his zest. He was the most "people person" I ever met. Wherever he was or whatever he was doing, if he saw a group talking, he'd walk over and join right in. He used to love to go on long car trips just to bring his friendly act on the road. He'd drive around the country and when he spotted families sitting on their front porches, he'd stop, get out of the car, go up on the porch, pull up a chair, sit down, and start schmoozing. Everybody knew who he was, and, as he himself admitted, it wasn't because he'd won an Academy Award for *Marty*, it was because they all loved *McHale's*. When he stopped the long-distance jaunts, he bought himself a Smart Car and tooled around Los Angeles. That was quite a sight. The car was just large enough to cover him; really, it looked as though he was wearing it. He never stopped working, either. He made appearances all over the USA from L.A. to New York. And right up to the very end, Ernie was on the phone with me trying to get me to go with him to some convention for people seeking memorabilia from old television shows.

"Ya gotta come with me, Tim," he'd implore. "Imagine, you just sign a piece of paper and they pay you five bucks."

Believe me, he didn't need the money. He simply loved to get out and socialize. He was a loyal guy, too. When Ernie was given the Screen Actors Guild Life Achievement Award in January of 2011, I was deeply touched that he asked me to bring him to the dais. I walked him up and said a few words. I told the audience that in order to get me there, Ernie had told me that the awards show was a pilot for a new series. I also mentioned that comedy was just one part of Ernie's wonderful career. "He's recently appeared in *Red*, an AARP action film." Ernie was roaring with laughter as I returned to my seat. I found out later he was mad as hell. He didn't want me to say a few remarks. He wanted me to introduce him and thought that was what I'd be doing. He didn't know that SAG had instead asked Morgan Freeman to do the intro. After the ceremony, Ernie came down to my seat, pulled me to my feet, and dragged me around the room to make sure that everyone knew who I was.

"This is Tim Conway," he bellowed. "Isn't he great!"

Correction, *Ernest Borgnine* was great. Of all the people I've known Ernie was one of those blessed ones who knew how to enjoy life. God love him, and He did.

From the very first show to the very last show, *McHale's Navy* was done with joy and ease, and it all began at the top. Without question, Ernie was the star and we all respected his position. He had that magic quality you find in the great ones. Plus he had the most wonderful sense of humor. He was like a big teddy bear; that's the best way to describe him.

I found out years later, though, that everything wasn't as hunky-dory with the production as I'd thought.

Ernie didn't like one of the producers who wasn't appreciative enough of the work we featured actors did, or so Ernie believed. Apparently Ernie told this guy that after the rushes were shown he at least should give all of us actors a pat on the back.

"I don't kiss up to anybody," the guy answered.

"I beg your pardon?" said Ernie.

"You heard me, I don't kiss up to anybody."

That did it. The next thing you know Ernie tore into him, and they had to be separated. Ernie later said that he was furious because he knew he was the only one making big bucks while the rest of us were getting AFTRA minimum wage. He felt that we deserved more respect for our work since we weren't getting dough.

All during the run of *McHale's Navy*, I never got over the fact that here was one of the biggest screen stars in the business doing a TV show with a bunch of crazies. Believe me, I wasn't the only cast member doing stupid things. Chief among others, I was aided and abetted by Joe Flynn playing Captain Wally Binghamton. Like me, Joe was an Ohio native; he came from Youngstown and, like me, he kept up with his hometown. I used to just visit Chagrin; Joe actually ran for a seat in the Ohio Senate in 1950. (He didn't win.) Joe was hilarious. My character, Ensign Parker, and his character, Wally Binghamton, aka Old Leadbottom, had certain catchphrases. Mine was "Gee, I love that kind of talk." When Wally got frustrated, he'd always say, "What is it? What? *What? What!*" Viewers picked up our expressions, and people all over the country were saying them. Joe Flynn became a friend. We worked together after *McHale's* ended. Joe had the distinct honor of appearing with me on *The Tim Conway Show*, one of the many bombs that bore my name.

The *McHale's* crew was a footloose gang of actors. Besides Ernie, Joe, and me, there were guys like Carl Ballantine, Gavin MacLeod, Bob Hastings, and Gary Vinson. Our rough and tumble way of acting brought a particular realism to the characters we portrayed. I'd known guys just like the fictional *McHale's* crewmembers when I was in the army. I'm sure that ex-service men watching the show felt the same, and that's one of the reasons the show was so popular. To my way of thinking, this sort of reality TV makes sense—actors playing real people. I did such a good job as a slow-witted, bumbling idiot that people thought I must be just like Ensign Parker.

One day Charles Laughton, the distinguished British actor, visited the *McHale's* set and sat on the sideline watching us shoot a scene. Laughton, an intellectual force in Hollywood, often appeared in classic dramas like *King Lear* on the legitimate stage as well in great movies like *Witness for the Prosecution*. I was in awe of him, as was Joe Flynn. Both of us were overwhelmed by his presence and neither of us could get over the fact that *he* was watching *us* perform. When we took a break, Joe convinced me that it was a good idea for me to go over and ask Laughton to lunch. I so wanted to talk to the man that I actually believed this was a good idea. I went over to the chair where Laughton was seated and said in the most refined tones I could produce, "I beg your pardon, Mr. Laughton. I was wondering if you would like to join Joe Flynn and me for lunch." I pointed to Joe who was standing there with an idiotic grin on his face.

Sophia Murgoi Conway and her son, Crown Prince Toma. I'm standing on the running board of one of Dan's second-hand Fords.

Sophia and Lawrence of Arabia on a Lake Erie beach.

Shore leave for the future Ensign Parker.

Have you heard the one about
the Irishman and the Scotsman?
Dan and his best friend, Bill Butler.

A boy's best friend is his dad.

In front of Mr. White's stables. I'm holding the whip Dan brought over from
Ireland. He left his shillelagh behind.

SUBJECTS	FIRST SEMESTER				SECOND SEMESTER				YEAR
	1	2	3	S	1	2	3	S	
English	C	D	c	c	c	D	C	D	c
Civics	C	b	D	D					
Commercial Law					b	C	c	D	
Public Speaking	B	B	c	B	B				
Shop	C	c	c	c	c	c	D	c	c
Phy. Cal.	A	A	A	A	A	A	A	A	A
Drama					C	c	D	c	c
Attitude	A	B	B		B	A			

ATTENDANCE RECORD

	1	2	3	SEM.	4	5	6	SEM.	YEAR
DAYS ABSENT				3½				5	8½
TIMES TARDY				0				5	5

A typical report card. Look closely and you'll see how I changed Ds to Bs and back again.

Graduating from Bowling Green State University. I would have gone to Harvard but the commute was too long.

The low-ceiling cellar on Orange Street. Even I grew too tall to stand up in it.

Rhett Butler, Scarlett O'Hara, and Ashley Wilkes seated in front of Tara. (Orange Street, Chagrin Falls.)

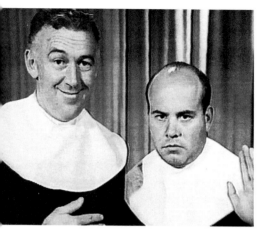

Mentor and friend, the multitalented and totally nuts Ernie Anderson, a television original.

My first appearance with television immortal, Steve Allen.

The incomparable Ernie Borgnine. His big grin reflects his zest for life.

Let's see, you put in the bullets, then you pull this trigger right here and . . .

LEFT: A publicity shot of me and some TV friends.
I just can't seem to recall their names . . .
RIGHT: Don't ask; don't tell.

LEFT: A drawing by Bob Mackie, given to me by Carol. He designed the costume for Mrs. Wiggins.
RIGHT: The Oldest Man and Mother Marcus, Canoga Falls' leading yenta.

Carol, I'd like to talk to
you about a raise.

Standing below my name in lights . . . sort of.

Five weeks after 9/11, Carol, Vicki, Harvey, and I appeared in *Carol Burnett: Showstoppers*, a twenty-fifth anniversary special. It became one of the most successful reunion shows ever; we actually beat out *Monday Night Football*. *TV Guide* called us "America's Secret Weapon." We were artillery, for sure, but the big gun was what the country needed most: laughter. *(Photograph © TV Guide)*

A day off and a chance to rest.
I'm somewhere in the middle
of my children.

Mary Anne Dalton, my first wife,
and I at our daughter Kelley's
high school graduation.

Recording a comedy album with Ernie Anderson. It looks like a dog is up
there with us but it's the back of a woman's head.

We have to dress up as what?
The Apple Dumpling Gang
(*Photograph © Walt Disney Productions*)

You make up a caption.
I'm speechless.
(*Photograph © Walt Disney Productions*)

The Shaggy D.A. Pie throwing at
the Disney studio was an art, but
only for the thrower. Whipped cream
doesn't hold up well under lights.
(*Photograph © Walt Disney Productions*)

With Don Knotts in
The Private Eyes. I helped
write the screenplay.
Basil Rathbone and Nigel Bruce
never had it so good.

STRIKE ONE:
Rango, not a hit show. "Listen,"
I'm whispering to the horse,
"I heard we're being cancelled."

STRIKE TWO:
Ace Crawford, Private Eye.
Likewise, not a hit show.

HOME RUN: *Dorf,*
the world's greatest golfer
and my greatest annuity.

Eat your heart out, Harvey.
(Like he didn't have
a roomful of Emmys.)

Charlene and her BFF, Carol.
Why are they wearing the same dress?

The marital score on our wedding day
was, and still is, Charlene: 3, Tim: 2.

It doesn't get any better.   It did!

Jackie, with her mom,
Charlene, and her
dad(s), Roger Beatty
and yours truly.

A view of one of our horses never seen by another jockey during a race.

With some of our dearest friends, Phyllis and Tony De Franco (in the bandana), and Doris and Bobby Schiffman at home in N.J. When it came to horse racing, Tony was the go to guy.

The Longshot. I actually did run onto the track at Hollywood Park to urge on my horse. Once, just once, I wanted to come in first.

Harvey, Carol, and
an unidentified couple.

More good friends: Debby and
Harvey Korman and Sheila and
Ron Clark.

A joint birthday party for Eydie Gormé, Mike Connors, and my wife. Hold on to your hat, here's the lineup, left to right. Bottom row: Pat Gelbart, Tom Rowan, Angie Dickinson. Middle row: Barbara Sinatra, Eydie Gormé, Michelle van Dyke, Dolly Martin, Marla Rowan, Ginnie Newhart, Charlene, Judy Tannen. Top row: Richard Crenna, R.J. Wagner, Jill St. John, Penni Crenna, unidentified woman, Merv Adelson, Mike Connors, Dick van Dyke, Steve Lawrence, Mary Lou Connors, Larry Gelbart, Grant Tinker, myself, Bob Newhart, Dick Martin.

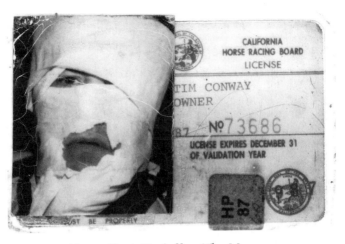

It's not Boris Karloff as *The Mummy*;
it's Tim Conway pulling off a complicated caper.

Pulling a plaid fast one on my friends with a jacket I made myself. Carol completely lost it when she discovered me plastered against—and blended into—the wall.

On stage with Tom Poston somewhere other than Broadway. I must confess I never made it to The Great White Way. But, I'm ready and willing.

The Dentist, a sketch that Harvey and I revived in our live shows on the road (1998–2005). I could still make Harvey break up every single time we performed it.

With Tim Jr. on his KFI AM radio talk show.

A jewel in my crown:
my granddaughter Courtney.

Another jewel,
granddaughter Sophia.

Taking orders for slipcovers.

Laughton slowly glanced up at me and said, "Kind of you to ask, young man, but what on earth would we talk about?"

I looked over at Joe, still grinning like the Cheshire Cat, then turned back to Mr. Laughton, and said, "Right."

One of the perks of doing *McHale's Navy* was the opportunity to play dual roles, which Ernie, Joe, and I got to do in a few episodes. I liked being a totally different character from the one everybody recognized. One of them was an English general. I think I did a pretty good job with the accent (I hope I did), and it was fun to step outside myself. But Ensign Parker was my bread-and-butter role. He was very real to me, too—so real that in the show he referred to his hometown, Chagrin Falls, quite a few times. Honestly, he could have been from Chagrin.

Everybody loved *McHale's Navy*. Yet, even though we ruled the broadcast waves, we were cancelled after a four-year run. The reason was simple. While we were shooting the first three seasons color television was on the rise, and by the mid-1960s, it had taken over. They could have shot the fourth season in color but, because the first three seasons were in black-and-white, they thought it would be a waste of time, and more important, of money. Basically, we got cancelled because people weren't watching black-and-white television anymore. Everyone was sorry to see the show end, and no one was sorrier than Ensign Charles Parker.

A Salute to Garry Moore

𝒟*uring my time on* Mc*Hale's Navy,* I did a lot of moonlighting on other programs. Variety shows dominated the television schedules, and I got to be on just about all of them. Why? Three little words: Ensign Charles Parker. I was a known commodity thanks to that guy. I appeared eleven times on *The Hollywood Palace*, both as a solo act and in comedy routines with Ernie Anderson. Billy Harbach was the producer and he was responsible for my gigs. I almost blew it at an early appearance when Kate Smith was the guest host. Kate was one of the most popular entertainers of her day; her day was more radio than television, but she did make the transition. She was a large woman with an imposing presence and a really great singer. Her rendition of "God Bless America" was one of the hit tunes of World War II. At the end of the show we all lined up for the finale; I happened to be standing near Ms. Smith.

I had no idea that she performed a ritual before her closing number. It seems that she always crossed herself before launching into her final song. I saw her make the sign of the cross, and instead of keeping my mouth shut, I chirped, "Sure hope you make the basket."

Kate Smith was not amused. If she had been the permanent host I might not have made any more appearances on *The Hollywood Palace*.

Joe Hamilton used to call me the Comedy Ambulance because when anyone dropped out of a spot on a variety show, they'd call me. I'd jump in the car, zip down to the studio, and fill in. I remember one time when I was involved in a sketch about chickens. The idea was to get me in a chicken suit, fill the stage with hundreds of live chickens, and put me in the middle of them. Unfortunately, some sort of strike was going on with poultry farmers, and they only managed to gather about ten live and clucking birds. This would never be as impressive as having hundreds of them. But we had to make do. Ultimately, it was a waste of time and costume. The studio audience consisted of elderly ladies with shopping bags, none of whom cracked a smile as I ran around in my chicken suit bumping into the few birds we'd scraped up. Some of the chickens laid eggs, and so did I.

Another time, I did a guest spot on a variety show, and one of the featured stars was John Wayne, a particular movie idol of mine. I was awestruck but still ready for some fun. Wayne's well-known nickname was Duke. I asked one of the producers, "Do you think Mr. Wayne would mind if I called him Duck instead of Duke?"

"Of course not," I was assured. "He has a great sense of humor."

In the scene we had together, Wayne was supposed to break things over my head to demonstrate how they use props that don't injure actors. Wayne said he would do the stunt only once. That put the crew on notice to get it right the first time. We took our places in front of the camera and as we prepared to demonstrate I said to him, "I just want you to know how great it is for me to be working with the Duck."

Wayne's eyes narrowed to a squint, he squared his shoulders, and hitched his thumbs into his belt. Immediately I knew I'd been set up but was helpless to do anything about it. The Duke grabbed a breakaway bottle and broke it over my head. He picked up a breakaway mirror and broke that over my head. He took hold of a breakaway chair and broke that over my head. It wasn't supposed to hurt but he smacked so hard it did, a little. The scene got big laughs from the audience. Fortunately, a still photographer was on the set and I got a set of pictures from him. To this day, three photographs of each of those breakaway moments are hanging on my den wall.

I did my stuff on *The Danny Kaye Show, The John Gary Show, The Dean Martin Comedy Hour, The Red Skelton Hour*, and, I had a bit part on *Channing*, a dramatic series. (*Channing* only lasted for one season, and I only appeared in one episode but, hey, a credit is a credit.) These shows came after *McHale's* aired in October 1962, but my most important appearance, the one that shaped the course of my future professional and personal life, happened before the *McHale's* premiere. On June 12, 1962, I guest starred on *The Garry Moore Show*.

Garry Moore was another major star of the 1950s and 1960s whose influence is felt right up to the present day but whose name is even more obscured than Steve Allen's. Garry's shows were variety programs that bore his name and featured a stock company of players performing comedy sketches, musical numbers, and monologues. Moore was a short, easygoing guy who did two things consistently—he wore his hair in a crew cut and he always sported a bow tie, both of which became his trademarks. He was about the most genial person you can imagine. He never needed to hog the limelight; in fact, he did just the opposite. He wanted to give audiences the best possible show they could get and to do this he'd hand over the biggest laughs to his cast and his guests (like myself) if it were in the best interest of the show. Case in point: A certain young lady, whose own trademarks included an earsplitting rendition of Tarzan's yell and a tug on her ear lobe, joined *The Garry Moore Show* in 1959 and stayed until 1966. To this day that certain (forever) young lady credits Moore with teaching her everything she needed to know about being a good performer and a good person—make that *great* performer and person. You know I'm talking about Carol Burnett, so let's get on with it.

Carol had put herself on the entertainment map with a comedy ballad, "I Made a Fool of Myself Over John Foster Dulles," especially written for her by Ken Welch. She first sang it at The Blue Angel, a popular Greenwich Village nightclub. Later she performed it on both *The Tonight Show* and *The Ed Sullivan Show* on CBS. For those who might not be up on the political scene of the 1950s, Dulles, the secretary of state from 1953 to 1959, was regarded as a bit stuffy and was really not that popular a public figure. The idea that this exuberant young woman had a crush on the stodgy secretary was so off-the-wall that people couldn't get enough of it. Not only did the song ignite Carol's career, it gave Dulles a needed political boost. She actually sang it to him on television and viewers were astounded to see the sour-faced secretary crack a smile. Carol then went on to appear off-Broadway and later on Broadway as Winifred in *Once Upon a Mattress*, a musical takeoff of Hans Christian Andersen's tale "The Princess and the Pea." Carol was a hit, and it was full speed ahead after that.

Phil Weltman arranged for me to fly to New York to film an appearance on Moore's show. I arrived on the set at CBS Studio 51 and was introduced to the regulars; Carol, Durwood Kirby, and Alan King. We really didn't have much to do with each other because they were doing their sketches and I was doing my own; a take-off on Superman that centered on his inability to find a phone booth to change back to Clark Kent or vice versa. As I remember the booth was too small for me to get out of my suit and into my Superman costume and ended with me emerging in my underwear. (What on earth would Clark and Supe do today? I dare you to find a phone booth in this cell phone world.) Carol later told me that she watched my act and thought I was really funny. However, in discussing my performance with Charlene Fusco, an assistant to producer Joe Hamilton, she found herself defending me. Ms. Fusco thought I stunk. Okay, how many Charlenes do you meet in a lifetime? I am talking about my own beloved future wife, and here she was making snide remarks about my comic ability at our very first encounter. She'd probably be dissing me to this day if I hadn't been asked to appear on *The Sammy Davis, Jr. Show* a few years later. Joe Hamilton was a producer on Sammy's show, a William Morris package. I was with William Morris as was Joe; we were members of the same fraternity, so to speak. When Charlene learned that I'd been booked, she remembered my *Garry Moore Show* appearance and went right to Joe.

"Tim Conway? Oh please. You booked that guy again? Didn't he do enough damage on Garry's show?"

"Sharkey, he's very funny," Joe said. "He's been a real hit on *McHale's Navy.*"

"McHale's what?"

My success had gone right by the lovely Ms. Fusco because, according to her, she didn't watch California sitcoms except for

The Dick Van Dyke Show. They were very snobby in New York City back then. And don't forget the East and West Coasts weren't connected the way they are today. There was much more local programming, and even though *McHale's Navy* was shown nationally, Charlene considered it a local product. Can you believe this? Not funny, huh? Well I showed her a thing or two! After my spot, she went to Joe and said, "Oh, now I get it."

And, happily, she's been getting it ever since.

It's time for a little background update which means I have to bring Carol into the picture, again. *The Garry Moore Show* was Carol's graduate school in entertainment. She sharpened all her skills on that program and later brought them into her own show. They were a close-knit bunch on Garry's show both behind and in front of the camera. Charlene and Carol were already buddies before I came along, and they still are. (To this day when we get together I feel like I'm along for the ride with those two. But it's a terrific ride.) Around the same time Charlene and Judy Tannen became friends. Judy's been managing Steve Lawrence and Eydie Gormé for nearly four decades. Carol and Joe Hamilton hit it off, big time, and eventually got married. The *Moore Show* trio—Carol, Joe, and Charlene—worked together so well it was only natural for them to continue their partnership. And so Carol led them out of New York and into the wilderness of Los Angeles where *The Carol Burnett Show* premiered on September 11, 1967 . . . without me. It's hard to believe but there are still people who think that I was a cast member from the very start. I made my first appearance on October 2, 1967, but as a guest, not a regular. Carol remembered me from the Garry Moore days and thought that I'd make a nice now-and-again addition to her show. And so I became a regular guest for seven years. I was so regular I was on the show at least twice a month. In 1974, Lyle Waggoner, the announcer as well as a performer, left the show. Lyle and I looked so much alike that I was asked to step in and take over his vacated spot as a performer. At the same time, Ernie Anderson, that well-known member of the studio audience, took over Lyle's announcing chores. Bottom line? *The Carol Burnett Show* was telecast for eleven years, and I was a regular cast member for only four.

All Roads Lead to Carol

Here's what I imagined heaven would be like when I was a kid. I pictured huge gates made of big white pearls and beyond them, fluffy clouds leading to a magnificent golden building that most resembled a humongous Falls Theatre. A smiling Eleanor Roosevelt was in the outside booth dispensing free tickets while inside, a smiling Franklin Delano Roosevelt gave out free popcorn. I'd take my seat and be treated to a newsreel, a Bugs Bunny cartoon, a Pete Smith special, a travelogue, and a double feature. After the show ended, I'd leave the theatre, wave good-bye to Franklin and Eleanor, and suddenly find myself on a racehorse competing against a bunch of jockeys with wings on their backs and halos on their heads. The vision ended with me in the winner's circle, one large horseshoe of red roses draped over my shoulders and another one hanging over the horse's neck as a crowd of spectators, which included Sophia and Dan, cheered wildly. Ah heaven!

Well, I grew up and discovered that heaven was nothing like that childhood dream. Heaven, in fact, was located in Los Angeles, California, at the corner of Beverly Boulevard and Fairfax Avenue in Television City's CBS Studio 33. That's where *The Carol Burnett Show* was filmed and that's where I spent the happiest days of my show business life.

What, you might ask, had I been doing between the time that *McHale's Navy* ended and my entry into the *Burnett* show? Actually, I kept pretty busy appearing on all those variety and sitcom shows, several of which I've mentioned, plus I had shows of my own. It's a sore subject, but I've got to get them out of the way before I further describe my heaven on earth. For the sake of full disclosure, here are some of the miss-terpieces I was involved in.

It was either Socrates or Milton Berle who said, "know thyself." And I knew myself. At least I knew my professional self. I was never deluded about where I stood in the entertainment world. I wasn't a star of the first magnitude. For that you have to look to someone like Carol. I didn't really aspire to superstardom. As long as I was working and doing what I liked I felt okay. What got me into trouble were all those producers who thought they knew me better than I knew myself. For a long time they kept coming up with projects that had me in the leading role. Look, I'd have to have my head examined to turn down opportunities like that when really I should have had my head examined for accepting them. It all started in 1967 with *Rango*.

You would think that the role of an incompetent Texas Ranger posted at a ranger station in the middle of nowhere would be a perfect fit for me. You'd think it, but you'd be dead wrong. Want proof? *TV Guide* rated *Rango* number 47 in the list of the fifty worst shows of all time. It just dawned on me that there were forty-six worse shows ahead of me. I was a mere three shows away from *not* being on the list at all. (In case you're wondering, *The Jerry Springer Show* topped the list.) Some of the stuff in *Rango* was okay, but basically the show didn't work. I think it had a lot to do with the fact that it was filmed without an audience. It was like making a movie, and I didn't have much chance to do any improvising or ad-libbing, which are my strong points. And, unlike *McHale's Navy*, I didn't have an Ernie Borgnine or a Joe Flynn to play off of, although as Rango, I did have an Indian sidekick named Pink Cloud. Guy Marks, the guy who played my Kimosabe, got some laughs by playing against type. Pinkie spoke in a highfalutin manner, more Noel Coward than Tonto. Guy was a good actor but occasionally unreliable. We were shooting one day and after lunch discovered that Pink Cloud had gone missing. We waited an hour for him to show. Now Guy was known to take puffs on his peace pipe from time to time and follow his inhalations with a catnap, which is exactly what had happened. Unbeknownst to us, he'd left the studio, gone to a nearby park, taken some puffs, and fallen asleep on a bench. Nothing unusual about that except that Guy was in full wardrobe, a headband with a pink feather, a hemp shirt, deerskin pants, moccasins, and a bag of wampum dangling from his snakeskin belt. Meanwhile, back at the set, more time passed and we got worried. Someone put in a few calls to local hospitals without success. They couldn't find anyone under the name Guy Marks. I suggested that they call back and see if an Indian had wandered in. We found him. Guy had gone to an emergency room where he'd tried to buy some medication to cure his headache. He wanted to pay with the wampum in his pouch. They hospitalized him. We asked them to keep him there and told them we'd be right over. I drove to the hospital with one of the producers and we picked up Guy, literally. He was in no condition to walk or work so we all took the day off.

Rango got pretty good reviews, yet the series only lasted for seventeen episodes. And the funniest moment didn't come in front of the camera; it happened in my dressing room as I was getting ready to go on the set. I didn't know that the decision had been made to cancel the show. None of the hotshots at the network wanted to be the one to tell me, so they got this kid who may have been working in the mailroom, put a suit on him, and sent him to me with the good news. I was pulling on my boots when I heard a knock at the door and told the knocker to come in. In walks this kid who introduces himself as someone from the ABC office. I could tell by his nervousness that he wasn't exactly from ABC's highest echelon so I tried to make him comfortable.

"Take a seat," I told him motioning toward a chair. "I'm just putting on my boots to go on the set."

"Um, um," muttered the kid. His face was red and sweat dotted his forehead.

"Look," I said, "is there anything I can do for you?"

"Yes," he blurted out, "stop putting on those boots."

That was his version of "your show is cancelled." I stood there with my boot half on and my mouth hanging open as the poor kid turned and raced out the door. The funny thing is, it was a Monday and not a Friday. I guess the network didn't follow the old fire-them-on-Friday convention.

Next up at the plate in my leading role series is *Turn-On* (1969), a show that has gone down in television history for all the wrong reasons. To this day *Turn-On* remains the shortest-lived television series on record. The producer was George Schlatter. George is forever saying that he loves me, but I think he hangs around with me because I'm the only one who's been cancelled more often than he has. He also likes to tell stories about me, some of which are true and others which are even truer.

George and his partner, Ed Friendly, along with NBC and Romart, Inc., produced *Rowan & Martin's Laugh-In*, a wildly popular show in the late 1960s. Inspired by *Laugh-In's* success, George and Ed came up with a new concept originally called *Cockamamie*. A natural successor to the Rowan and Martin juggernaut, *Cockamamie* was an electronically inspired, multimedia show, with cartoon sets and a moog synthesizer as the audience. *Cockamamie* was so outrageous and so hard-edged it made *Laugh-In* look like *The Waltons*. We did a pilot, and George brought it to the ABC network. (Okay, he brought it to them after NBC and CBS turned it down.) ABC, in its infinite wisdom, thought it was the funniest thing they'd ever seen and sold thirteen episodes to Bristol-Myers. The total was upped to eighteen when the company's top brass saw the pilot. By that time, the show had been rechristened to *Turn-On*. To give you an idea of what *Turn-On* was like, in one sketch I was arrested and brought to a police station where I was allowed to make one phone call. I picked up the receiver and made an obscene call. In another, I was doing a commercial for a man's deodorant. I was working out with weights and ended by saying, "When I'm all through, I smell like a lady." Then a shot of me in drag flashed on the screen. And, in another scene, I was a spokesman for the "Citizens Action Committee of America," the acronym for the group was, of course, CACA. Basically, *Turn-On* was caca.

Turn-On premiered on February 5, 1969, with me as the guest host, and was on the air from February 5, 1969, to February 5, 1969. You heard me; the show was pulled midway through the first and only episode and replaced by some affiliates with organ music. It was never seen in many West Coast cities. Picture this, while *Turn-On* was being turned off, the cast and crew were gathered in a New York hotel enjoying a premiere cast party for a show that didn't even make it through the first episode. It's the only television program that had a combined premiere and cancellation party. Very economical don't you think?

I recovered from my *Turn-On* experience and by January of 1970 I had another show of my own, a half-hour comedy sitcom with the very original title, *The Tim Conway Show*. The best thing about the show was that it reunited me with Joe Flynn. We played a pair of owner-pilots of an airline, an airline with only one plane, a Beechcraft 18. One episode was entitled "All of Our Aircraft Is Missing," which is amusing if you're old enough to remember the British World War II movie *One of Our Aircraft Is Missing*. The show was funny, but it's hard to come off a highly popular series and create another character who can make viewers forget the first one. Viewers looked at me and saw Ensign Parker. We managed to squeak out twelve episodes from the basic premise. But again, the show was filmed, which made even bantering with Joe a bit too confining for my taste. Although we had our fans, there weren't enough of them for the show to be renewed. My memories of *The Tim Conway Show* are bittersweet; it was the last opportunity I had to work with Joe. Tragically, he drowned in his swimming pool in 1974. He was fifty years old and apparently had suffered a heart attack. All I can say is it was a privilege to work with a master of subtle humor who died way too young.

Regarding my starring vehicles, any way you slice it I'd had three big strikeouts. Did the producers who thought I was the greatest thing since Wonder Bread give up on me? Nope. The next thing I knew I was sitting across the desk from the president of CBS. He loved my work on the *Burnett* show and offered me an hour variety show of my own. I'd been burned so many times I was wary of jumping into the flames again, but who was I to argue with the president of CBS? I said okay. So, what should we call it? Why not *The Tim Conway Comedy Hour*? Here was I, a humble permanent guest on *The Carol Burnett Show* about to star in his second eponymous vehicle. Ron Clark and Sam Bobrick, established comedy writers, were the producers. Any way you looked at it, my comedy hour would appear to have been a natural. There was that little, itsy-bitsy, teeny-weeny hitch, though. I never was comfortable doing a show where I was the head honcho. Give me a chicken outfit and a sketch and I'd be glad to do a guest spot, but being the captain of the ship was not in my DNA. Despite my misgivings we taped our first episode in September, which happened to be a Christmas show. When friends asked why I was doing a Christmas show in September, I told them that I was sure the show would be cancelled by Christmas and I wanted to get my kids on before it went off.

On September 20, 1970, *The Tim Conway Comedy Hour* premiered. It wasn't exactly an extravagant production. We didn't have an orchestra, just Art Metrano humming his signature tune, "Fine and Dandy." And we only had one dancer, Sally Struthers, who did all the moves the June Taylor Dancers used to do, only she did them solo. If you need further proof that it was impossible for me to have my own show, cast your eyes on the following guest stars who were willing to appear with me: Steve Allen, Dan Blocker, Walter Brennan, Imogene Coca, Joan Crawford, Barbara Feldon, John Forsythe, Eydie Gormé, Merv Griffin, Dorothy Lamour, Steve Lawrence, Janet Leigh, Audrey Meadows, David Janssen, Dick Martin, Tony Randall, Carl Reiner, Mickey Rooney, Dan Rowan, Connie Stevens, Lana Turner, and Shelley Winters. Let me see, did I mention everybody? Oh, I almost forgot, that kind lady, Carol Burnett, volunteered to try to save my sinking ship. I think it was a very funny show if I must say so myself, and I must. It could have gone on for years if it hadn't been cancelled.

In 1983, the old Punching Bag was again wooed by CBS for a series called *Ace Crawford, Private Eye*. This, too, looked good on paper; it was a parody of the hard-nosed detective stories that were so popular. I got to wear a trench coat and a Stetson hat; trouble is I only got to wear them for one season of five episodes. Like its predecessors, *Ace Crawford* bit the dust. Have I told you that the minimum commitment of episodes pledged by a network is thirteen? As you can see by my record, I never quite got there. For a while I had a license plate that read 13WEEKS. Truer words were never embossed. My experiences were pretty embarrassing, or would have been if I had invested much ego in them. But I don't hold grudges or harbor bad feelings; I had my chances and I had fun with them. Like I said, I'm not superstar material. Come to think of it, I probably should have gotten a license plate that read 2BANANA. Okay, that's enough of this. Dry your tears and let's move on.

Heaven

This is the chapter where I'm going to go behind the scenes and blow the lid off the myth of Carol Burnett. Did that statement grab you? I just wanted to see if you were paying attention. The truth is Carol Burnett is even better than the myth surrounding her. The myth is that she's simply the best at what she does and who she is. (Does that sentence make sense? According to spell-check it's okay, but I don't understand it myself.) Let's put it this way, there's no more talented entertainer in the world and there isn't a better friend in the universe than my dear, dear Carol. Did you notice that she wrote the foreword to this book? It was a Friday when I called and asked if she'd do it. I told her there was no big rush; she had months in which to write it. It arrived the following week. I didn't even have a book written and I already had a foreword. That's Carol Burnett. Look, she's been the other woman in my life for nearly half a century and it's not a problem because I think my wife likes her better than she likes me.

It all began in 1962 when, as you might recall, Joe Hamilton, a producer on *The Garry Moore Show* and Carol's future husband, requested me as a guest. At that first meeting, Carol was a delightful, kind, brilliant comedian, and nothing's changed. Even though we didn't actually appear together, she took a shine to me, and filed "short, funny man" somewhere in the back of her head. Then when *The Carol Burnett Show* began broadcasting from CBS in Hollywood in September of 1967, she remembered that short, funny man. She also knew that I had relocated to Los Angeles and also knew about my work on *McHale's Navy*.

Since my honorable discharge from the *Navy*, I had won the Tour de France and the Nobel Peace Prize and was kicking around the variety show circuit when, out of the blue, Carol and Joe called.

"Why don't you come over to our show on Stage 33," she said. "You can try it on and see if it fits."

So I dropped into Television City and tried on the show. It was a 34 short, a perfect fit, and I was booked for a guest appearance. At the same time, Carol asked me if I knew a guy named Harvey Korman. I told her that I'd never met him but that I'd seen him many times on *The Danny Kaye Show*.

"Well, I'd like you to meet him," Carol said, "because you're going to be doing a sketch with him. I have a feeling that you two might work well together. Let's go see him."

We hopped on an elevator and went down to the subbasement. Carol led me into the furnace room, and there, handcuffed to a water pipe, was Harvey Korman.

"Don't get too close to him," she cautioned, "he can be dangerous."

Despite Carol's warning, Harvey was as nice as pie and even offered me some moldy apple crumble from a tin plate that was on the floor next to him. I took a bite, and we chatted about comedy and the interwoven dialectics of what we thought was funny. I thought it was funny to put on a white wig and pretend to be an addled old man. He thought it was funny to dress up as a meddling old Jewish woman. We were made for each other.

I did my first sketch with Carol and Harvey that week and immediately was asked back as a guest star. And that's how it went for seven years until they broke down and asked me to be a regular. By then they were doing twenty-three shows a year.

"Well I don't know," I said playing it cool. "I don't want to be a regular because that doesn't leave me open to do other things. I tell you what, I'll do twenty-two shows and be a guest on the twenty-third."

I still haven't figured out their thinking. It must have had something to do with paying me health benefits. Why didn't they make me a regular from the beginning? I mean I did everything they asked of me—well, almost everything. I balked when they wanted me to sing in one of the big musical numbers Carol loved to do. You've heard of a tin ear? I have no ear. I said I couldn't sing. They wouldn't believe me. I was brought over to a rehearsal piano, and Peter Matz, the musical director, sat down at the keyboard.

"Look, Tim," Pete said, "let's make it easy. You know 'Row, Row, Row Your Boat,' don't you?"

"No, no, no I don't," I protested.

Pete wouldn't take no, no, no for an answer. He started playing and I started (trying) to sing. It was torture . . . for everybody. At last, Pete took his hands off the keys and looked over at me.

"You really don't know it, do you?"

"No, I don't. I can't sing."

Pete stood up, closed the lid over the keyboard, shook his head, and walked off.

So don't look for me singing in any musical numbers in Carol's show. I only agreed to try it because I would do anything for her.

From the beginning, I realized that there was something special about this Burnett girl. When Harvey and I ran through our routines for that week's show, those watching would laugh, and that included Carol. Let me tell you, most stars would have been surveying the scenes to see how they could appropriate the big laughs for themselves. Carol, the PhD graduate of the Garry Moore University of Good Clean Fun, never did that. Like her mentor Moore, she always put the show and the other performers first. In the eleven years I was with her, I never heard a guest express any dissatisfaction with the way they were treated. That's a record.

The routine for doing *The Carol Burnett Show* was pretty simple. We had a sit-down reading on Monday, we'd rehearse on Tuesday, we'd learn the lines, and on Wednesday we had a run-through for the network and the staff. Thursday was for blocking, so we couldn't do much rehearsing, and Friday night was the show. When you think of it, the whole thing was so quick. We had cue cards but we didn't use them in the sketches. Actually, I was on the show for years before I realized that the cards they held up were the script. Even though the show was filmed, Carol wanted it to have the feeling of a live performance. That's why viewers saw so many instances of the cast breaking up on camera. I know that there are viewers out there who still believe that many of those moments weren't really spontaneous. I assure you they were never staged. What I'd sometimes do was go to the director and ask him to keep the camera rolling even if I departed from the script. My pals never knew what hit them. We had a real audience, two of them, since the show was taped twice, and I had the freedom to do what came naturally. I never got the feeling that I was overstepping my bounds when I took advantage of situations that were ripe for improvising. I give you my word, I could not, and would not have done it, if Carol and Joe hadn't let me.

By the way, Carol is no slouch when it comes to ad-libbing, either. She's quick, really quick. When we get together and talk about those days, certain moments in the show always resurface. We've given most of them code names. All you have to say is "The Curtain Rod," "The Dentist," "Nora Desmond," "The Elephant," or "The Horse" and everyone knows exactly what sketch we're talking about. "The Horse" provides the perfect example of Carol's ability to take charge of any situation, no matter how off-the-wall. The sketch was a take-off on the old-fashioned Judy Garland and Mickey Rooney musicals that were set into motion by the immortal line, "I know a barn where we can put on a musical." In the sketch, Carol was singing a song in front of the barn while outside a real horse stood behind the fence. As Carol warbled, the horse felt the call of nature and answered it. When a horse makes a decision like that, it doesn't go unnoticed; he began to pee, big time. The wrangler in charge of the gallant steed rushed out and put a pail underneath him. Meanwhile, unaware of what was happening behind her, Carol kept singing as the horse kept peeing. She wondered why the audience was laughing hysterically and glanced over her shoulder to see what was going on. She saw the horse (still going), the pail, and the wrangler. Carol sized up the situation and, instantly, worked out everything in her head. After the audience calmed down, she turned to the wrangler and asked, "Is he through?"

The wrangler nodded. Carol then turned to Peter Matz and said, "Okay, Pete, let's start again. Do you want to take it from Number One or Number Two."

I'm sure I don't have to tell you how the audience responded, that is, how every single person in that studio, from the control booth, to the stage, to the audience, erupted. You could have passed the pail around the entire room. You have to be a special performer to top an impromptu animal act like that, and that's exactly what Carol was, and did.

Here I am telling Carol stories again. Maybe I'll wire the keyboard and every time I type "Carol Burnett" I'll get an electric shock. Better not do that. Chances are I'd electrocute myself within two paragraphs. Much as I love her, I have to banish her for a while. Who I really want to talk about now is Harvey Korman.

Harvey

Harvey Korman and I were much more than friends. We were much more than brothers. I don't know what the next step on the relationship ladder is, not including "don't ask, don't tell," but whatever it is, we were it. He was my partner, my friend, and my target. With the exception of height and religious persuasion—Catholic vs. Jewish—we were the same person. To this day, I have no idea exactly how tall Harvey was, but he seemed to be around ten feet. We saw eye to eye on everything, except I had to stand on a chair to do it. We were as close as the pages in this book. We even had the same personal problems. Both our first marriages ended in divorce and both our second marriages endured. We loved our children and devoted our very beings to them. We had the same car troubles—dead batteries. You name it, we were the same. Wait—except for the fact that we dressed differently.

Harvey, in fact, may have been the worst dresser in the world. I purchased my clothes at Carroll and Co., a men's clothing store in Beverly Hills. Harvey took clothes off the costume rack from Carol's show, combined them in a helter-skelter way, and called the result a wardrobe. His number one outfit was his go-to ensemble for semiformal occasions, which included anything that fell between loungewear and black tie. The first time Charlene saw his number one outfit in all its glory was during a weekend trip to San Francisco where Harvey and I were doing a benefit. Charlene and Debby Korman joined us. We were going out for dinner, and Char and I waited in front of the hotel for the Kormans. They walked out the door and as they approached us, Charlene grabbed my arm.

"What on God's earth is Harvey wearing?" she gasped.

He was, of course, in his number one outfit. I shall now attempt to describe that ensemble without gagging. It began with a multicolored shirt that had as much going on in the pattern as Dan's mosaic cellar floor on Orange Street. None of the shirt's colors matched anything else he was wearing, which included a yellow tie and a brown sports jacket, both lifted from a "Carol and Sis" sketch on *The Carol Burnett Show*. The jacket had some sort of crisscrossing pattern; the cut was of a style that had definitely gone out of style. His double-knit pants were brown but not a complementary shade to the jacket. They were flared at the bottom, and the hem on the left leg had come undone leaving the cuff flapping in the wind. On his feet he wore brown loafers with white cloth inserts on the upper vamps. To top it off, a gold chain-link ID bracelet, that must've weighed five pounds, circled his right wrist. And that's how my friend Harvey appeared when he got dressed up, except for black tie events when he had to wear a tux. Oh, I almost forgot, sometimes he sported a Dodgers baseball cap that he'd received on Fan Appreciation Day at Dodger Stadium. He'd even wear his Dodgers cap with his tux.

One sartorial occasion is forever etched in my brain. Harvey and I were invited to be Cary Grant's guests at the Hollywood Park racetrack. We were thrilled at the invitation and equally thrilled to learn that Grant was a huge fan of our show. Some of you may recall that, besides being a great actor, Cary Grant was just about the best dresser in show business. Harvey picked me up to go to the track and, of course, he was wearing his number one outfit. We met Mr. Grant in the dining room for lunch before the races began. I wasn't sure how Mr. Grant would react to my pal's bizarre attire. I should have known that he was too much of a gentleman to show anything. I'm happy to report that Cary Grant didn't blink an eye when he shook hands with "Nicely-Nicely Johnson." We sat down at a prominent table and had lunch. Every time Harvey brought his fork to his mouth his sleeve would draw back revealing the chain-link ID bracelet in all its glory. Cary Grant had to have seen it—the people across the dining room could see it—but he said nothing. Knowing Harvey, he probably was waiting for Grant to compliment him on it. We we're sitting there eating and chatting when Grant dropped a little salad dressing on his jacket. As he brushed it off with his napkin, Harvey did a double take and cried out, "Oh, I don't believe it, Cary Grant dribbles, too!"

Along with his eccentric way of dressing, Harvey had an eccentric way of doing almost anything. For instance, he drove a car that had a small hole in the roof. Rather than lay out the few bucks it would have cost to have the thing professionally restored, he did his own repair by taping a plastic Dodgers baseball helmet over the open space. You could always spot Harvey's car in traffic. By the way, Harvey's thrift was legendary; he could be suckered into any deal that promised a bargain. And I could come up with those deals at the drop of a hat. We were sitting around at rehearsal one afternoon when Harvey commented that he'd gained a few extra pounds and was looking at various diets.

"The best one I know is the Gavin Diet," I told him.

"What's that?" Harvey asked.

I had made up the name on the spur of the moment and, prompted by Harvey's query, I immediately made up a diet to go with the name.

"Well, it was created by a Dr. Gavin and the best thing is you don't have to eat anything special or count calories or anything like that. And it doesn't cost anything, either."

At the words "doesn't cost anything" Harvey leaned forward. I had him hook, line, and sinker. All I had to do was reel him in.

"What are you talking about? How can there be a diet that doesn't cost anything and lets you eat anything?"

"I know it's hard to believe, but I've been on the Gavin Diet for years to keep my weight constant. It's so simple I don't know why everybody doesn't go on it. It's based on the fact that your body burns up the fat to keep the body temperature at a constant ninety-eight point two degrees."

"How the hell do you do that?" demanded Harvey.

"Well, it all happens at night. When you go to bed you have to sleep in the nude, without blankets, and you've got to keep the windows open."

"That's it?"

"That's it. It's that simple."

"And you've done it?"

"For ten years."

"And that's all you have to do?"

"That's all."

That evening Harvey went on the Gavin Diet; he went off it the next morning after his wife asked him where he got the crazy idea that sleeping in the nude with the windows open had anything to do with losing weight. The funny thing is, he never said a word to me about what happened. I only found out because Debby told Charlene.

Another time while we were on the road, his suitcase, a beat-up imitation leather knock-off that he'd owned for years, split open, forcing him to buy a new one. He purchased a cheapie with a three-dial combination lock and brought it to my room.

"I can't figure out how to open this thing," he said tossing the suitcase on the bed. "I pushed the dials around but nothing clicks."

"I know how to open it," I replied.

What I didn't tell him was that the combination dial usually was preset to 0-0-0 and opened automatically. Inside the suitcase the instruction booklet told you how to set your own code. Harvey never saw the instructions because he had messed up the preset. I picked up the case, held it up to my ear as though I were listening to the clicks on the lock, and put 0-0-0 on the dial. Then, I put the case on the bed and opened it. He was dumfounded.

"How did you do that?" he asked.

"Well, I knew this guy who'd spent a lot of time in prison and he taught me how."

I shut the case and gave the lock a spin.

"Stop!" Harvey cried, "Don't lock it. I've got to open it."

"Ah," I answered, "that's where I come in. I'll open it for you, but each time I do, it'll cost you two dollars."

"You're kidding me," said Harvey.

"Try me," I said.

I made eight dollars on that trip; eight dollars from a guy who could name all the presidents of the United States in order but couldn't figure out how to open a simple lock.

The cornerstone of our relationship, professional and personal, was my ability to make Harvey laugh just by looking at him. While I got a real kick out of getting any of my colleagues to crack up during sketches, I *lived* to break Harvey. He was the easiest target in the entire ensemble, which was ironic because he was, excluding the lady herself, the most professional actor in the company. Harvey prided himself on being a comedic actor, which is not the same as being a comic. He considered himself to be a really good straight man, that is, someone who is funny himself but who knows when to shut up and serve the star. Harvey acted funny but he could have acted serious, too. He knew a lot about acting, and if you don't believe me, ask Vicki Lawrence.

In case you don't know how Vicki became part of *The Carol Burnett Show*, it happened when Vicki was a high school senior. The media had reported that the *Burnett* show was looking for someone to play Carol's kid sister. Vicki sent a letter and a picture of herself to Carol and, by golly, she got the job. Fine, except that Vicki was a teenager and had no experience. Carol had faith in her, but there was talk of letting her go after a few episodes. Vicki's job was looking precarious when Harvey pulled her aside and took her under his wing. He worked with her on accents and building believable characters. He worked her hard and whipped her into shape. Such good shape that she was the only cast member, except for Carol, who was on the show for the entire eleven seasons. (Have I mentioned that it took seven years for me to become a permanent cast member?)

When it came to getting Harvey to crack, I had a distinct advantage because I also was one of the writers on *The Carol Burnett Show*. Over the years there were easily fifty writers, not including the ones who did special material like the musicals. People who watch *Carol Burnett and Friends*, half-hour syndicated shows cut down from the original *Burnett* shows, don't get to see those amazing production numbers since they were edited out. Honestly, they were like Broadway shows. We had dancers, and singers, and guest stars. Everyone was in those numbers except Mr. Tin Ear. If I appeared, I didn't sing and you can thank your lucky eardrums I didn't. (Happily, in 2012, when Time Life released a comprehensive collection of *The Carol Burnett Show* DVDs, those lost musical numbers were included. Now, you can see me not sing.)

Back to my writing. I'd write a sketch, they'd print the scripts, hand them out, and we'd go over them in rehearsal. Half the time I'd put in things that I never intended to say or do during the actual performance. For me the script was a trampoline from which I could jump into the unknown. Harvey tended to walk the script like it was a tightrope. That's not to say that he couldn't improvise; he certainly could, and he certainly did. The difference is I was constantly on the lookout for opportunities to do things on the spur of the moment; grabbing and using any situation was at the core of my performances. Not Harvey. He was content to stay in character. But if an opening presented itself, he'd go with it.

Harvey was quick, a great ad-libber, and a real natural. He said a lot of funny things in the forty-some years we were friends. A couple of them come to mind; one involves Louise DuArt and Marty Klein, and the other involves Elizabeth Taylor.

Louise is one of the greatest comedic impressionists in the business. She was on the road with Harvey and me for years, and then when Harvey left she continued to tour with Chuck McCann and me. Listen, seeing Louise alone is worth the price of admission. She is amazing. A lot of mimics do Streisand and Joan Rivers, you name it. But how many *women* do you know who can do a George Burns that's more George than he was? That's Louise, a master of her art.

Louise, Harvey, and I were performing in a Canadian casino, and Charlene and Marty joined us for lunch at the casino deli. We were halfway through the meal when, all of a sudden, Marty said, "I'm going down." With that, he leaned to one side and slid onto the floor where he lay unconscious. It happened fast, but fortunately a couple of paramedics were at the counter ordering sandwiches. (Paramedics should be on staff at any establishment serving corned beef and pickled tongue.) They rushed to Marty's side and began taking his pulse and all that stuff. By then Marty had come to and was looking rather annoyed that his lunch had been interrupted. One of the paramedics turned to the rest of us; we were seated around the table eating our salads.

"Does he have a history of heart trouble?" the EMS asked.

"He's an agent," said Harvey, "he doesn't have a heart."

The other time came during an interview we gave on TV. We were talking about the *Burnett* show spoof of *Gone with the Wind* when the interviewer asked what our own favorite movies were. I forget what I said, but Harvey mentioned *A Place in the Sun* as one of his. You may recall the film starred Elizabeth Taylor, Montgomery Clift, and Shelley Winters. Briefly the story is, Monty's going with Shelley, gets her pregnant, but in the meantime he's met and fallen in love with Elizabeth, and decides he has to kill Shelley in order to be with Elizabeth.

"Tell me," said the interviewer to Harvey, "would you kill your wife to be with Elizabeth Taylor?"

"I'd kill my wife to be with Shelley Winters," shot back Harvey.

He could toss off impromptu remarks with the best of them, but he wasn't hell-bent on digressing. I was. Whenever I deviated, Harvey was left hanging in midair. How I loved to watch him struggle to stay in control. His lips would start to quiver. He'd clamp them together and draw his mouth tight. His eyes would roll up and begin to tear; his face would turn red. His cheeks would puff up. He could hold on for just so long, and then he *had* to laugh. It wasn't a question of *if* Harvey would break up; it was a question of *when*. A betting pool flourished during the *Burnett* show taping sessions. People would put money down on the exact time that Harvey would go up. One sketch perfectly illustrates what I'm talking about.

I got the idea for "The Dentist" from talking to my own dentist. While in dental school he accidently stuck the needle into his own thumb when he was administering Novocain. He carried on with a numb thumb without telling the student patient. That was the barebones outline of the sketch. Harvey was the patient, and I was the novice doctor reading from an instruction manual as I went about my work. There was no mention of Novocain in the written sketch. It was pretty simple, so simple that Harvey spent the week telling me that it wasn't that funny and was going to bomb. I told him not to worry. I was going to do something at the very end that would tie everything together. He replied that nothing could save this "piece of crap." I didn't tell him or anyone else that I planned to stab myself in the hand with the Novocain-loaded hypodermic needle and then go to work.

During the rehearsals, I fumbled around looking first in the book and then into Harvey's mouth as he sat in the dentist's chair. When we began taping the scene on Friday, Harvey got in the chair and I began my watch-out-Harvey-here-it-comes routine. If you view the video, you can tell exactly when I start to move away from the script just by the expression on Harvey's face. I intended to stab my hand with the needle but I didn't stop there. I jabbed my hand, I jabbed my leg, and I jabbed my head. Harvey sat there in the chair ready to explode, which he did. The poor guy actually wet his pants by the time the sketch ended. (I think people who worked with me should have taken out bladder insurance.) What amazes me is how I was able to keep going without breaking myself. Just the sight of Harvey in torment was enough to get anyone going.

Harvey loved that sketch, the two of us used to sit and watch it over and over and laugh just as hard each time we viewed it. Later, a friend of mine told me that she saw Rowan Atkinson do a sketch on London television that was just about a duplicate of what I did with Harvey all those years ago. I was flattered.

The Oldest Man, a recurring character I played, caused Harvey no end of pain. The Oldest Man was a senior, senior citizen who wore a wild white-hair wig and was completely bewildered. I could get Harvey going just by walking across the set at an unbearably slow pace. The Oldest Man was billed as the "world's oldest something-or-other" in various sketches. In one of them, I was the world's oldest fireman called to a fire in Harvey's apartment. I entered the room to find Harvey on the floor overcome by smoke and crying for mouth-to-mouth resuscitation. In the script, The Oldest Man looks suspiciously at Harvey and then, shrugging his shoulders, takes out a breath spray. First I squirted it in Harvey's mouth, and then in mine. Harvey knew I was going to do this. He also knew that the Oldest Man was going to think further about this mouth-to-mouth business and take out a pocket comb. While combing his white locks, the Oldest Man would sing a bit of "Kiss of Fire," a song popularized by Louis Armstrong. Harvey was fairly composed as I sprayed his mouth and then mine. I leaned over him and began croaking, "I touch your lips and all at once the sparks go flying / those devil lips that know so well the art of lying . . ."

"Hurry, hurry," Harvey cried.

At that moment I left the script. I got down on my knees on the floor next to Harvey. I put my right arm underneath his shoulders and pulled him up in a we're-about-to-kiss embrace. Harvey began to giggle. Then, I brought my face closer to his and said softly, "Where are you from?"

At which point, Harvey utterly and completely lost it.

Harvey wasn't any safer off camera. I got that guy so many times it was embarrassing. And I got him on land, on the sea, and, once, in the air. We were flying from the East Coast back to L.A. on a small plane and had to refuel somewhere in Arkansas. The plane landed and taxied over to the fueling station. I was in the window seat and watched the procedure while Harvey read a magazine. Once the refueling was over, the plane turned around and began moving toward the runway.

"Hey Harvey," I said, 'I don't think they put the gas cap back on."

Harvey was always a little leery of flying so, naturally, he was put out by what I said.

"What are you talking about?" he asked.

"Well, when we pulled up to the gas truck, the guy took off the cap and put it on the wing. I didn't see him put it back on. I think it fell off."

Harvey paled.

"Gee," he said, "you better go tell the pilot."

"Not me," I answered, "I don't want to get involved."

"Are you nuts? You've got to tell him. We could lose fuel and crash."

"You go tell him," I said.

"I will," said Harvey.

He got up, went to the front of the plane, and knocked on the cockpit door.

"Yes," came the voice of the pilot.

"Excuse me," said Harvey, "my friend noticed that when we re-fueled they forgot to put the gas cap back on. I thought you should know."

There was a long pause.

"Sir, there is no gas cap on the plane. Please, sit down."

Harvey stood there for a moment. He turned and came back to his seat. Before he sat down he looked at me and mumbled something about my being a son of a something.

While I could get him nine times out of ten, there were occasions when he'd turn things back onto me. One Friday, we were having dinner in the green room between the tapings. (Green rooms are so rarely painted green. This one had beige walls.) We both ordered roast beef au jus (that's French for brown stuff that's supposed to be gravy), and it was served on paper plates. In those days paper plates were really flimsy. They weren't heavy enough to be called cardboard but were more like four of five layers of paper towels pressed together in the shape of a plate. While we ate, Harvey was busily telling me how stupid I was about politics. I didn't know anything about an upcoming election and this incensed Harvey. I was uninterested in politics, and he was politically active. As he spoke he was trying to cut through the meat but he never looked down; he was too busy staring me down. I noticed that while ranting at me, he had cut through the meat and the bottom of the plate. He finished his comments on my stupidity and, without looking, put the fork full of beef into his mouth. Along with the meat came a nice piece of the paper plate. He chewed and continued to berate me on my stupidity. Finally, he took a breath and I said to him, "I may be stupid but I'm not so stupid that I would eat my plate."

Harvey looked down and saw the hole in the bottom of his plate; some of the au jus was trickling through it onto the table. He realized what he'd done and paused for moment. Then he continued chewing, swallowed, and looked at me.

"See, that just shows how stupid you are," he said. "You don't know how delicious this plate is."

With that he cut another piece of roast beef and paper, and continued eating. If I hadn't started laughing he'd have eaten up the whole thing.

Harvey and I were inseparable. When I think of all the time we shared together—the phone calls, the emails, the dinners, the ball games, the horse races, and the drinks while watching ourselves on tapes and DVDs—I don't know how I've managed to get along without him all these years. I guess it's because when you have the kind of friendship we had, the essence remains. We had very few disagreements but when we did have a tiff, I had the advantage. His arguments lost their bite because I was often in costume and he couldn't keep a straight face. It's hard to yell at a guy in an ape suit so our quarrels usually ended in shared laughter. I can be in situations today and know exactly how he would react.

We were interviewed together on a television show, and the host asked when we became a team. We told her it just sort of happened. We did so many sketches together that people began to think of us as a comic duo and then we sort of fell into it. We did our individual thing, but there was something special in our joint appearances. Harvey said he wasn't so sure that he'd have been inducted into the Comedy Hall of Fame on his own. Ha, that's a laugh.

For a few years, Harvey and I played badminton with the Emmy award for Outstanding Regular on a Comedy Show. Either he won or I won. The first time I received the award I went up to the mike, pulled out a blank piece of paper, and pretended to read from it. The acceptance speech went something like, "I would like to thank everyone at the Tarzana Pitch and Putt" and from there I went into a commercial for the "new Mark Twain Hole. The rotating paddle wheel will test your timing skills. Thirsty? Stop by the nineteenth hole for a Big Gulp, small, medium or big gulp.

Babysitting problems? Not to worry, the little ones will be waiting in the tot's nineteenth hole. See you on the carpets." I took the Emmy and returned to my seat. Thank goodness my fellow performers appreciated the joke. It's always a gamble when you put yourself out there. I'm not complaining, but you'd have thought the Tarzana Pitch and Putt people would at least have written me a thank-you letter.

I was nominated again the following year but was unable to attend the award ceremony because I was working in Vegas. I asked Harvey to represent me and gave him a sealed note to read should I win. I didn't expect to, but by golly I did. Harvey took the stage, ceremoniously opened the note, and read, "Harvey, thank you so much for accepting for me. By the way, you know when I said if you vote for me, I'll vote for you? I lied."

I won again the next year and was running out of people to thank. As I told the audience, "I would like to thank my agent but he's at the Dodgers game. I'd thank my wife but she's playing bridge. And all my kids went to see *Superman*. So I hope you folks will accept my thanks to you. It's good to be with friends."

In 2008, I appeared on *30 Rock*, thanks to the extremely talented, attractive, and most humorous Tina Fey. I was lucky enough to be nominated for an Emmy for that guest spot. At the awards ceremony, Jack McBrayer, a member of the *30 Rock* cast, was to present the award in my category. Jack read: "For outstanding guest appearance on a comedy series, the nominees are, Tim Conway, *30 Rock*."

At that point I got up, went onstage, and stood next to him. Jack was a bit thrown by my move. He had four other nominees to name. I smiled and explained that I'd come up because if I won, I'd be there and they wouldn't have to wait for me to get up there to receive the award. I was saving them time. Jack accepted my reasoning and read the rest of the nominees. He opened the envelope.

"And the winner is, Tim Conway."

I took the Emmy and without a word returned to my seat. If I had lost, I'd have checked the card Jack was reading from to make sure he hadn't gotten it wrong. Truthfully, as always, I was amazed that I won.

Of all the award shows, the one I enjoyed the most was the year that both Harvey and I were nominated for our work on Carol's show. We were seated next to each other and when the presenter said, "The winner is Harvey Korman," Harvey leaped up and headed for the stage. I followed and stood next to him on the podium. I kept giving him disappointed looks as he thanked Carol, Vicki, Lyle, and his family. He began to walk off and then returned to the microphone to say, "Oh, and by the way, I'm thankful to be able to work with nuts like this."

We walked off together. Whether he won or I won, we both won.

I could go on about Harvey, but there's really no need. All you have to do is watch him on those videos to know how brilliant he was. He was one of the smartest guys I knew. He could do *The New York Times* crossword puzzle in ten minutes, in ink. But he couldn't tie his own shoes. I took advantage of him on the screen and I took advantage of him in real life. I loved him and I miss him. But I know we still have many laughs to share. God has a sense of humor; why else would He have let me enjoy life so much? I know He'll put us together again.

Save me a seat up there, Harvey. I want to be right next to you so I can crack you up through eternity.

The End of the Affair

*O*ne evening, *Mary Anne and* I, Charlene and Roger, and Carol and Joe went out for dinner. We went to a small restaurant where we could eat in peace and quiet. Not an easy place to find considering the popularity of our show and the resulting recognition factor. Carol wasn't her usual peppy self. Her eyes were red, she'd obviously been crying. I had an awful feeling in the pit of my stomach. We gave our orders. Then Carol took a deep breath and told us that, after eleven years, she and Joe had decided not to continue with the show. Silence fell. Nobody could speak. We'd just heard the news that we never wanted to hear. Carol was in tears and asked to be excused. She left the table and headed for the ladies' room. The rest of us sat there trying to absorb the enormity of Carol's words. I waited for a bit and then leaned in and said, "Okay, here's the plan. We go to CBS, tell them Carol has gone crazy and that in order to keep this from the public she's been institutionalized. In the meantime, we'll do the show until she comes to her senses. Then she can join us. Desperate times call for desperate measures."

Nobody said a word. It looked to me as though they were thinking about it seriously, but as you know, my plan wasn't adopted. The show ended, and part of my heart went with it.

The last week of filming was sad. We went through the motions and gave it our all; still, it was tough going. It would have been even tougher if Harvey had still been with us. He'd left after the previous season to star in his own sitcom, *The Harvey Korman Show*. Like my solo ventures, it was in and out in a season. (Do you need any more proof that even the greatest of straight men needs to work off of a star rather than as a star?) We'd already said a major good-bye, but now the parting was total and catastrophic. A world without *The Carol Burnett Show* was inconceivable to me.

In my memory, Carol and I never had a serious exchange that lasted longer than a few sentences. We always knew what the other was thinking; there was no need to express it. But I wanted her to know how much she meant to me. Rather than tell her, I thought it would be easier to express my feelings in a familiar form. So I wrote my good-bye as a *Burnett* show sketch, not for us to perform, just for her to read. It was published in *Variety*.

The Good-bye Sketch (*Carol and Tim*)

The set: *Two stools in front of an eleven-year-old flat. Carol is dressed in an evening gown. Tim is in a tux.*

Music: *"I'm So Glad We Had This Time Together"*

TIM

(Pause.) Well, I guess this is it.

CAROL

I guess so.

TIM

(Pause.) Eleven years together, and you come up with, "I guess so"?

CAROL

It's a little late for a raise, isn't it?

TIM

It's never too late for a raise. Can I tell you something before I say good-bye?

CAROL

It's a little late to get serious isn't it?

TIM

It's never too late. I just want to say thank you. Not just me, a bunch of us. Just for a minute I want to be one of the many that have watched and laughed at you over the past eleven years. I want to thank you. I want to thank you for the times you have changed my mood from sad to happy. The times you have been silly just for me. The times you made me sing along with you. The times you have cared. The times you have helped. The times you have looked absolutely ridiculous just to make us see how absolutely ridiculous we look. The times that you have answered our needs, to smile at something that we thought was so untouchable, and for the times when you were just you.

CAROL

It's my job.

TIM

No. A job is something you work at. You've

never worked at being you. You are something
special. You never smiled because someone
cued you. You were always you. And I don't care
how many times you've heard it. You're going to
hear it again. You're the nicest person anyone
would ever want to know.

CAROL

Tim, I think you better say good-bye.

TIM

I don't think so.

CAROL

We're running a little late.

TIM

I don't care. Do you realize how many times
we've spent together? Do you realize how many
times we've laughed together? Do you realize
how many dumb sketches we've done together?

CAROL

I know.

TIM

No you don't, 'cause if you did, you wouldn't
make me say good-bye. I don't want to say good-
bye to the best times of my life. Let me put on
my chicken outfit and do one more sketch with
you. Please?

CAROL

Tim, we have to go.

TIM

Just one more . . .

CAROL

No, Tim. Now say good-bye.

TIM

Maybe.

CAROL

No.

TIM

I love you.

CAROL

Please.

TIM

All right . . . Good-bye.

CAROL

Good-bye.

TIM

I think I'm going to cry.

CAROL

You never could be serious.

TIM

No, Carol, I'm serious.

(Fade to Black)

Old Friend, New Beginning

It all began in Paterson, New Jersey, where Charlene Fusco was born in 1938. My Char is Italian on both sides. Her dad's family was big; her mother's family, the Gigantes, was bigger. Her dad, Angelo, was a trumpet player who blew the horn for the likes of Harry James and the Dorsey Brothers. That is, he played with them whenever they performed in New Jersey. Back in those days big bands traveled all over the country and they couldn't take along more than the minimum of players. So, wherever they appeared on the road, they'd pick up local musicians or sidemen, and that's how Angelo Fusco got to play with Harry, Jimmy, and Tommy. Charlene remembers her dad taking her to a rehearsal in Meadowbrook, New Jersey, when she was five. She sat on Harry James's lap and, urged on by her father, hummed James's theme song to him. She was pitch perfect and the bandleader was very impressed. Char hung around musicians so much she grew up thinking that she was in show business.

After Charlene graduated from high school she had two educational choices: she could go to Paterson State College and become a teacher, or she could go to Ridgewood Secretarial School and become a secretary. That's what young women were offered in those days. She felt that she didn't have the patience to be a teacher (I'll second that) and she didn't want to be stuck in a classroom all day. So she went to secretarial school where the guarantee was that in one year she'd learn typing and shorthand. Furthermore, at the end of the year she'd have a job waiting for her. Sure enough, by the end of the school year she'd learned typing and Gregg shorthand and was offered a job at the Nabisco offices in New Jersey. My little Ginger Snap, however, didn't want to work for Nabisco in New Jersey; she wanted to work for TWA, NBC, or CBS in New York City. (You'll have to ask her why she picked those three companies; I have no idea.) On a sunny November morning in 1957, she took the train into Manhattan, got out at Penn Station, got into a cab, and told the driver to take her to CBS at 485 Madison Avenue. Okay, you have to understand a few things:

1. She'd never been to New York before.
2. She hadn't made any appointments.
3. The only reason she went to CBS was because she knew the address from watching Arthur Godfrey and Garry Moore. The announcers always said, "Write to us at 485 Madison Avenue" at the end of the programs. And you thought I had chutzpah.

Charlene marched into 485 Madison Avenue, went to the CBS Personnel Department, and announced that she wanted a job.

"And do you have an appointment?" asked the assistant to the assistant to the assistant personnel director, the designated receiver of girls who came in off the street looking for jobs.

"No," replied Char, "but I came in from New Jersey."

Maybe it was because she was from New Jersey, but whatever the reason, they let her take a typing and dictation test. She aced the exam. Unfortunately, she was told that there were no openings for an executive secretary, her level of expertise. There was, however, an available position for a junior secretary.

"You're overqualified," said the assistant to the assistant.

"I'll take it," said Charlene.

And she started work the next day.

For the next couple of years Charlene rode the intercity bus to the Port Authority on West Forty-second Street and walked to the CBS studios on West Fifty-seventh Street. Then, she bought a car and drove in every day. The man she worked for liked her very much and appreciated her skills. (That's what she told me.) He kept telling her she was overqualified for the job. (That's what she told me, too.) One day, he asked her, if she had a choice, what she would prefer doing at the network. Char said she would love to work in the programming department. Bingo. Whatever Charlene wants, Charlene gets. She was hired to work for the writers on *The Garry Moore Show*. Among the writers was Neil Simon who, during his off hours, typed his first Broadway play, *Come Blow Your Horn*, on the *Garry Moore Show*'s typewriter. When Simon left, another writer joined the crew—but Woody Allen didn't stay long. He left, too, and Buck Henry replaced him. And when Buck left, George Bernard Shaw replaced him. Just kidding, but you get the drift. Those really were the Golden Years of Television, and a lot of the luster came from the camaraderie that existed within individual programs. Charlene describes CBS in those days as "love city."

You may remember that when I appeared on *The Garry Moore Show*, Charlene thought I stank, which didn't affect me in the slightest because I didn't know who she was or care about her opinion. My, how things change. Today, there's nothing I value more than Charlene's opinion, but I've managed to convince her that I'm terrific. Here's the thing, Charlene knows the real me and knows better than anyone how shy I am. If I could only sing I could make that my theme song: "How shy I am, how shy I am, nobody knows, how shy I am." C'mon, would you have thought I was shy if I didn't tell you? Here's something else you might be surprised to hear: most of my performing life, I'd just about throw up before I went on stage. And there were many times when I actually did throw up. (I can't believe I'm telling you all this stuff. Writing is like going to confession. I only hope I get absolved at the end of this.)

Charlene became Joe Hamilton's secretary on *The Garry Moore Show*, and her friendship with Carol began. Then Joe and Carol got married, and when they went to Los Angeles in 1967 to begin *The Carol Burnett Show*, Charlene tagged along. No wait, I meant to say that another important member of the production staff went with them. It was while working on the *Burnett* show that Charlene, by then divorced from her first husband, met a guy named Roger Beatty who was a writer, associate director, and stage manager on the *Burnett* show. Charlene and Roger married in 1971 and had a daughter, Jackie, in 1974.

Roger Beatty and I became pretty good buddies during those years. He, in fact, directed most of *The Tim Conway Show* episodes and was a writer for that series as well. In 1977, we wrote a film together called *The Billion Dollar Hobo*, and he directed the very first Dorf video, *Dorf on Golf*, in 1987. Roger also directed the *Tim Conway & Harvey Korman: Together Again* tour, which began in 1999. He was our road manager and production manager. Harvey left the show in 2006 for health reasons, and when we resumed the tour with Chuck McCann, Roger again called the production shots. Oh, I should mention that the road staff expanded in 2004 when Roger's daughter, and my stepdaughter, Jackie, joined the tour. Are you confused? Be patient.

Charlene and I led parallel lives for two decades. Professionally, we worked together on the same show. Personally, along with our respective families, Carol and Joe's family, and Harvey's family, we spent a lot of our leisure time together. Charlene and I were friends for years before romance entered the picture. She even managed to break into the exclusive men's club that the guys on Carol's show had formed.

Here's how she came to be one of the boys.

Joe Hamilton, Harvey Korman, Roger Beatty, Dave Powers, and I stuck together in that male chauvinist way that we used to keep out the girls. We had wives but went our own way a lot of the time and one of the ways we went was to the racetrack. Who'd have thought a girl would want to join us. Well, Charlene did, and she kept nagging.

"Come on, let me go to the track with you," she'd beg every time we were setting out for Del Mar or Santa Anita.

"Naw," was the answer she got, over and over. A lesser person would have stopped pestering us.

"Come on," she pleaded one day practically falling on her knees, "I won't bother you; just drive me there. I just need a ride. I'll get my own seat at the track. Just give me a ride. I know how to bet."

"Yeh, yeh," I thought, "she knows how to bet and I'm Eddie Arcaro."

She broke us down with her pleading, and we gave her a ride to the track. The minute we got there, she jumped out of the car and ran off. We couldn't believe it. She sat all by herself a few rows away, and we watched her go back and forth to the window to place her bets. She never threw us a glance. Talk about independence.

At the end of the afternoon, we all met back at the car and piled in. Charlene sat in the backseat, all five feet one of her squeezed between Dave and Roger. I was on the window side next to Roger. Joe was driving, and Harvey sat next to him. We pulled out of the parking lot, and Little Miss Marker pulls out a wad of bills from her purse and starts counting.

"Where'd you get that money?" I cried.

"I won the last race," she answered, coolly. "I had a hunch."

That did it. That fateful afternoon Charlene became one of the boys. The funny thing is, all those years before the two of us got together, she was my go-to person and the one I really could talk to. I made her my confidant. I told her stuff I never told the other guys, and some of it was pretty personal. Char accepted me warts and all. Later, she told me that when I was making the confessions she used to think, "Thank God I'm not married to this guy."

Looking back, I'm still amazed at the way things evolved. Because we were co-workers, Charlene and I were together a lot. I'd always drop by her desk to talk. We were definitely drawn to each other but as friends. Here's one for the books. In 1973, I went to Australia to do the *Burnett* show at the opening of the Sydney Opera House. Charlene, who was pregnant with Jackie, went along. Char says she had the happiest baby in the world because she spent her pregnancy with Harvey and me and all she did was laugh. She got so huge I used to make fun of her and get her giggling. She begged me to stop because I made her stomach ache. I tried not to be funny; I really tried.

A while after we returned, Charlene went into the hospital for a C-section. Mary Anne and I were at a tennis tournament when we got the news and we called to see how she was doing. I was the first on the phone, and when Char heard my voice she shouted, "No, no, no, I can't talk to you, I can't laugh, it hurts!" and she hung up.

Even after Mary Anne and I, and Charlene and Roger were divorced, we all continued to see each other. Char and I remained buddies. Carol swears that she saw the relationship shift before we did. And, the relationship did shift. Gradually I began to realize that my buddy was very dear to me, so dear I couldn't imagine not being with her. Thank God, she felt the same way. In 1984, I asked her to marry me. The truth is Char and I were made for each other; it just took us a while to find out. One thing's for sure, Charlene never dreamed that the expression "for better or worse" would come into play as often as it has in our lives.

When we decided to get married I asked her if she wanted a ring. She thought about it and came up with a pretty original idea for a betrothal token. We were very into horse racing at the time, and Charlene said she would rather have a horse than a ring. So I bought her a wedding horse, and she named her Bossy Knickers. She turned out to be one of the few horses we owned that actually won a couple of races. We were in Chagrin Falls one summer when I got a call from the vet in California. He informed me that Bossy Knickers had come down with a serious case of colic. When a horse gets colic the intestines become knotted and food can't pass out of the stomach. The animal is in terrible pain, and even if you operate the surgery doesn't always resolve the problem. The vet felt that Bossy Knickers would be in agony for the rest of her life. I felt bad but I told the vet to put her down. I had the sad task of telling Charlene. She was sitting outside, reading a book. I went over, knelt down in front of her, and gently took the book out of her hands.

"Honey," I said softly, "I am so sorry to tell you this, but your engagement ring just died."

Close friends are amazed that Charlene has put up with my nonsense all these years. Considering the fact that I grab any opportunity to drive her crazy, I am, too. No matter how many times I pull the wool over her eyes, she comes back for more. Although I have to admit it's getting harder to deceive her. I long for the good old days when bamboozling her was a piece of cake. Like the time I was doing summer stock and we were staying at a hotel in Connecticut. The first two nights we were so tired, we were asleep by the time we hit the mattress. The third night, we'd caught up, and leisurely prepared for bed. I got in first. While propping up the thick, fluffy pillows behind me I discovered a switch on the wall near the top of the headboard. I flipped it to the on position and what do you know, the hallway light went on. Charlene was busy in the bathroom as I began plotting. I moved one of the pillows in front of the light switch, hiding it from view. Then I slipped my hand in back of the pillow and placed my finger on the switch. Poised and ready, I awaited my lovely wife. The second phase of the let's-mess-with-Charlene caper began when Charlene emerged from the bathroom and got into bed.

She settled in on her side, took a book from the night table, and began reading. As she read, I schemed. I waited for the moment, and soon it happened. Charlene closed her book with a soft bang, and, at that noise, I flipped the hidden switch. The hallway light came on, and I was in business.

"What was that?" said Charlene.

"What was what?" said I.

"The light went on in the hall."

"So, turn it off."

"I didn't turn it on. It turned on by itself."

"That can't be," I said solemnly. "You must have done something to turn it on."

"I just shut the book I was reading."

"That's it," I cried, "the light is connected to the book."

"What are you talking about? How can the light be connected to the book?"

"Do it again."

The book was on Charlene's lap. "Do what again?"

"Open the book," I said.

She flipped it open.

"Okay, now close it."

She closed the book and at the slight *pop* sound of the pages coming together, I flipped the switch. The light went off.

"There you go," I said. "The book did it."

"That just can't be!"

"Do it again."

She opened and closed the book, and I flipped the switch at exactly the same moment.

"Happy?" I asked.

"I don't believe this," she said.

"Slam the book and go to sleep."

She slammed the book and I turned out the light.

"This is nuts," grumbled my wife. "I'm going to watch TV."

She turned on the television and I said, "You can't watch TV because the hall light will go on and off."

"What are you talking about?" she said.

"I think it's probably one of those Clapper lights. You know you clap your hands, and that controls the on and off for the light. You banged the book shut, and the noise acted like a handclap."

"Oh, I get it," said Charlene. "But what does that have to do with watching television?"

"Well," I continued, "The commercials have a higher sound level than the regular programming so when they come on the light's going to react."

"Get out!"

"Okay, turn on the TV and you'll see what I mean."

Charlene pressed the remote, the television turned on. After five minutes or so, the commercials began. The minute they did, I turned on the hallway light.

"See," I said.

"This is the dumbest thing I ever heard of."

"Well, you can call Maintenance in the morning and get them to fix it."

"I'm not waiting until morning, I'll call now."

Charlene picked up the phone, called the front desk, and said, "This is Mrs. Conway. May we have somebody up here to fix our hall light? No, not tomorrow morning," she said after a pause. "Tonight. It's flashing on and off."

Half an hour later a guy appeared at our door with a tool belt wrapped around his waist. He could have built the Empire State Building with all the equipment he was carrying.

"You need something fixed?" he asked when Charlene opened the door.

"Yes, we would like our Clapper turned off."

The maintenance man looked at her quizzically as he entered the room.

"Your what?"

"Our Clapper. We would like it turned off."

The guy continued to stare.

"Let me show you," said Charlene.

She stood under the hall light and said, "Watch."

She clapped her hands. Nothing happened. Charlene clapped again. Still nothing. I had removed my hand from the switch.

"That's strange," she said.

The maintenance man looked over Charlene's shoulder at me. I took my index finger and made little circles at the side of my head. He looked back at Charlene who was still clapping. Finally, she gave up.

"Well I guess it fixed itself," she said dropping her hands.

"Right," said the maintenance man. He looked over at me and said, "Anything else I can do?"

I just gazed sadly at Charlene and slowly shook my head.

"No," I said forlornly, "there's nothing anyone can do." He gave me a knowing nod and left.

Charlene remained in the dark about the Clapper light for months. Then, I appeared on *Live with Regis and Kathie Lee*, and when one of the hosts asked me to reveal the craziest stunt I'd ever pulled on my wife I told the story of the mysterious hall light. Later, Charlene and I had a lively conversation about my revelation on the show, really lively. I was lucky to get out of it alive. But, you know, some things are worth the price you have to pay.

All I can say is if laughter is the key to youth, Charlene and I are approaching twelve again. It is one delightful path we take together, my dear. I love you, Char. Thanks for all the smiles.

They're Off and Running!

When the Burnett show came to a close I decided to take a few years off. I couldn't look into another camera. Fortunately, I had something to fall back on—horses. As you've probably surmised I was, am, and always will be a racing nut. So is my better half. I'm not saying I married Charlene because she knew how to handicap, but it didn't hurt. (Even the judge who married us in the Los Angeles County Courthouse was a tracker. He kept his eye on the clock during the ceremony to make sure our 'I Do's' were in before the 2:00 post time at Hollywood Park.) We're both committed devotees of the sport of kings, and racing continues to enrich our lives. Once you've got racing in your bones, it's the same as golf: You have to participate.

In the past, Char and I had owned a couple of horses. Now we decided to buy a bunch of them and start a small stable.

Eventually, we owned eight. We had a beautiful cabinet made (not by me) where we planned to display the trophies we'd win. In the end, the only display was a bowl of artificial fruit. Who cares? We had the time of our lives. We were serious about the racing game. We even had our own jockey silks designed with the words "No Passing" embroidered on the backs. Unfortunately, the other jockeys never read those words because our gallant steeds were never in front of any other horses. Losses aside, I've had more darn fun with horse racing. I doubt I could have had a better time had I actually been a jockey.

Also thanks to racing, I've met some swell people, and one of the most memorable was Marje Everett. Marje was a major racing figure and, at different times, owned the Washington and Arlington parks, and the Balmoral Track in Chicago. She also owned Hollywood Park, which was where we got to know her. Marje was the hostess with the mostest. One weekend Charlene and I were invited to a big party she threw for her friends and for the jockeys who raced at Hollywood Park. When we arrived, the front lawn was full of guys talking into their sleeves and coat lapels, so we knew someone important was attending. As it turned out, the someone was President Ronald Reagan. Nancy Reagan and Marje were good friends. The party was underway when it was announced that the president was about to arrive. Guests were told to form a welcome line in the house. I jumped in and stood at the ready. Charlene, however, wasn't there; she had sneaked into the garage and was having a cigarette with the jockeys. The president and first lady came in and began walking down the line. I realized that Charlene wasn't going to make it back in time, so I improvised. I grabbed a tiny uniformed woman who was serving canapés on a silver tray and pulled her into the line next to me just before the Reagans reached my place. I was introduced to them and exchanged handshakes. I stepped back, turned first to the woman with the tray, then back to the Reagans and said, "May I introduce the First Lady of the Canapés?"

The Reagans smiled and the little lady did what she was trained to do. She presented the tray and said, "Cheese puff?"

The Reagans continued smiling and moved on.

Charlene hit the roof when she returned from her cigarette break only to learn that the canapé server had been introduced to the guests of honor instead of her.

"If you stopped smoking, this wouldn't be a problem," I said.

Char did stop smoking, and while I can't say for sure that this incident was the reason, it couldn't have hurt. How can you justify missing a chance to meet the president of the United States face-to-face because you have to have a lousy cigarette?

Meeting people like the Reagans was only one of the benefits of knowing Marje Everett. Marje was a philanthropist of the first order and a loyal supporter of the Don MacBeth Memorial Jockey Fund. Wait, have I told you about the Fund? It all started when I made an appearance at Canterbury Park in 1987. I wanted to donate my fee to a fund benefiting jockeys and was shocked to discover that no such endowment existed. The idea that there was no organization to take care of ill or injured riders, most of whom made precious little money during their careers, was appalling. I wanted to do something about it so I talked to fellow racing enthusiasts, Judy and Chris McCarron. In 1987, we established the DMMJF in honor of a well-known rider who died of cancer at the age of thirty-seven. His widow, Jo Ann, worked with us. For twenty-five years, the fund provided services for more than two thousand riders all over the country. Tony DeFranco was the fund's first and only director. I met him and his delightful wife, Phyllis, through Charlene and the four of us became family. Tony was a character straight out of *Guys and Dolls.* No one knew more about betting than Tony. He was the inspiration for a movie I wrote called *The Longshot.* Tony died in 2011, and his passing plus the economic downturn, forced us to disburse all remaining funds and to shut down operations. I'm sad that the DMMJF had to end, but I'm very proud of what we contributed all those years.

You meet all sorts of people when you're involved in racing. Most of them are down-to-earth, but here and there you'll come across some real snots. Charlene and I were at the opening of a new racetrack and seated at a table with all the big shots—track owners, racehorse owners, and officials of the racing community. Char and I didn't have that much to add to the conversation because we didn't own a farm, quality horses, or even a box at the track. One of the women, a real "fauwfeefon," as Charlene calls snooty ladies, started questioning Char as to whether her family was in racing.

"Well," answered my wife, "we were kind of connected."

"How is that?" asked Madame Fauwfeefon.

"My dad was a bookie," said Charlene.

I honestly thought that poor woman's hair was going to blow off. Charlene's bluntness broke the ice. The others at the table began laughing. Everybody wanted to talk to her and get an inside look into the world of bookmaking.

Probably the most amazing episode in my jockey/racing life came decades after I'd given up any hope of being a rider. Dick Van Patten was hosting a TV program where performers were challenged to compete with professional athletes in various sporting events. I was asked to ride against Lafitt Pincay, one of the best jockeys around. Was I wise enough to think, gee, the last time I was on a racehorse I didn't even make it out of the starting gate so maybe I'd better decline? Sure, that's exactly what I said. Ha! Who could turn down such an opportunity?

I trained for a few weeks and my pal Chris McCarron helped whip me into whatever shape I could achieve at that stage of the game. Lafitt and I met at the Hollywood Park. I noticed an ambulance parked on the side, and the thought crossed my brain that maybe someone would need it. Had I thought further, it might have occurred to me that between the two of us, I was the more likely candidate. Lafitt was in his jockey silks, and I had managed to squeeze my carcass into something resembling the proper attire. We mounted our horses, two old racing steeds who'd been put out to stud for years, and steadied them as the starter made ready to call.

"They're off!" he shouted.

And we were. For a while, our horses were running nose to nose. I was on the rail and thought I'd pull ahead a little to create some excitement. I tapped, and I mean tapped, my horse with the whip. Big mistake. He must have had a flashback to his racing days because he took off like a rocket. Lafitt thought I was pulling a fast one; we were only supposed to lope around, so he snapped his whip. His horse took off. Now we were at a full gallop. I've mentioned that your legs have to be in top-notch condition in order to ride jockey style. They're the only communication between you and your horse. My legs were way over al dente and in the next fifty feet they went to mush. I was no longer in touch with my horse. The only thing I could do to keep from falling off was to wrap my arms around the horse's neck and hang on for dear life. Lafitt took a look at me and started laughing hysterically.

"Da es fonny," he cried in his best, broken English.

I tried to explain that I was going to die, but he zipped by me and crossed the finish line. I was hanging on with my last bit of strength when my horse crossed the line. We zoomed by the outrider who was on the track to help out in case of an emergency. As we flew by I heard him call into a two-way radio, "You want me to pick him up or are they going to go around again?"

"*Help!*" I screamed just to make it clear that I didn't want to go around again.

The outrider took off after me and, grabbing hold of the reins, brought my horse to a stop. It took three people to help me slide off. They had to hold me up because I could not put one foot in front of the other. I was dragged to the ambulance and told to lie down for a minute. I closed my eyes and did as I was told. For nearly a week, I couldn't get my legs into my pants. It was impossible to lift and push them. Fortunately, my permanent trainer, Charlene, was there to help, otherwise I'd have been walking around in shorts for days. I donated my fee from the show to the Don MacBeth Fund. In case I ever decided to ride again, I wanted to make sure I was covered.

Excluding my "ride of death," I had a ball with horse racing and my utter delight with all things racing was evident to my friends. Harvey Korman, Joe Hamilton, and Ernie Anderson saw what fun I was having and wanted in. They asked if we could buy a horse together. Charlene wisely sat this one out. I had Jude Feld, the trainer who worked for Charlene and me, purchase a horse for the four of us. Jude found Hail Columbus, an eighty-thousand-dollar investment that would surely prove its worth. (By the way, I know there's a patriotic song called "Hail, Columbia" but the song was not related to our horse.)

What's that old saying about never going into business with friends? Truer words were never spoken. When Harvey put up his twenty thousand, the pained expression on his face told me I was in for trouble. I knew horses, Harvey didn't, and it would take an awful lot to get him to understand that, basically, it's a crapshoot and there's only so much you can do. Hail Columbus didn't really understand the sport, either. Oh, he got the eating and sleeping part of it, but not the running. He went no place fast. In one race, Jude told the jockey riding Hail Columbus to go right to the front after the break and stay there. The jockey happened to be the great Bill Shoemaker.

"So," concluded Jude after expounding on the strategy, "do you think you can do that?"

"Sure," said the Shoe. "I can go to the front but what do you want me to do with the horse?"

That exchange perfectly illustrates the respect that Hail Columbus and his owners inspired in the racing community. Hail Columbus ran a few times and each time came in last, by a lot. We owners weren't happy, but only one of us gave voice to his displeasure.

"How long is this crap going to go on," demanded Mr. Korman who was desperately trying to recoup his money.

I asked Jude Feld what could be done to improve Hail Columbus's chances of finishing in the front of the pack. Jude thought a bit and then offered his suggestions. The first was to geld Hail Columbus, which meant removing his testicles. I pointed out that if we did that we'd have a perfect product, a horse that couldn't race and couldn't breed. The word "worthless" came to mind.

"Look," I said to Jude, "why don't you have a conversation with Hail Columbus. Tell him what's in store for him if he doesn't start running faster. Trust me, that's all you'd have to say to me to get me going."

"I'm only suggesting this," answered Jude, "because I've been trying to figure out what's holding Hail Columbus back. I've looked that horse over top to bottom and I've come to the conclusion that his testicles are the problem; they're just too big and they're hindering his running potential. Look, if you don't want to geld him, the only other thing I can suggest is that he wear a supporter when he runs."

Picture this, my friends. The race is about to begin, the horses are led out, and the crowd sees that one of them is wearing a large, custom-made jockstrap. A quick check of the program reveals that Tim Conway and Harvey Korman are among the owners. The crowd roars and then the race begins. Hail Columbus does his best, but neither the jockey nor the jockstrap can help him improve upon his customary position, last place.

This is not the end of the story. Now comes a tale in which Tim Conway, once again, gets the better of his friend and pawn, Harvey Herschel Korman. The catalyst for this tale is none other than the late, great Dick Clark.

At the same time Hail Columbus was doing nothing on the track, Dick Clark was doing a *Candid Camera*–type show called *Super Bloopers and Practical Jokes*, where practical jokes were played on unknowing celebrities. He called and, after telling me that he'd been a big fan of the *Burnett* show, asked if I'd be willing to do his show. He wanted me to pull a gag on Harvey. This was a gift from heaven. I told Dick that not only would I do it, I had the perfect gag for them to use, one in which that great stallion, Hail Columbus, would be prominently featured. Briefly, I explained the situation and then suggested that we tell Harvey that a gentleman from Australia wanted to buy a breeder for his granddaughter and was interested in Hail Columbus. I let Jude, Ernie, and Joe in on the joke and they agreed that it was a perfect setup. I called Harvey and told him the good news. He was elated at the thought of getting rid of our four-footed fiasco. I told him to come over to the Burbank stables where we'd meet the grandfather and his granddaughter and introduce them to Hail Columbus. When I told Jude where we were going to meet, Jude said he didn't want to ship H.C. all the way to Burbank because it would be too expensive.

"Jude," I laughed, "just pull out any horse from the riding stable. Harvey doesn't know one from another."

So, one fine day, Dick Clark's crew set up an area at the Burbank Riding Academy, with two-way mirrors, cameras, and mikes, before Harvey, Joe, Ernie, myself, Jude, and a horse named Howard gathered there. The actors portraying the Australian grandpa and granddaughter arrived, and Harvey was introduced to them. Believing they were going to take Hail Columbus off his hands, Harvey was at his most charming. He chatted about our trip to Australia with the *Burnett* show and what a wonderful country it was, and how adorable kangaroos and koala bears were, and how he'd love to go back. Meanwhile, Gramps and his granddaughter smiled and nodded. For the record, neither of them had ever been out of California and didn't know what Harvey was blathering about. Gramps asked to see the horse. Jude went and got him and led him into the area where we were standing. Just as I predicted, even though Howard was a hundred times sleeker than Hail Columbus, Harvey believed it was our horse and kept commenting on how great looking he was. Gramps appraised the animal in a very professional manner; he looked him up and down, felt his legs, opened his mouth and looked in at his teeth, then stepped back and said, with a terrific Australian accent, "Well, he certainly is a fine-looking animal."

"He certainly is!" Harvey said, jumping in.

Gramps took out a checkbook and said, "As you know, I'm interested in a purchase for breeding purposes and I realize this horse has a glorious pedigree. (I wondered what he'd have thought if he had been confronted with Hail Columbus in his jockstrap.) Since that's my main interest, I'm prepared to offer you ninety thousand dollars."

"Sold," cried Harvey. He practically went into a jig he was so excited.

The actor started to make out a check and that's when I stepped in.

"Hold it," I said, "let's talk this over for a minute."

You cannot believe the look of horror that flashed over Harvey's face.

"What talk? There's no talking. The horse is sold."

I excused myself and called my fellow owners over to one side. We stood in front of a window that was actually a two-way mirror behind which Dick and the camera crew were positioned.

"What's the matter with you?" Harvey whispered in fury.

"Look," I said, "this is horse trading. I think we can get this guy up a few bucks."

"If you screw this up," whispered Harvey, "I'll never speak to you again."

I told Harvey to calm down; I was just going to test the waters. So the four of us went back over to the horse and the prospective buyer.

"We've thought about it, and we feel the horse is worth more than your offer," I said politely, but firmly.

The actor looked at a paper he was holding and said, "Well, the information here does show that he's from fine breeding stock." He looked at me, shook his head, and smiled.

"You, sir, are a true horseman," he said admiringly. "You know value all right, and I'm not going to quibble. Let's make it an even one hundred thousand."

"Sold. Sold. Sold," cried Harvey, staggering forward.

"Hold it, hold it, hold it," I countered. I turned to the actor and said, "We have to discuss this."

Once again the four horsemen stepped over to the window; I practically had to drag Harvey there. Meanwhile the actor made out a check for a hundred thousand dollars—from a fictional account, of course.

"We have got to take this offer," Harvey was positively threatening, but I managed to convince him that we had nothing to lose by going for more.

We strolled back to Gramps and told him we really were looking for a better deal. He gave us a long, serious look. Harvey began to tremble.

"I'll give you a hundred and twenty thousand, and that's my final offer," said the actor.

"*Sold*, and I mean it!" cried Harvey.

We all smiled, shook hands, and confirmed the deal. The actor wrote out another phony check and was about to hand it over when his "granddaughter" spoke up.

"Grandpa."

"Yes, honey."

"Don't you remember? I told you I wanted a black horse; this horse is brown."

"You want a black horse," cried Harvey, "we'll paint it!"

"Honey, now that you mention it I do recall that you asked for a black horse. Okay, sweetheart, we'll find you one."

Turning to us he said, "I'm sorry, gentlemen, but my little girl here has to get what she asked for. It was delightful meeting you and I do thank you for your time." With that, he took his granddaughter's arm and they walked off.

Harvey was in shock. I had to get him back to the window, so

I took him by the arm and led him over. As we walked, I started to let him in on the gag.

"Harvey, you know the show Dick Clark has that's—" I didn't get a chance to finish the sentence. Harvey cut me off as we reached the two-way mirror.

"Dick Clark, that cheapskate," said Harvey. "He does all those shows where he gets people to do stuff and never pays anybody for doing anything."

Before I could stop him, Harvey went on a tirade about Dick Clark's cheapness. Finally I managed to inform him that we were on Dick's show and that the whole thing was a televised stunt. Harvey was furious. He didn't speak to me for weeks, but it was worth it! When he finally thawed, I gave him the two phony checks and he kept them in his desk drawer for the rest of his life. By the way, I can't let this story go without adding that, contrary to what Harvey said, Dick Clark was a very generous producer.

A Little Friend-Dropping

While I sometimes think that I may be possessed, I know for certain that I've always been blessed. My pals are blessings, and I don't think you could find a more wonderful group of people than those whom I call friends. Because I've been in the business for so long, most of them are entertainers. You'll recognize some because they've entertained you for years but, whether or not they are familiar names to you, my life has been enriched by knowing each and every one of them. Years ago, a core group of us—Bob and Ginnie Newhart, Mike and Mary Lou Connors, Dick and Dolly Martin, Charlene and I, and, on occasion, Barbara and Don Rickles—formed a dining club. (Carol and her husband Brian Miller and Steve Lawrence and Eydie Gormé drop by whenever they're in town.) Bob and I were the founders of the club. Just to show you how nice Bob and I are, we chose Tuesday night because we didn't want to interrupt anyone's weekend. We're still at it, but now that Dick's gone, Dolly comes on her own. And she can hold her own with any of us. Having that Tuesday dinner is a tradition that we all want to keep up. While a few things have changed, mostly dietary ones, the fun remains.

Now, I'd like to introduce you to my circle of friends, not alphabetically or in order of importance, just as they come to mind.

I've known Steve Lawrence and Eydie Gormé, The Duke and the Duchess of Vegas, about as long as I've known my own wife. We were never formally introduced at the time, but they were on *The Garry Moore Show* when I went on. We became pals when we all appeared on Steve Allen's show. Steve and Eydie are great performers individually and together. He's a terrific comic and a helluva singer. She was a spectacular singer and a darn good actor as well, but she retired in 2009. Steve will still trot out for a gig. Enough of this, I feel like a press agent.

I have to credit Steve and Eydie for bringing me to Las Vegas. They talked me into opening for them at Caesars Palace. Vegas is where all entertainers eventually want to play. Really, you have to play there if you want to round out a career. Frankly, I don't think there's a more threatening place to perform than that desert city. There aren't many second chances in Vegas. You go on and if you stink you go home—usually before the second show. There are too many acts waiting in the wings to take your place for you to be less than good. The first time I appeared, Steve had to push me onto the stage. I managed to start talking and somehow thirty minutes passed and no one threw anything at me. I left the stage with applause ringing in my ears and sweat rolling down my back. Steve and Eydie gave me my standup wings, and thanks to them, I've played casinos all over the States and in Canada, too.

Eydie and Steve have been part of my life for many years. I was asked to speak at their twenty-fifth wedding anniversary celebration. I thought about the two of them and their lasting relationship, and I wanted to contribute a serious note to the occasion.

Here's my tribute:

In the beginning God created heaven and earth. And on the seventh day he rested. He stood upon a hill and looked out on the wonders he had wrought. He looked at the beautiful mountains and the lush prairies and flowing waters. A peaceful silence enveloped the earth and God said, "Let there be noise." And God created Eydie. And Eydie sat by a creek, babbling and alone, not the creek, Eydie. "Create for me a companion," Eydie said unto the Lord. "A man who will make beautiful music for me to enjoy." And God created Mel Tormé. And Eydie said, "No, Lord, I want a man who will make me laugh when I am sad, a man who will bring joy into my life." And God created Steve. And Eydie looked upon Steve and harkened unto his songs and his humor. Then Eydie said unto the Lord, "Could I see Mel, again." But the Lord said, "Mel is booked at Caesars." And so Eydie said, "Okay, give me Steve." Thus they were united and lived happily ever after and brought joy and laughter and music to us all.

After Steve and Eydie brought me into the wonderful world of Vegas, I met, if not the greatest entertainer of the day, then a top contender. I was standing in line at a charity banquet honoring Lucille Ball when someone behind me rested a hand on my shoulder.

"Where're you sitting, Tim?" said a very familiar voice.

I turned and looked into the blue, blue eyes of Frank Sinatra. In a million years, I wouldn't have expected the Chairman of the Board to know who I was. As always, when I'm confronted by my idols, my response came out as though I were speaking a foreign tongue. I wanted to say, *From Here to Eternity, Come Fly with Me, I Did It My Way*, stuff like that so he'd know I knew who he was. What I said was, "Maaurn . . . ffrna . . . onekkd."

"Nice talking to you, kid," said Sinatra over his shoulder as he turned and walked away.

Despite the pathetic beginning, I did become friendly with Old Blue Eyes. And, I got a chance to tell him how I felt about him at a couple of poker nights at his home. (I'm pinching myself remembering that Tommy Conway from Chagrin Falls played poker with Mr. Frank Sinatra from Mt. Olympus.) I also attended a special birthday dinner for Sinatra at a beach restaurant. There were maybe fifty people gathered to fete him. We finished the meal, Frank blew out the candles on his cake, and then he, Steve, and Eydie stood up and began to sing. Fifty people went crazy. We were cheering them on and they kept on singing right up to the moment when half a dozen cops walked in. Someone in the neighborhood had complained about the noise and the police came to quiet things down. The cops caught sight of Sinatra, Steve, and Eydie singing their lungs out. They looked at each other, pulled up some chairs, and fifty-six people enjoyed the rest of the concert. This is a perfect illustration of star power.

Here's another example, from a different vantage point.

After Sonny and Cher got divorced in 1975, Sonny asked me to join him at Harrah's in Lake Tahoe. I was pleased to be asked and delighted to go. By then I had some casino experience under my belt. I'd played to packed houses at Caesars Palace with Steve and Eydie and with Carol. Because of their star power, I was used to a certain way of being treated, a deferential one. Whatever I asked for I got; fast. Sonny without Cher was a different story. We were playing to less-than-full houses, way less. One night I was between shows and wanted to refresh my drink. A waiter walked by, and I called out, "Could I please have some ice?"

"Get it yourself," he told me.

Sic transit gloria mundi. Sonny, however, managed to regain some glory. He reinvented himself. He went into politics and was elected to the U.S. House of Representatives. Tragically, in 1998, Sonny Bono was killed in a ski accident.

I've worked with many wonderful performers over the years. And that includes Betty White. She is a standout. Betty's more fun than a barrel full of monkeys. She's kind of old now, and it's sad that she doesn't get the recognition that she deserves, I mean you barely hear about her anymore. Unless you watch television, that is.

Dick Martin was the personification of carefree. He was the insane half of the Rowan and Martin *Laugh-In* comedy team. Dan Rowan was a funny guy but a sobersides compared to his partner. When Dick arrived in Hollywood, his first job was at Paramount Studios—as a janitor. He had a snappy uniform, carried a portable vacuum cleaner, and was assigned to straighten up the offices on the second floor. A vice president at Paramount occupied one of those offices. Dick worked the night shift and had some spare time during the hours between 10 P.M. and 3 A.M. He got in the habit of looking through the manuscripts that were piled on the vice president's desk. Near the bottom of the pile, he found one script for an upcoming feature film that intrigued him. In looking it over, he found a number of places where the script didn't stick to the story line. So the janitor pulled the script from the pile and began editing it, making copious notes in the margin. He did this for about three nights and then slipped his corrected script back on the pile. Months later, the film went into production and when it was released, Dick went to see it. He was delighted to discover that all his suggestions had been used. It was a shoemaker-and-the-elves situation and nobody ever found out that the janitor was responsible for the final script and not the VP.

Dick Mr. Happy-go-Lucky Martin and his wife, Dolly, were regulars at our Tuesday night get-togethers. The Martins' presence made it a little difficult for us to find a feeding place. Dick and Dolly were barred from at least five restaurants in the Malibu area. Dick claimed that they were the victims of bad restaurant management. I have to say I never saw any restaurateur force vodkas down Dick's throat—the result of which was a profound increase in the volume of his conversation. That increase did not sit so well with fellow diners. Consequently, when Dick was along with the Tuesday Diners' Club, we'd usually end up at Chez Mimi, where the sympathetic owner put us in a backroom. There, Dick could express himself without fear of someone punching him in the nose or tossing him out on his butt. Dick's another friend who is gone, which feels so unfair; there were a lot more laughs to be shared with him. Fortunately, Dolly has kept his voice on the answering machine, so we do get a chance to say hello when we call.

Would you believe that I acted opposite Henry Fonda? Well, I did, in a commercial for a camping trailer. Amazing isn't it, that a great actor like Hank Fonda and a schnook like Tim Conway got to work together? What united us? Money, my friends, money. You can make a nice bundle doing commercials, and Papa Conway was always looking for ways to add to the family fortune to keep his family going. The commercial was an advertisement for a trailer, and Mr. Fonda and I played campers. In the shoot, he was seated on the steps of the trailer while I was standing nearby, busily engaged in trying to set up a tent. He sat there calmly watching me go through the frantic motions of putting up a tent that was not cooperating. Pegs were flying, poles were breaking, and canvas was tearing, all to illustrate the superiority of the camper. I was working my buns off trying to make the scene humorous. Mr. Fonda looked on. When they finally said, "Cut," I was exhausted. I wandered over to the camper and sat down next to the movie star. I was hoping for an expression of approval for what I'd just done. He looked at me, smiled, and said, in his perfect Henry Fonda drawl, "Tell me, do you make a living doing this crap?"

Another friend, Pat McCormick, was a writer on *The Johnny Carson Show*. He was six foot plus, somewhere in the Korman stratosphere. Pat got away with a lot because his size was so intimidating. Among other things, he was famous for streaking on the *Carson* show. I know he was wacko because I experienced his irreverent behavior firsthand. One afternoon, we got on an elevator together. A Hindu woman wearing the red dot on her forehead stood in the back. Pat looked at her, pointed his finger, gently poked the dot and said, "Four, please." I don't remember who laughed more, the lady or me.

Here's a paradox: one of the sweetest, kindest, most loving men I've ever known is the sharpest tongue in the business. He is the grand high master of the insult and holds nothing back. The fact that Don Rickles has remained out of the emergency room all these years is one of showbiz's great mysteries. He was Frank Sinatra's opening act for years, and even Sinatra wasn't safe from Don's jibes. No one except Don Rickles could mess with Frank Sinatra and expect to keep his nose in the center of his face. When you put your money down for a ticket to Don's show, you have to leave any psychological problems at the door because, if he decides that you're going to be a target, you will suffer, my friend, you will suffer. I recall one performance in Vegas when Don, microphone in hand, patrolled back and forth along the apron of the stage, looking for prey. He hit on a few guys in his travels, but the funny thing was he kept walking by a prime target seated dead center in the first row. The spotlight fell on the back of this guy's head. I should say more precisely that the spotlight was on one of those masses of synthetic threads that some guys think pass for hair. It was the worst toupee imaginable, and as the show progressed and Don kept on the prowl, the question became when was he going to pounce? He'd pause and look at him and then move on. Then he'd come back from the side of the stage and stop again, look down at the guy, and move off without a word. People in the audience were on the edge of their seats. And then it happened. On about his fifteenth crossing Don stopped directly in front of the guy and stood there looking down. Then he crouched, leaned over, and whispered into the mike, "Sir, let me ask you something. Do you really think you're fooling anyone?"

Without waiting for an answer, Don stood up and walked away.

The great thing is the guy with the lousy rug laughed as loud as everyone else. The truth is most of us in the business are highly insulted if we go to Don's show and he doesn't come after us. It's a badge of honor to be badgered by him. He's banged me on many occasions when I've been in the audience. He just loves to tell everybody about all my cancelled shows.

"Tim," he cackled a while back, "Carol's been off TV for a hundred years. It's over for you; stop calling her. She can't do you any good now. Get a job. You need money? Go to an ATM machine and leave that poor woman alone."

Here's a guy who rips you to shreds in public and then, without any publicity, is always first in line to contribute to worthy charities. With apologies to Rudyard Kipling, this is what I say to you, Mr. Rickles, "Though you've belted me and flayed me, by the living Gawd that made me, you're a better man than I am, Gunga Don."

Tuesday nighters Mike Connors and his wife Mary Lou have been dear friends for more than twenty years. Mike was the star of the popular TV detective series *Mannix*, the last series from Desilu Productions. Mike was an action star, but the guy could have been a stand-up comedian. When the Television Academy honored Bob Newhart, I wrote a routine for Mike and me to perform, and that son of a gun got all the laughs. For reasons I don't care to go into, because they cast aspersions on my skills at the wheel, Mike has become the designated driver for the Conways and the Connors on our Tuesday night excursions. We pile into his car and before the doors close, we're reminiscing. We do have a little trouble talking while we're driving because the cars behind us keep honking their horns to get the old geezers moving. We spend a lot of time talking about the good old days on those journeys. There's quite a bit of repetition, so much so that Mike suggested that we number the stories and rather than repeat them, we just call out the number. (Mike, number fifty-two. I can't print it, but I can hear you laughing.)

Do you watch the TV series *Mad Men*? Well, those guys aren't mad men. There's only one really mad man, and his name is Jonathan Winters. Jonathan was my teething ring for comedy. He is nuts and I mean that in the kindest way. He thinks funny, not just when he's on stage entertaining, but when you run into him on the street. On the stage, he doesn't need a script because he's much more brilliant than anything a script holds. All you have to do when you're working with him is jot down an idea and stand back. I did a TV special one time and asked him to join me as guest star. We met for rehearsal and someone handed him a script. I turned to Jonathan and said, "Leave it on the table, we'll figure out something to do."

He dropped the script and we started talking.

"I got it," I said, "I'll be a drill sergeant in the Marines and you'll be a recruit trying to put your rifle together."

That was the entire script. And from it came ten minutes of virtuoso comedy as I fired question after question and he fired back comic gem after comic gem. Jonathan is one of those guys who has the right words and perfect timing, and both come out of whatever unique character he is occupying at the time. His uncanny ability to react is matched by his talent at creating his own material.

When Jonathan moved out of L.A., we began communicating via telephone. I miss his presence, but the phone calls are a goldmine of Jonathan at his freewheeling best. I've kept all his recorded messages and, every so often, when I want to be inspired, I'll sit down and listen to a few of them. It's my version of going to comedy school. Speaking of telephone calls, I'd made a few of them to him not long ago and got a bit concerned that he wasn't answering. I called and when I got an unfamiliar hello, I asked, "Is Johnny there?"

There was a very long pause.

"Oh, I guess you haven't heard."

My heart sank. "Heard? Heard what?"

"Johnny passed away two days ago, I'm his brother Frank. I've come in from Ohio to take care of his affairs."

I was in shock and went into a serious string of "Oh my Gods." Then I got control and asked how it happened.

"Well," said Frank, "he was out on the lawn in back when a ground squirrel jumped up and grabbed him by the throat and that was the end."

In a second I realized that brother Frank was fiction and that, in fact, I was talking to Mr. Jonathan Winters. He'd fooled me big time.

"You son of a gun." I cried into the phone. "You really had me."

I'm telling you I was still in mourning when I finally hung up. It just shows how deep his comic skill goes. To come up with a routine about such a dark subject and to bring it off requires absolute conviction and total commitment. But that's Johnny. I don't think I've ever come within shooting range of what he's recorded in the comedy world. I am in awe of him.

I'm pretty sure Bob Newhart and I were twins separated at birth. We may not look exactly alike but our personalities are definitely identical. The only difference is that Bob keeps up with the news of the day and I ignore it. We're Midwesterners and we have a similar take on life: We want to make people laugh but we don't want to hurt anyone while we're doing it. We want people to like us and we'll do anything to make that happen. And, even though we're out there on a stage in front of millions (well, thousands; okay, hundreds) of people, we're both basically shy. As alike as we are, our performance backgrounds are quite different. Bob started out on the road doing his routine in nightclubs. As you might recall, I tried to start out on the nightclub circuit in Seattle but failed. I'm a studio-bred comic and Bob's a roadman. I can't remember how we met and I don't think he can, either. (He can't. I just called him and he doesn't remember.) I do recall that Bob appeared on the second episode of *The Carol Burnett Show*. He was supposed to do a sketch in which he played Tonto in a phone booth talking to the Lone Ranger. I found out later that he took one look at the sketch, said it was awful and that he didn't want to do it. Naturally, when he passed, I wound up as Tonto in the phone booth. During the taping Joe Hamilton said over the intercom, "Newhart was right, it isn't funny." It wasn't, but I had to plow through it anyway.

I told you that Bob is Mr. Nice Guy and never wants to offend, but he also doesn't like to admit that he's wrong. He takes a lot of heat for the wrong things he's said (but won't admit to). At one Tuesday dinner, we all were looking over the menu when someone asked Bob what he was going to order. Bob glanced at the menu, looked up and said, "I think I'll have the tripe."

The rest of us were surprised that Old Meat and Potatoes Bob was ordering something so exotic. Ginnie was the first to question his selection.

"Bob, you don't eat tripe," she said. "You don't even know what tripe is."

"Yes, I do," he responded, "and I like it. It's just that it's not available that often."

Sure enough, when the waiter asked what he wanted, Mr. Nice Guy ordered the tripe. When the bowl of tripe was placed in front of him, he stared at it. So did we all. He picked up his fork and gingerly put it in the bowl and pulled forth what looked like a large, pale tapeworm from a swamp of white sauce. We all knew he didn't know what tripe was and he knew we knew. That didn't stop him from taking a healthy bite of the delicacy. We waited for his reaction. He chewed. He paused, chewed again, paused, chewed again, and finally swallowed. He took the napkin from his lap and gently patted his mouth. We waited.

"You know," he said at last, "this is just about the best tripe I've ever had."

Sure, I thought to myself, it's probably *as delectable as Harvey Korman's paper plate au jus.*

The occasional stubborn stance aside, Bob Newhart is one of the nicest guys you could ever hope to meet. He brings smiles to all of us on our Tuesdays. By the way, whenever tripe is on the menu we always order him a side dish. And by golly, he eats it. None of the rest of us will.

I hate to close this chapter on a sad note, but my dear friend Jonathan Winters really did die on April 11, 2013. *Ave atque vale* to a true comic genius.

Golf

$\mathcal{D}$*on't ever pick a up* a golf club and hit a golf ball unless you are willing to devote the rest of your life believing that you can beat the game. Not only that, you must be willing to dress in outlandish outfits, spend megabucks on equipment, swear, lie, and cheat, and finally, you must be able to afford a divorce. That's what the future holds when you start chasing a little white ball around the course. I was a victim of that wonderful challenge in life called "golf" and experienced all the shortcomings listed above. Thank God, three other fellows, equally mad about the game were my accomplices. Harvey Korman, Ernie Anderson, Joe Hamilton, and I comprised a foursome that met every Monday morning, come hell or high water. (In case you were wondering, we all swore, lied, cheated, and ended up divorced.) Harvey, as always and however unintentionally, provided most of the amusement. I cannot begin to describe his golfing attire which only stopped short at those old-fashioned knickers called plus fours. He was the tallest of us by a vertical mile, and to watch him tee off was excruciating. He'd wind up like a pretzel and swing away at the ball, which, more often than not, remained at his feet. He looked like a whooping crane. Eventually, Ernie, Joe, and I had to look the other way when Harvey began his game; none of us had the bladder to handle it.

Joe Hamilton was both the best golfer and the best-dressed of our quartet. He belonged to the Bel-Air Country Club and on one occasion invited us to play there. Later that same week, he received a letter from the front office suggesting that he not invite his friends to return. The fact that it took Harvey something like twenty-eight strokes on the ninth hole to get the ball into the cup, had a lot to do with the management's request. Behind us was an extended line of golfers, all club members, waiting for our group to move on. The problem stemmed from Harvey's first shot, which rolled off the green and into a sand trap. I can still see him standing in that trap whacking away at the ball, sand flying all over, until the green looked like the beach at Santa Monica. As if that weren't enough, his next shot landed on a drainage ditch and rolled back down toward the previous hole. To top it off, when he finally got the ball back on the green, he had the nerve to ask the caddy which way the green broke.

Ernie spent most of the game in the woods because that's where his ball usually came to rest. When he went searching for it, he never came out of the woods until he'd found at least three other balls. One time, the ball rolled under a thorn bush. When he reached in to pick it up, he stabbed his thumb. Ernie yanked his hand away and pulled out the thorn. But he didn't get it all out. A small piece broke off and remained embedded in his flesh. Holding the damaged hand out in front of him, he emerged from the woods, told us what had happened, and announced that he was afraid that his wound would become infected.

"Someone's got to drive me to the doctor's to get it out."

The three of us looked at him.

"What?" he said after a while.

We continued to stare.

"Ernie," I said breaking the silence, "we're just on the third hole."

"So?" he said.

We kept staring. Then my better nature took over. I felt sorry for the guy.

"Okay," I said, "you can take my golf cart back to your car."

"You mean to tell me, " he said slowly, "that nobody is going to drive me?"

We continued to stare until again, I broke down.

"All right, I'll drive you," I said. Adding, "to your car."

So Ernie and I got into the cart, I drove him to his car, and he drove himself to the doctor. Harvey and Joe were furious with me for interrupting the game, but I felt it was the right thing to do. (Perhaps only a golfer can appreciate this story.)

I really was crazy about the game; I think everyone who plays is crazy about golf. The idea gets in your head that all you have to do is get that ball into the cup. Eventually you do, but you've taken so many strokes to do it, it doesn't matter. Also, the grand game of golf became a worthwhile means to an end for me. For the twenty-five years that I worked with the United Cerebral Palsy Spastic Children's Foundation, I sponsored a tournament at the Westlake Golf Course. Once a year, some of the nicest people in the business would show up on a Sunday afternoon to play eighteen holes of the wackiest game in which they were ever likely to participate. But charity was the name of this game. We got Roger Barkley, a local disc jockey, the old-fashioned type of DJ—who makes sense and is funny—to interview the celebrity participants. The first year of the tournament, we set up a two-man tent at the first hole. Roger interviewed the players as they teed off. That's right, he talked to them while they took their swings. Again, golfers will read this and cringe. Nobody's supposed to talk to a golfer teeing off. But this was a charity tournament, and the idea of someone forced to chat while he swings is funny. Well, it's supposed to be funny.

Roger was Don Rickles–like in his confrontations. One time he asked Sammy Davis Jr., who had a glass eye, which eye he kept on the ball. Another time he arranged for "The Star Spangled Banner" to play when President Gerald Ford went into his swing. The president stopped the club in midair to stand at attention while the entire anthem blasted from the loudspeaker. Dick Martin didn't need Roger's kibitzing; he sauntered on the green with a martini in hand, took out the olive, shook it, and placed it on the tee. Handing his glass to Roger, he took his swing. The olive went a little farther than his usual drives. And when the chief of police got ready to swing, Roger asked him how often he had dinner at Hugh Hefner's house and did he have any phone numbers to share? The biggest laugh of the day didn't need any prompting from Roger Barkley. All Harvey Korman had to do was show his golf swing, and the thousands in the galley burst into laughter. Juvenile? Silly? Definitely. The outcome? People had a good time. More important, we raised enough money to provide care for the kids we were swinging for.

The Birth of Dorf

In the summer of 1987, Harvey and I were trying to salvage a sketch I'd written for the *Burnett* show. It was a take-off on the popular dramatic series *Fantasy Island*, which starred Ricardo Montalban and Hervé Villechaize. The former played Mr. Roarke, the tall, handsome host, and the latter played his assistant, Tattoo. Villechaize was barely four feet tall. Can you guess who was going to play whom in our sketch? In order for me to look even shorter, I knelt on the floor and slipped a pair of shoes under my kneecaps. I didn't look like a little person; I looked like a man on his knees. The sketch wasn't clicking. About all we had was me yelling, "Boss, da plane, da plane." After that, it was downhill. I was on my knees pondering, when I looked down at my knee-feet and something occurred to me.

"You know," I said to Harvey, "if they cut two holes in the floor,

I could put my legs through them up to my knees. And I could cut out the center of the shoes so it would look as though my legs ended at my knees."

"Are you nuts?" said Harvey.

That's all I had to hear. Anytime I had an idea and someone asked me that question, I knew I was on to something. So, instead of making a trap door, the carpenters drilled a couple of trap holes in the floor of Studio 33, and I was lowered into them. There was a platform beneath the surface on which I actually stood. It was just the ticket. I fell into place and so did everything else, including the sketch. The audience laughed it up. Everyone was talking about the "little fellow," whom I'd dubbed Dorf. Why Dorf? I don't remember. Maybe it was because it sounded like dwarf. Whatever the reason, a half-star was born.

Once I'd created the weird little guy with the weird toupee and the weird accent, I began to think of all the different situations I could put him in. I didn't have to think for too long. Dorf and I went to the Westlake golf course where we filmed a video, in which Dorf demonstrated his golf skills. I'm almost embarrassed to tell you that the resulting DVD, *Dorf on Golf*, has sold millions of copies. It was a super success and spawned many, many more discs, with Dorf as a fisherman, a hunter, a baseball player, etc. The one I loved doing best starred Sam Snead as Dorf's golfing partner.

We called Snead out of the blue and asked if he'd come in for a couple of days to film a video with Dorf. We were thrilled when he said okay. He arrived the night before the shoot. Lang Elliott, with whom I'd worked on *The Private Eyes* and other films, was the producer. He and I invited Snead to join us for dinner. We met at a local restaurant and had a drink in the cocktail lounge. About twenty minutes into the cocktail hour, Sam asked if Dorf was going to join us for dinner. Only then did Lang and I realize Sam didn't know who or what Dorf was. All he knew was that he was going to make a golf film with him. (We must have paid him a lot of money.) Neither Lang nor I was sure about what to do. How do you explain to the most well-known golfer of the day that he was going to be horsing around with a four-foot clown? Lang and I looked at each other. Implicit in our respective gazes was the shared notion to say nothing.

The next day when Sam appeared on the course, I was already buried in the ground on the eighteenth hole. Lang brought him up to me. Sam leaned over and shook my hand. He took in everything, from my height, to the square moustache under my nose, to the bad rug on my head, and made a pleasant comment about what a beautiful day it was. He had no idea that we'd had dinner the night before.

"Sam," I said looking up. "It's Tim Conway."

He looked down again, checked under the toupee, and with a grin a mile wide, grabbed my hand and, laughing aloud, shook it again.

We began shooting and came to the scene where I was to hit the ball across a pond. The ball was supposed to ricochet off a tree and bounce back into the water. In the past, without wanting to, I'd hit that tree dozens of times and watched as the ball caromed into the water. This time I didn't even come close. I could not hit that tree. We even tried it with special effects by shooting the ball out of an air gun. But nothing worked.

"What are you trying to do?" Sam finally asked.

"We're trying to hit that tree with the ball and have it drop back into the lake."

"Oh," said Sam, "give me the ball and turn on the camera."

I handed him a ball. Sam put it down, stepped back, took a beautiful swing, and hit the ball. The ball soared across the water, hit the tree, and bounced back into the pond. Sam turned around and said, "Like that?"

What a terrific guy Sam Snead was. We had a blast that afternoon. I've never heard anyone tell as great a bunch of golf stories. And, boy, have I dined out on my Yes-I-played-golf-with-Sam Snead experience. That day will always be special for me and for my annuity, Dorf.

Trodding the Boards

While I've alluded to my theatre experiences, it might come as a shock to learn that I've been working on the legitimate stage for almost as long as I've been on the illegitimate stage, if that's what you call television and movies. I've appeared quite a bit on the summer stock circuit, in regional theatre, yet, for a number of reasons, I've never appeared on Broadway. First reason, nobody ever asked me. I guess you don't need any more reasons than that. Then, too, there's an important word connected with the theatre. The word is discipline. You really have to have it when you're performing on the legitimate stage. It was different on the *Burnett* show. That's not to say we weren't disciplined; we were, but only up to a point and, as I've pointed out, we had permission to vary the script. But you can't mess with words when you're on the stage. Never mind the playwright, it's not fair to your fellow actors.

Despite the restrictions, I enjoy working in the theatre because I get an instant reaction and every performance is different in some way. I never know what's going to happen. And, whatever does happen, I'm stuck with it. In my legitimate career I had to impose a lot of discipline on myself and I did, most of the time. There were, of course, moments when I strayed.

I was appearing in a three-character comedy called *Wally's Cafe* by Sam Bobrick and Ron Clark. It opened on Broadway in 1981, without me in the cast. I did it a few years later in summer stock.

I made my entrance in the first act and was given my cue by Yvonne Wilder, who played a waitress.

"What would you like to drink, Wally?" Yvonne asked.

"I'll have milk," I said.

Yvonne looked at me. I could tell by the way her eyes suddenly opened wide that something was wrong.

"Wally, wouldn't you rather have orange juice?" she asked.

"No, why?" I responded, innocently.

What I had done was take a line from the second act and plunk it in the first. My response was supposed to be, "I'll have orange juice." The orange juice line in the first act was essential to the plot and would be used again in the last act to bring the play to its conclusion. Bringing the play to a conclusion one minute into the first act was a bit premature. Poor Yvonne had to prompt me a couple of more times before I realized what I'd done. I recovered brilliantly by saying something like, "Wait a minute, I think I'd rather have orange juice." We were back on track. Over the years, whenever I run into Yvonne, we exchange those lines before we even say hello.

I went up on my lines in *Wally's Cafe*, which isn't quite the same as deliberately mucking with the script. As you might guess, I did that, too. One summer, I appeared in *Mr. Roberts* at the

Chagrin Falls Little Theatre. I was in *McHale's Navy* then, and it seemed a natural for Ensign Parker to play Ensign Pulver in his hometown. The director was wonderful. However, during rehearsals he did suggest that it would be a good idea for me to stick to the script. Obviously, he knew my work. I agreed and promised to be on my best behavior.

In the 1950s, *Mr. Roberts* was a huge success, first on Broadway and then as a movie. Hank Fonda played the title role in both instances. Mr. Roberts was a good man who protected his crew from the tyrannical Captain Morton. Ensign Pulver was a good man, too, but a jackanapes. (Do you like this word? I do. I'm going to look it up now.) The play was so popular, productions blossomed everywhere: from Broadway, to regional theatres, to summer stock, to schools. Audiences were so familiar with it people could recite the lines along with the performers, and they often did. Near the end of the play, Mr. Roberts has left the ship to join a combat troop. Pulver is standing on deck with the other members of the crew. He receives a radiogram and learns that Mr. Roberts has been killed. One of the crew sees the pained expression on Pulver's face, and asks, "What is it?"

"It's Mr. Roberts."

"What happened?"

"He was killed in action," says Pulver.

"Oh no," cries the crewmember, and he buries his head in his hands to hide his tears. It's very moving, a foolproof scene. Ah, but things can happen when a fool is involved.

One evening we got to the big scene. I took the radiogram, read it to myself, looked up, and projected a pained look of disbelief. Jack Riley, who was playing the sailor, said his line.

"What is it?"

"It's Mr. Roberts," I said slowly.

"What happened?"

"They repossessed his car."

"Oh no," Jack responded. His eyes widened.

"What?" he asked again.

I looked down at the radiogram.

"Oh, and he was killed in action, too."

Let me assure you no one in the audience caught my improvised remark. They were too busy saying the lines to themselves, as I knew they would be.

I spent several summers appearing in *The Odd Couple* along with Tom Poston and Pat Harrington. Those two brilliant actors were from Steve Allen's stable of funny guys, and we had a ball during the show's run. Trust me, audiences were treated to performances of *The Odd Couple* that will never be duplicated. That is if Neil Simon has anything to say about it.

Speaking of Neil Simon, I've written a few plays myself. One was called *Just for Laughs*, and Tom Poston starred in it opposite me. In the play, Tom portrayed my partner, but he didn't want to be my partner in backing the play. He wouldn't invest his money because he didn't think the play would make it. But he was willing to appear in it as a paid performer. Tom was no dummy. We opened in Florida at the Burt Reynolds Jupiter Theatre. After the first week, we decided to take it on the road. Tom suggested that when we got it on the road, we run over it. I stonewalled that proposal. That's a key to my personality; the more people say something can't be done, the more I try to do it. It makes for an interesting life.

With the exception of Connecticut, we played to audiences that enjoyed and applauded our efforts. Connecticut is too close to New York; they know good theater when they see it. The best week's run was in San Antonio, Texas, except for the fact that we arrived with a bang and left with a whimper. Our sets were carried on a large truck that had been parked outside the theatre all week, waiting to reload after the final performance on Sunday evening. From there we were going to Vegas. We did the afternoon show and went out for an early dinner. We returned, did the evening performance and then, carrying our luggage, we went outside to supervise the loading of the sets. Surprise! There was no truck. It seems that a new driver had come in the night before. He didn't realize there were two Sunday performances and thought everything had been loaded after the matinee. He didn't bother to check the back of the truck but just hopped into the cab and drove off. We stood there on the sidewalk when someone said, "Tim, do something."

"What?"

"Call the driver and tell him to come back for the sets."

"Great. Who's got his number?"

Would you like to guess the answer to that question?

"Well, call the company and tell them to get a hold of the driver."

"Tim, what's the name of the company?"

"Aaah," I began, "I don't know the name of the company."

There followed a series of mild expletives and suggestions as to what I should do with myself. There seemed to be nothing else to do except wait to hear from the driver. We returned to the hotel and checked back in. The next evening around ten, the driver called. He was at a weigh station two hundred miles outside of Vegas. He said that the guy at the station noticed that the weight listed on the papers was way more than the truck actually weighed. So they opened the truck doors.

"You'll never guess what," said the driver.

"Oh, I think I might have a good guess," I replied. "I'll just betcha the truck was empty."

"Hey, you're right," said the astonished driver.

So he turned around and drove back to San Antonio to pick up the sets. We were a day late for the Vegas run, but everything ran smoothly after that. The play was successful, I made back the money and then some. On Broadway they call this a Happy Ending.

Epilogue

Hey, look at the title of this chapter. I can't believe I've already gone through my whole life (to date, at least). I know I've reached the stage where a lot of people look back and dream about living their lives over again. Some become obsessed with wishing they'd done things differently. People, including yours truly, can do some mighty dumb things on the way from the cradle to the you-know-what, but that's what makes one guy's life different from the other guy's. In my case, right from that cardboard polo box that Dan made for the infant Toma, I did what I wanted to do. Sure, I wish I could do it all over again, but I can honestly say, I'd do it exactly the same way.

I've always viewed life through Coke bottle lenses. That distortion, that visual twist, brings into focus the things that made me laugh, and, even better, the things I can use to make other people laugh. For me, the world is composed of props. I simply cannot resist them. Most people walk into a room and take an overall view. Are there windows, who's in the room, where's the nearest place to sit down, things like that. I walk into a room and right away I'll look for something usable. It could be a chair, a vase, a curtain, a paperweight, or even a doorknob; whatever it is, I'll find it. I never met a prop I didn't like or that I didn't try to use. I can't help it; it's just the way I am. I used to think I was possessed. After writing this book, I know I'm possessed. Why else would I do the things I do? I really owe a debt of gratitude to whoever is watching over me; it can't be an easy job. My nature is to amuse, and I'll grab any opportunity to do it.

While being an entertainer can make you totally happy, it can also completely annoy you. You can spend precious time asking, "Why didn't I get the part? Why don't I make the money he makes?" I never asked those questions because I was too busy enjoying my life in the biz.

I remember the first time I ever saw television. It sure wasn't at home; very few people we knew, including us, could afford a set. My first TV sighting came courtesy of Ken Shutts. He put a set, rabbit ears and all, in the window of Chagrin Hardware. I parked myself in front of that hardware store window whenever I could, and so did a lot of other people. Usually a small crowd would gather on the sidewalk and watch whatever happened to be broadcast. Often it was the test pattern. There was a communal feeling that went with television viewing especially standing on the sidewalk with your neighbors. Dan finally got a TV when we lived on Orange Street. Just like the radio that preceded it, that twelve-inch box brought the family together. Most homes only had one set and there were only three channels to choose from. Forget downloading, or on demand; you either saw a show or you didn't. If you wanted to talk about what you saw the night before, you had to watch the broadcast in real time. One of the unwritten laws of television viewing was, thou shalt not call anyone for the duration of *The Texaco Star Theater*, *The Jackie Gleason Show*, *The Toast of the Town*, or any of the other really popular programs. Even if you did telephone someone during the broadcast, no one would answer. I miss watching those worry-free television programs, the kind you could view with the whole family without hearing foul language or seeing too much violence or too much skin. Wow. I sound like an old geezer. Well I am an old geezer, but that doesn't prevent me from knowing what's worthwhile viewing and what isn't.

Television was the backbone of my performing life. I still can't get over my good luck in choosing my career. Actually, my career chose me. Growing too big prevented me from being a jockey; the inability to match patterns in wallpaper prevented me from being a paperhanger. Forget delivering papers, that was never going to last; the early hours required prevented me from being a baker. Lack of stamina prevented me from being a track star, and my big mouth kept me from having a military career. Show business was the only thing left. If you're reading this book you're one of the people who made, and make, my life so worth living. I love to stand behind the curtain in a theatre waiting to be introduced. I can't wait to get out onstage to meet all of you in the audience. The instant I walk out I forget my troubles and get happy. It's such a comfort to be entertaining you. And I love it when you let me know you're having fun. Laughter has always been what I was after; it's the key to my career and it's the key to my life. Believe me, whatever laughs you had were given with great pleasure and much joy.

Hey, wait a minute! Here I am in the epilogue and I haven't told you the elephant story yet, and it's one of the biggest laugh-getters I ever got. It also was one of the few times that I ever completely lost it and the only time I wound up on the floor laughing.

"The Family" was one of the most popular sketches on *The*

Carol Burnett Show. Carol played Eunice Harper Higgins; Harvey played her husband, Ed; and Vicki played her mother, Mama Harper. Those three characters were the nexus of those sketches. A whole bunch of other characters wandered in and out. I played Mickey Hart, one of those wanderers. Mickey was an employee in Ed's hardware store and always wore a baseball cap. He also wore an old-fashion hearing aid with a long, oversize wire attached to an amplifier in his pocket, but I don't remember why.

In November of the show's last season, we were taping a Family sketch in which Mickey had dropped by the house and was asked to play a word game with Eunice, Mama, and Ed. Harvey had left the show by then and Dick Van Dyke had taken over. In the sketch, Carol was to look at a card and give me a key word; I was to answer "elephant." Before the taping started, Joe Hamilton took me aside.

"Tim," he said, "the show's running a little long, so please when Carol gives you the cue, just say elephant, nothing else."

I smiled and nodded my head. I knew what Joe was up to. He was politely telling me to stay on script. That's all I needed to hear.

I walked onto the set and found Carol and Vicki sitting on a sofa. Dick was draped on one arm of the sofa, and I took my place on the other. Carol held up the card, gave me the cue and, instead of saying "elephant," I said something like, "Oh, elephants. See uh, there was this elephant that had a dwarf trainer and he used to put a little ballerina skirt on that elephant, and he'd go around dancing. I thought it was so laughable at the time. There was a rumor going around the circus that the dwarf and the elephant were lovers."

At this moment Carol buried her face in her hand. She was still clutching the card. Vicki's head had dropped to one side and Dick was wiggling all over the arm of the sofa. I continued.

"The elephant squashed him though," I said after a long pause. "So they had to shoot the elephant."

All three of my colleagues were in various stages of suppressed laughter. I didn't even look at them. I just went on.

"I don't know whether it was because of the rumor, but they were buried together. It was a great big tombstone . . ."

Carol cut me off by whirling around and hitting me with the card, and Joe stopped the taping. Carol, Vicki, and Dick collected themselves and we began again. Carol gave me the cue and this time, instead of saying "elephant," I said, "I guess it's not 'elephants,' huh?"

Carol said, "No!"

And I continued. "I was at a freak show one time 'n I saw two Siamese elephants this circus trainer had. They was uh joined at the end of their trunks. 'N this trainer'd make 'em stand on their back feet with their trunks stretched. Then this little monkey would go out on their trunks and dance a merengue. Those elephants couldn't trumpet like the other elephants 'cause they were joined at the trunk. All they could do was blow 'n go 'huh-gnorly.' One'd see the other's eyes get real big.

While I'm embellishing my one-word line, Carol, Vicki, and Dick were struggling to control themselves. Which only made me embellish more. Carol tried to get me on track, but I went on and on about the difficulties of being joined at the trunk and concluded with, "Then one day, one elephant sneezed and blew the other one's brains out."

The audience went wild.

In a desperate final attempt at restoring order, Carol thrust the white card in front of Vicki. Her voice trembling, she pleaded, "Go on, Mama."

Vicki pulled herself up, slowly turned to Carol, and said calmly, "You sure that little asshole's through?"

Guess what, folks. I am.

Fooled You!

I don't care if the Epilogue is supposed to be the end of a book, I've got more stories to get off my chest and I'm not leaving till they're told. Are you surprised? You shouldn't be. If you've been paying attention you know that once I get started, I can't stop. So sit back, relax, and enjoy (I hope) a bonus look at some random acts of mischief that have brightened my days.

I've already mentioned that I was a pretty good tailor, and this tale illustrates my skill with needle and thread. Ever since Charlene and I moved into our Encino home nearly three decades ago, we've given an annual Christmas Eve party for close friends. Our place, a sprawling combination English country house and Western ranch, is great for giving parties. I swear there are rooms I haven't discovered yet. The Christmas party guest list includes Carol and her family, other people from the *Burnett* show, and everybody's kids. (In the past, we entertained good buddies like Harvey Korman, Don Knotts, and Steve Allen. I still miss them.) It's a fun time, but neither Charlene nor I want it to go on too long. To make sure it doesn't we set all the clocks ahead by an hour so that everyone's out by 10 P.M. Charlene cooks most of the food; I assist her. The night before Christmas 1984, I greeted all the guests, served them drinks, and then slipped away. Carol noticed that I was missing, as I knew she would, and after a while, suggested that everyone go and find me, which I also knew would happen. They checked the kitchen, the bedrooms, and then went to my office where the walls were papered in a plaid design, the rage in those days. Without telling anyone, I had purchased material in the same plaid as the wallpaper, and had tailored myself a jacket. After I skipped out on my guests, I put on the jacket and went into my office. I stood with my back up against the wall and spread out my arms, aligning myself with the wallpaper pattern. I knew my pals eventually would get there.

"Come in," I called out when the search party finally knocked on the door. They walked into the room and found plaid-jacketed me plastered against the plaid-covered wall. All Carol and the others could see were my head and hands; the rest of my upper torso blended seamlessly into the paper. I'd been standing for quite some time, but it was worth it to see the looks on their faces, and to hear Carol shriek with laughter as only she can shriek. (Charlene took a photo; it's in the picture section.)

On a Monday evening in the mid-1960s, Ernie Anderson, McLean Stevenson, and I were in the City Slicker, a watering hole near CBS TV City, waiting for the Monday Night Football game to begin. That night the Los Angeles Rams were at home playing the Detroit Lions. The three of us were primed and ready when, suddenly, the screen went blank and a voice announced that the game would not be shown. Even today, if a home game isn't sold out in advance, it will not be broadcast over the local affiliate. You really can't blame the football leagues for imposing local blackouts; they want to sell the seats in the stadium. On the other hand, why would you pay to go to a game being held in your city if you could watch it for free on television? Ernie, McLean, and I were bummed. We'd looked forward to seeing the game.

This is the perfect spot for me to illustrate how I get, and put into action, my ideas. In order for you to follow my precise thinking, I'm going to take you into my brain at the exact moment that I heard the television announcement.

> *Newscaster:* The Rams game has been blacked out. Stay tuned for the Monday Night Movie.
>
> *Inside Tim Conway's Brain:* Nuts. I want to see that game. What am I going to do? (*Jumbled thoughts follow.*) Wait. The Rams are playing the Lions. There were three lions in the sketch we just did on TV. That means that three lion costumes are available.

> (*We now leave my brain.*)

"Hey guys, I just got an idea," I cried to Ernie and McLean. "What if we went over to the studio costume department and got those lion costumes from the sketch? We could go to the stadium and say that we're three mascots from Detroit."

Ernie and McLean were all for it, although I have to add if you've been at the City Slicker for a while, a preposterous plan like that might seem more plausible than if it were presented cold. We finished our drinks, paid the tab, and returned to the CBS studio. We went to the wardrobe room, took out the three lion outfits, and hit the road. On the way to the stadium we stopped at a diner, went into the men's room, and changed into the lion suits. It was a little cramped for three costume changes, but we managed to get them on. I wondered what the diner customers would think after watching three guys walk into the toilet and then see three lions walking out. No one looked twice, a phenomenon that could only take place in two cities, Los Angeles and New York. The three of us piled into the car and drove down the 101 to the Coliseum. I was at the wheel. I wondered what others, this time on the highway, might think upon seeing three lions driving along with them. Again, no one seemed to notice. As for the journey, I'll only say that it's not easy to drive a car with paws.

Our plan was to go to the stadium tunnel entrance. If we were questioned, we'd tell them we were the Detroit mascots. If they didn't let us in, then we'd gun the car and drive down the tunnel. I pulled up to the entrance, and a guard came over. I rolled down the window and said, "We're the lions."

"Right," said the guard, "we've been expecting you. Park over there, then go down the tunnel, and wait in the room with the band."

We were dumfounded. Why was he expecting us? Why didn't he question us? Little did we know that the San Diego Zoo had been asked to send up some caged lions for the halftime show. Apparently, the guard had been told to expect lions, but he didn't know whether they were real or not. I didn't ask any questions; I just did what he said and pulled the car over. The three of us got out, waddled down the tunnel, and went into the room already occupied by the USC band. We took seats along the wall and waited for instructions. A guy came in and announced that the band would be playing at halftime and that he'd come back closer to the performance to get them organized. I looked at the lion to my left and he looked at the lion to his left. We all had the same thought. Why should we miss the first half? We got up and walked out of the room. We huddled near the door and decided to continue down the tunnel. Soon we were at the entrance to the football field. The Detroit team was gathered there waiting to run onto the field. The three of us sauntered over and joined the group. The Lions looked at the lions; one of them, Alex Karras, came over to us.

"What are you guys supposed to be?" he asked.

By a stroke of luck, Ernie knew Alex.

"It's Ernie Anderson in here," he said. "And these are my friends Tim Conway and McLean Stevenson."

We shook hands and paws as Ernie told the Lions' defensive tackle what we were up to.

"You guys are nuts," Karras said laughing. "But hold on a minute."

He walked over to his teammates, told them who we were and why we were there. The Lions thought it was a hoot. They insisted that we come out on the field with them. We didn't argue. What better place to watch the game?

"Sports fans, let's welcome the Detroit Lions!" blared the voice from the loudspeaker. With the crowd's cheers and jeers ringing in our ears, we costumed lions led the playing Lions onto the field.

After our entrance, Ernie, McLean, and I went over to the side where we expected to watch the game. Unfortunately the fans seated in the section behind us couldn't see over our outsized lion heads. They complained to the ushers, one of whom leaned over the rail and told us that we'd have to lie down or get off the field. We weren't about to leave, so we got down on our bellies and watched. It was an exceptionally warm evening and the temperature inside the lion outfits was somewhere in the high nineties. Plus, our elbows ached from supporting our heads. In the middle of the second quarter, we decided that we'd had enough. Putting our tails behind us, we left the stadium and returned to the City Slicker where we spent the rest of the evening musing on our dumb luck. I've been fortunate to have happenstance on my side on many occasions; that Monday night was one of them. I still don't know if the San Diego Zoo lions ever got there.

I was eating in a restaurant when a lady came over to my table and asked for an autograph. She handed me a paper napkin indicating where I should sign. I wrote my name and handed the napkin back to her. She took a look and said, "I can't read this."

"But," I answered, "that's the way I sign my name. That's the charm of an autograph."

"Well," she replied indignantly, "Nobody's going to believe it's you. You can't read this thing."

Usually, I cut people slack when they're nice enough to ask me for an autograph, even when I'm eating. But this lady was terribly aggressive, and it got to me.

"I tell you what," I said. "You give me back the napkin, and give me your name and address. I'll go home and type my name and send it to you." She did just that. She returned the autographed napkin and gave me her name and address. When I got home, I typed "Tim Conway" on a piece of paper and sent it back to her, just the paper, not the napkin. I only wish I could have been around when she showed her chums my autograph.

One evening in the early '80s I went to a party at Ernie Anderson's. A lot of people from *The Carol Burnett Show* were already there, including Harvey, a few of the writers, and a group of regulars, dancers, and singers. At some point, I believe it was after I visited the punchbowl, I got a flash, an entire scenario popped into my brain. I had no choice but to enact it. I went into the bathroom and took a roll of toilet paper from underneath the sink. I opened the roll and wrapped the paper around my head until it was completely covered except for slits that I left for my eyes and my mouth. I looked like a mummy, but I could breathe, eat, and drink. I went back into the living room, got a glass of punch, and sat down on the couch. I was seated there, sipping punch and chatting with one of the dancers from the show, when Carol and Joe arrived. By that time everyone at the party was comfortable with my getup and treating me quite normally. Carol took one look and started shrieking. But I wasn't doing this to get a rise out of Carol. I was doing it for myself and it was just the beginning.

Toward the end of the evening, I asked Ernie to take a picture of me with his Polaroid camera; everyone had a Polaroid then. In the picture, my papered head was pretty near the size of the photos used in drivers' licenses. I asked Ernie for a pair of scissors, which I used to trim the print until it was just the right size. I took out my license and slid the photo under the plastic sheath on my license so that my official picture was completely covered. (You couldn't do this today because licenses are laminated.) I said good-night to everyone, got into my car, and drove off.

All this took place in the San Fernando Valley where I live, and I knew the streets like I knew the back of my hand. My destination was a particular intersection with a four-way stop sign. A cop car was always in hiding at that corner. As I drove into the intersection, I checked carefully to make sure no other cars were coming. Then, I went through without coming to a complete stop. I hadn't gone far when I heard a siren and saw a red light flashing in the rearview mirror. The plan was working perfectly. I pulled over to the side, turned off the engine, rolled down the window, and waited for the officer. He pulled in behind me, got out of the patrol car, and walked over to my window. He leaned over, looked at me, took a breath, and said, "May I see your license?"

I reached into my pocket, took out my wallet, pulled out my license, and handed it over. The cop never said a word. He looked at the license, then looked at me, then looked at the license, and then looked at me. He threw his head back and burst out laughing. Ta da! I pulled it off. I realized I was taking a chance. I could've hit a humorless cop, or one who didn't recognize the name on the license, but, oh boy, was it worth it. Warning: Do not attempt this stunt on your own. You have to be a licensed nutcase to do it. I am a licensed nutcase, and I have the photo ID to prove it.

When it comes to dealing with our wives, guys never understand that the truth will eventually come out. I avoided the truth here and there with my first wife. I was young and, in some instances, foolish. I thought I could get away with a few things, mostly when it came to answering the question, "Where have you been?" This never happened with Charlene. I was older and wiser. What's more, her family would destroy me if she caught me in a lie. That's the thing, though—wives call it lying, when I prefer to think of it as trying to save your marriage. In the B.C. era (Before Charlene), I was a little more of a scamp, especially when it came to hanging around at the City Slicker with the guys from the *Burnett* show. Truth to tell, I went across the street from the CBS studio to the Slicker every Thursday night. That's when we prerecorded all the music for the show. I implied that I was needed at every music rehearsal. Mary Anne never questioned me, which was strange since I never sang a note on air. We guys would while away a couple of hours and then wend our way home.

One night we whiled away a lot longer than usual. Mary Anne even made some calls to a couple of hospitals to see if maybe I had been brought in. By the time I got home, she was sitting in the living room waiting. She looked at me and said those words that men never want to hear.

"Where have you been?"

I was now on the clock, as they say, and had a split second to gather my thoughts. You can borrow a little time if you cough, but that's about it. I had to explain. Telling the truth—"I was at the Slicker with the boys, dear"—was the furthest thing from my mind. So, I began the story.

"Well, I was on my way home hours ago but I took the freeway and got behind a truck on the 405. It was a big tank truck from the Sea World in Burbank that was transporting a new Shamu whale to the San Diego Sea World. I was passing the truck when I noticed that the tank was leaking water on the left side. I blew the horn and signaled for the driver to pull over. He pulled over and I pulled in behind him. I got out and told him that I had noticed a leak. He checked and said we had to do something or we were going to lose a whale. He said he would call the fire department and have them come and fill the tank with water. In the meantime he asked me to go get salt because whales are ocean creatures. I drove around to restaurants and bars asking the managers for salt. Some gave me boxes and some just took saltshakers off the tables and put them in plastic bags. I promised I would return the shakers. I went back to the truck. The firemen were already there. They'd rigged up a hose that was pumping water into the tank. After they were through, I climbed up the side ladder. When I reached the open top I began pouring in the salt. I finished and came down the ladder. The driver was waiting at the bottom. He thanked me and said so long. As I drove off, I saw him get back on the highway through my rearview mirror. I guess they made it to Sea World all right because I didn't hear anything on the news. Anyway, by the time I returned all the saltshakers it was really late. I headed straight home and ran into some traffic. But here I am safe and sound."

I stood there staring down at Mary Anne waiting for the verdict. It was unanimous: *guilty* as charged. The jury also said I was full of crap. It's funny, when I told Harvey the story he said he didn't see a hitch in it. Of course, both of us did get divorces during the *Burnett* Show. I'll never understand why. Must have been the salt.

This next story might better fit in a chapter called "Stupidity," but since there is no such chapter in this book, I'm going to stick it here. The first thing you have to know is that I frequent a drive-in diner down the street from me. The food is good, really good, but the owner is crazed, really crazed. He purchased a small area in the back of the building that is reserved for patron parking only. "Reserved" is too feeble a term to describe how completely sacred to his diners that lot is. That little parking lot has everything but a dress code. Signs are plastered all over the wall beginning with a mild PATRON PARKING ONLY and culminating in a threatening THE MANAGEMENT RESERVES THE RIGHT TO REMOVE ANY VEHICLE THAT DOES NOT BELONG TO A PATRON EATING AT THIS ESTABLISHMENT.

Trust me, if the owner had his way the sign would read THE MANAGEMENT RESERVES THE RIGHT TO DISEMBOWEL ANY NON-PATRON WHO PARKS HERE.

In a way, I don't blame the guy. A lot of non-patrons use the lot because it's attached to several small stores, the kind that people run in and out of to make a quick purchase. Rather than wait for a meter, or park illegally, they use the diner parking lot. I only used it when I ate in the diner. Until one day when I had to drop off some information at a lamp store in the same strip. In my defense, I tried to park legally. I circled and circled and circled. I had a two-minute errand and had already spent twenty minutes looking for a parking spot. I gave up. I was going to park in the lot, run in and out, and that was that. I pulled into a space in the Forbidden City, grabbed the papers, jumped out of the car, raced around to the front, ran into the lamp store, threw the papers at the clerk, sprinted out the door, ran around the block and into the parking lot. I was heading to my car when I saw several cops crouched behind some parked cars. Their guns were drawn and pointed in my direction.

"Get down! Get down!" the cops yelled at me.

I stood there in disbelief. I'm thinking to myself that the guy who owns the diner *is* crazy. I was in and out in under two minutes and he called the cops?

"Officer, I was just here for five minutes," I shouted to one of them. "Look, I'll go in and buy a bagel. Would that take care of the problem?"

The cop looked at me and yelled again. *"Get down!"*

I was not going to argue with drawn guns, so I slowly got down on the ground next to my car. I knelt there as the cops kept their guns pointed. I had made up my mind I would never illegally park in that lot again when a couple of other cops came out of a building escorting a guy in handcuffs. At this point, one of the gun-wielding officers put his weapon away and came over to me.

"Are you nuts?" he asked.

"Everyone asks me that," I answered.

He took a good look at me.

"Are you the guy on the *Burnett* show?" he inquired.

"Yes."

"Then you are nuts."

He was kind enough to explain that in the few minutes I'd been away from my car, they had cornered an armed robber on the roof of the building next to my car. Yours truly had wandered into what could have been a shootout at the OK Corral.

"I wonder," asked the officer after he finished explaining. "Would you mind autographing one of these traffic tickets for me?"

"Sure," I said. I took the ticket, wrote my name, and added a ten-dollar tip. I don't usually tip that much but I felt he deserved it.

One year, I bought a fancy foreign car. It was painted racing green, but it should have been painted yellow. It was the lemon of lemons. I hated that car. Why wouldn't I? I'd owned it for only six months, and it was in the repair shop for almost four. Once, on a rare occasion when it was out of the shop, I drove to a party in Beverly Hills. I arrived late, gave my keys to a parking attendant, went in, and was one of the last to leave. When I got out on the street, I looked around for the valet parker. I couldn't find him so I went back in and asked where I could find him.

"What parking attendant? We have no parking attendant," answered the host.

It seems that I'd given my keys to a kid who looked like a parking attendant but who, in fact, was a car thief. With great joy I reported my car as stolen and awaited the insurance settlement. That was the good part. Here's the bad part. A day and half shy of the settlement date, the car turned up around three blocks from where the guy stole it. I think he dumped it because he didn't want a lemon, either. I was bummed.

Imagine for a moment that you are a member of a jury and I have been brought to the witness stand on a charge of indecent exposure in a public place. Before you come to a verdict, here are the details.

I was waiting for Charlene in the men's department of a well-known specialty store. I was minding my own business, leaning up against the shirt display case. A lady came over to me and, assuming that I was a clerk, said, "Pardon me, where is your underwear?"

I showed her.

Ladies and Gentlemen of the jury, I rest my case.

Speaking of resting my case, I think I'd better wrap this up. I don't want to overstay my welcome even though I have many more stories to tell. Maybe I'll save them for a sequel. How does the title, *Son of What's so Funny?* strike you? Think about it. Meanwhile, take good care of yourselves till we meet again. Good-bye for real, but just for now.

Acknowledgments

Writing a book is no joke. I want to thank everyone who's helped me, my family, my friends, and my colleagues. Thanks also to Steve Tellez and Jim Stein at Innovative Artists Agency and to Jennifer Gates and Todd Shuster at Zachary Shuster Harmsworth Literary and Entertainment Agency; my editor, Becky Nesbitt, and her associate editor, Amanda Demastus, and all the other wonderful folks at Howard Books. Jane Scovell was a pain in the neck, but she tried hard.

Tim

I did try hard and had the time of my life working with Tim & Company. (Even Dorf was helpful.) I especially want to thank my rival Sharkey and Jackie Beatty, whose cheerful nature and thoughtful assistance was invaluable.

Jane